LEADERSHIP
ABOVE & BEYOND
THE CROWD

by James E. Melton, PhD

Global Publications
P.O. Box 340 • Yucca Valley, CA 92286
760.365.4552

ISBN 978-0-9604752-2-3

Cover design by Mark Biley, One by Design, Inc.
Cover author photo by Dana Eastman Melton
Interior design and layout by Quality Printing & Design
Editing by Noal McDonald, Just Write

For information about additional products and services, including
speaking, speech coaching, or consulting, please contact:
James Melton
info@ChallengeTomorrow.com
www.ChallengeTomorrow.com

To Dana...
my professor of patience.
I fear that I have not been the best student,
but I marvel at your ability and sensitivity
to hold fast to your values
and watch the imagined emerge.
Your love sustains me.
My love to you then, now and always.

PREFACE ON LEADERSHIP
FROM PEOPLE WHO LIVE IT:

This section reveals thought-provoking comments from my personal conversations with individuals who have been a catalyst for growth in the lives of countless people. My interviews with them relate essential leadership qualities that can be effectively utilized by anyone seriously seeking positive change. Their sincere desire, and mine, is that the reader will benefit from their personal insights and words of wisdom.

ALAN BEAN, Astronaut
Lunar Module Pilot on Apollo 12
Fourth man to walk on the moon

"I believe that leadership can be taught. My life path is a perfect example. I was not born with leadership skills. In high school and college no one looked at me as a leader.

When I entered the Navy I felt I was deficient in leadership skills and had little if any charisma, and I needed to improve both. I read a number of books on leadership. I studied the principles and I learned that what you consciously study you improve upon. If you work on it, the things you concentrate on will improve.

Pete Conrad was a natural leader and I watched him close on the Apollo 12 Moon Mission. I applied what I observed and the things he taught me when I was assigned to the Sky Lab 3 Mission.

You can learn to be better if you are willing. "Willing" is the key word here. It takes time. You don't have to be 6' 4" tall, or have any other physical attribute to be a leader. It evolves through study and acquiring better ideas and ways to express them. But, the person who wants to step forward to assume the leadership role has got to be thinking ahead of the people he is trying to lead. This means time spent in study and thought.

I now think that charisma is more a result of leadership than the reason for it."

HOWARD BEHAR
President, Starbucks Coffee International, retired
Author: *It's Not About The Coffee*

"Often people aspire to a leadership position because of the power they have over people; in reality great leaders flip that on its head. Great leaders empower people. I think it's most important to serve others. Sometimes it is difficult for young leaders to appreciate this, they look at getting the corner office and think it will make them special. That does not happen. What will make them special is their service to others.

Leadership is not as much about leading others as it is about leading yourself. If you are clear about your own values and goals and lead yourself well, then you will be better suited to serve others.

Can leadership be taught? Absolutely! Someone does not come out of the womb as a leader. Granted, we are all born with certain personality traits, but most of our influencing is environmental, our parents, our teachers, our friends and we're not always in control of those things.

We do, however, follow the example of others. All too often we are not aware of this, but then someone may catch your eye and say, 'Oh, he has skills that I would like.' You watch, you read, and you most definitely learn to lead yourself. You work on what matters to you. People can spot a fake leader easily. True leadership comes from the soul; it's not just learning the words.

Also, management and leadership are so closely woven together that sometimes it's often difficult to distinguish between them. A good enduring leader has to be both manager and leader. A coach can motivate, certainly that's an aspect of leadership, but a leader helps people to become better human beings. As a leader sometimes it is necessary to step into a management role, into the details and the muck. You may have to manage to the goal, you may have to step in, but as a leader you must also know when to step out."

SCOTT KASTNER
Senior Manager, IT System Operations
JetBlue Airways Corporation

"In my opinion, leaders need to have empathy... to be able to relate to another person's feelings. With empathy a leader will be able to convey his vision in terms that can be understood. He must accomplish that vision with a set of values that are consistent with the process and the outcome.

As a child and young man, empathy and character ethics were instilled in me by my mom. Often it was tough... doing the right thing is not always easy, but I learned that it's also about caring for other people. It's not always about *'me'*. I believe I learned that from my mother. I have had many opportunities to practice that on the job and I have seen it be very successful.

Leadership instills trust and confidence in others. In the words of General Colin Powell, 'The day soldiers stop bringing you their problems is the day you have stopped leading them. They have either lost confidence that you can help them or concluded that you do not care. Either case is a failure of leadership.'

A leader helps to remove the road blocks. A leader sets goals and objectives and then steps out of the way. A manager may be more hands-on in accomplishing each successive step along the way.

When I learned to fly, I did so because I was intrigued with the technology. I like to immerse myself in things, kind of like when I wanted to sell my home I became a licensed realtor so I could know the inner workings of the process. What I realized about flying was that it was not about being a pilot or the actual flying of the plane, it was not about fueling the aircraft, or baggage handling, (which were all respectable positions that I held in the industry,) it was more about being enamored with what it took to get an airplane in the air ... the technology, the avionics, the systems. I knew then that that's the direction I wanted to go."

NANCY KIRCHEN, CTC
Manager, Operations and Infrastructure Support
Walt Disney Travel Company

"Leaders lead by example. You can watch them get results. A leader is someone whom you admire and aspire to be like.

Managers, on the other hand, make a solid connection with people and doing this takes a lot of listening. Listening goes deeper than just hearing. You need to get to know someone before you can manage. You must have a variety of people to pull from to build a top-flight team. You pull the right people together and help them find their strengths. Everyone has strengths, some of which are not seen by the person himself. A manager helps to locate those strengths and bring them to light.

My dad and I used to joke when I told him that I was promoted to another leadership position. I never asked for a leadership position; he said that they are obviously seeing something in you that you don't see in yourself. But I always wanted to learn... anything I could. I never said that's not my job; I feel that is a key to success for everyone.

I've been known as a Switzerlander—someone who is neutral. One who doesn't take sides, but allows everyone to express themselves. Even after 25 years with Disney I still look at myself as a manager, but in reality I think that some people do look to me for leadership. I can see a mile down the road whereas some people will only look a few blocks. To be a real leader, however, one needs to take a more distant view by looking 15 to 20 miles into the future. They need to stay way ahead of the game."

HOWARD PUTNAM
Former CEO of Southwest Airlines
Former CEO Braniff International Airlines
Author: *The Winds of Turbulence*

"A leader must have passion to lead anything. Also, some people just seem to be born with leadership skills, but I feel that it can also be taught. It does help if you are able to refine and tap into your sense of intuition.

I was born on a farm in Iowa. My dad bought an airplane and I learned to fly when I was 12. He let me drive tractors at night when I was only 10 and 11 years of age. He taught me accountability and responsibility. He put his trust in me and I respected that and responded accordingly. A leader has to step in and be up for the challenge.

Eddie Carlson of United Airlines once told me, 'Some people manage and some people lead.' A manager runs the department. A leader moves you to the next level."

PROLOGUE ON LEADERSHIP:

Even before we get into the introduction of this book I thought it might be a good idea to share some of the common beliefs, definitions, traits, myths, and rumors about this aspect of life called leadership. Leadership plays a role in all that we do as a child, a father, a student, a manager, and in married life just to name a few.

In my view, leadership is the education, training, and experience gained in life. It is based largely on proper implementation of the "soft-skills" that make up our daily activities, whatever role that may be at any specific time. In other words, leadership seems to evolve as we as individuals go about our activities. It is a collection of a multitude of messages, insights, sensitivities, and intuitions. You might say that Management deals with the "hard-skills", the process, the implementation, and the direction, and Leadership evolves through the "soft-skills" by acting, reacting, and being sensitive to the forces in and around us. Leadership may play a role in some parts of our lives, and not in others, which means that "following" could very well be part of the leadership process. People may be leaders in one organization and have quite ordinary roles in another.

This book identifies many of the tools and processes that build leadership. In themselves they are applicable for personal use; as a whole, they embody true leadership. Briefly, here are some of the myths and traits as related to leadership:

MYTHS OF LEADERSHIP

1. *Leadership is a rare skill.* While great leaders may be as rare as great athletes, musicians, or artists, everyone has leadership potential.

2. *Leaders are born, not made.* I believe that leaders evolve through education, training, and experience.

3. *Leaders are charismatic.* Some are, but most aren't. For the most part, we are all too human. Charisma is rather the result of effective leadership, not the reason for it.

4. *Leadership exists only at the top of an organization.* We may have unintentionally supported this myth by focusing exclusively on top leadership. Elements of leadership exists in all jobs.

5. *Leaders control, direct, and manipulate.* Not really. Leadership is not so much an exercise of power as it is the empowerment of people. To get power, you give power.

TRAITS OF LEADERSHIP

I like to think of a person who demonstrates leadership as one who possesses emotional wisdom. Emotional wisdom reflects itself in the way people relate with others.

1. *The ability to accept people as they are, not as one would like them to be.* In a way, this can be seen as the height of wisdom—to enter the "skin" of someone else, to empathize, to understand what other people are like on their terms, rather than judging them.

2. *The capacity to approach relationships and problems in terms of the present rather than the past.* Using the present as a starting point for making fewer mistakes is more productive.

3. *The ability to treat those close to you with the same courteous attention that you extend to strangers.* The reverse is also true.

4. *The ability to trust others, even if the risk seems great.* Withholding trust is often too high a price to pay if it means taking for granted that everyone is incompetent.

5. *The ability to do without constant approval and recognition from others.* Particularly in a work situation, the need for constant approval can be harmful and counterproductive.

INTRODUCTION:

ROME, ITALY: He was on center stage. Eight thousand people were riveted to his words, locking them to their seats. It was as if they were hypnotized. A cloud of optimism settled on the audience as Lee Iacocca spun his magic for the absorbent crowd. Silence filled the arena and rested on all ears waiting for his next insight.

I was sitting three rows back, stage left. How would I follow this—yes, I was the next speaker. How many were Italian? Would they understand me? Would they care?

A rush of applause filled the center and the crowd rose to their feet as one giving a well-deserved standing ovation to one of America's most profound leaders of our time. Eight thousand people stood to applaud. More than five thousand did not return to their seats. For them, they had achieved what they came for—an audience with Lee Iacocca.

I, however, was left with less than three thousand people in an arena which seated eight thousand. To say—empty—would be an understatement. I felt humbled, but inspired with the thoughts and comments of Mr. Iacocca, and in those thoughts, I proceeded to deliver what I felt was a solid presentation on leadership to those few who chose to remain.

With that in mind, this book is about what can be done. So often we hear "You'll never be able to do that." "Others have tried, but failed." "It's beyond you, why even bother?"

Well, I was told many of those things, and for a long time I believed them. It's been said that we are a product of the books we read and the people we meet. To some degree that is true. Oh, you'll find those who say, "It's our upbringing." Yes, it is. But that falls into the category of those with whom we meet and associate. Others will say, "It's our education." Yes, but consider that education is derived largely from books and experience. Of course, the combination of the two is in constant play, but you get the point—don't you?

When I failed kindergarten. Yes, that's right, failed kindergarten, the message I received was that the opinions of others were more important than my own. I bought it—totally, completely, and without question. Later in my years I realized that I was wrong, terribly, terribly wrong. But I will never regret those many years of feeling inferior, of feeling that someone else had all the answers and I had none. Why? Because the process of discovery has led me to some highly unconventional methods of personal and professional fulfillment.

My social patterns as a young man, with friends and school mates, work habits as a teen-ager, musical endeavors, aviation career, romantic relationships, and education all followed the circuitous path of non-tradition.

I look at the statement of my teacher in 12th grade English who said, "Jim, don't ever attempt college—you'll never make it." And I say to myself maybe these types of statements have caused me to look between the clouds where most people would never think of looking.

There are many ways to achieve an end, some better, some worse. The creative and entrepreneurial spirit, which is often developed in people who get bounced around through the air pockets of life find their greatest development in the very essence of challenge and disappointment.

This book was written for those who want a departure from the norm. "Leadership Above & Beyond The Crowd" directs itself toward the ultimate goal for which we all strive—the process of making life more productive and enjoyable for ourselves, for those with whom we associate, and for the ones we love. It is about relationships in life itself. It is, in a very personal way, a process of addressing and re-engineering the beliefs and values each of us have formed at an early age. The conscience that tugs at the very fiber of our being.

Each of us has made a series of choices in life to bring us to this moment today. Your determination and commitment to a new direction will be challenged by many, but cannot be squelched by anyone but you. There is no such thing as failure, unless we quit in our minds. To unlock our unlimited wealth of potential and drive we must look toward what we can accomplish, not toward what we can not. We must look at what will work, not at what will not work. We must focus our minds on the positive and seek out new and productive methods for life enrichment. Our success, then, will be determined not so much by what we do, but by how we do it. Success will not be so concerned as to what you are, but by who you are. Ultimately, the choices you make will create your experiences. Choose your direction wisely for you are about to cross the threshold into your future.

Taxi into position and hold . . .
James Melton

TABLE OF CONTENTS

PEOPLE MAKE IT HAPPEN

THE SERVICE EDGE

THE SALES LEADER

REACHING HIGH

GETTING RESULTS
THROUGH PEOPLE

SECTION I:

PEOPLE

MAKE IT

HAPPEN

Enhance your communication ability
and you will elevate your career
and your position in society.

CHAPTER 1:
TO RELATE—COMMUNICATE

Lee Iacocca once noted that ". . . there's one phrase that I hate to see on any executive's evaluation, no matter how talented he may be and, that's the line: 'He has trouble getting along with other people.' To me, that's the kiss of death. 'You've just destroyed the guy,' I always think. 'He can't get along with people? Then he's got a real problem, because that's all we've got here. No dogs, no apes—only people."

To me, your skill in dealing with people is essential. Whatever your product is, how well made, cost efficient or how great a need you supply to the community at large, if you don't effectively talk, listen, work, play, in short: if you don't relate to people well, employees as well as customers, it all goes out the window.

Good people skills begins and ends with relationships. So, let's start by asking, what is a relationship? According to the second edition, Random House Dictionary, a relationship is: ". . . a connection, association or involvement between people."

Now, that can cover anyone from the janitor in a building to the CEO of the corporation and in many cases, that's the same person!

But let's start at the beginning. It is difficult to have a good relationship with other people until you have a good relationship with yourself. So, how can you tell if you have a good relationship with yourself? Simple. A relationship is like a mirror. What do you see in the people you work with? What do you hear, from yourself as well as others? Is there a lot of complaining? Blaming? Do you hear the critical or negative words being spoken?

The first step in developing a relationship with yourself is to begin by taking responsibility for what you say and what you do.

Here's an exercise for you. Select a partner (a spouse or co-worker) and ask him or her to actively listen to you throughout the day for any of the following words: *can't, try, if only, but, however, difficult, ought to, should, doubt,* any words that tend to judge, condemn or limit yourself or another.

─────── **LIFE LINE** ───────

*"Everything that seems to happen to me,
I asked for and I receive as I have asked."*

In order that we might develop a better relationship with ourselves, we must first become aware of, and accept who we are at this moment. Sort of a mini-evaluation, a reality check, so to speak.

At the end of the day, sit down with your friend and listen as he or she tells you the words you used. This might surprise you. That's okay. Learn to recognize yourself right where you are so you can begin to make changes.

Start by making a declaration to yourself right now: "Right now, I am responsible for what I see. I select the feelings I experience. I choose the goal I want to achieve." Now, here's the tricky part: "Everything that seems to happen to me, I asked for and I receive as I have asked."

By learning to first take responsibility for what we say and do and then becoming aware of this, we can see where we would like to make changes. Then, begin to make those changes accordingly.

Be easy with yourself. If you find yourself continuing to use a lot of negative words, merely regard them as a mistake to be corrected and choose not to feel guilty about making a mistake. It takes time.

LIFE LINE

If we consistently speak in negatives we will see negative situations around us.

If we want to experience better relationships we have to start by accepting ourselves right where we are, and be willing to change what is not working for us. This begins with our thinking. The words we use every day are a direct reflection of our thoughts. If we consistently speak in negatives we will see negative situations around us. Positive words will generate positive experiences. It's up to us!

Start by taking a look at yourself. If we don't have a high regard for ourselves then how can we have a high regard for others?

The premise of this concept is based on five simple points:

1. *Choose your thoughts.* Ultimately, you choose your thoughts. No one else does. So, choose positive ones.

2. *See the image.* Construct a picture in your mind of the positive experiences you want and make it real by adding details to it.

3. *Develop your feelings.* Develop a feeling to match the picture in your mind. Maybe it's a great feeling of accomplishment that you experienced in the past. Remember it and use it.

4. *Your body responds.* Your body responds to outward situations. Observe how you begin to respond to the images and feelings you create. Go with it.

And finally:

5. *Produce the results.* The results will show up as you keep working the process.

——— LIFE LINE ———

What you think about,
you bring about
——— ✍ ———

That's it, in a nutshell. If you want to begin to change the way you
see yourself and the way others see you, you must begin by changing
your thinking. Then, you need to see yourself in your mind the way
you want to be seen. Next, develop a feeling to match the image.
Wind this up by outwardly responding positively to others, co-
workers, clients, anybody and everybody. Then, the results you're
looking for will emerge. They have to. What you think about, you
bring about.

Okay, let's move the focus toward relationships with others and so
that you understand, when I refer to relationships with others, I'm
speaking about those with whom we work: co-workers, bosses,
executives, clients. Anyone with whom we have some kind of
working relationship.

The business environment can give you opportunities to grow and
expand. It can bring you to a level of creative satisfaction that is not
experienced quite the same way in your personal family life. It allows
us to share, be supported and contribute ideas toward one goal.

What an opportunity! So, how do we start?

Communication

Well, communication is the basis for any relationship, but becomes
absolutely essential in the work environment if the needs of the
workers as well as the company are to be met.

We have a tendency many times in work relationships to react
rather than to act. It's a common problem and it doesn't have to exist.
Let's get something clear from the start. *Reacting is not
communicating*. It's reacting. You are not communicating with
anyone if you spend most of your time reacting to what someone has
either done or not done.

"Okay, I got that. So, what is communication?" Simple. It's talking and listening. You listen while I talk and I listen when you talk. In between, we may ask each other questions about what has been said, but basically it's talking and listening. So, let's break it down. Here are some points to keep in mind when talking:

1. *Be clear.* Know what you want to say and say it. Unless you're involved in a brainstorming session, talking in complicated paragraphs can be confusing and exhausting to the listener. And he may not understand you. Short, simple thoughts work best.

2. *Be concise.* This relates directly to the first. Maybe you have clear thoughts but now you go on and on so much that you're putting everyone to sleep. Stop. Don't do it. Learn to be quiet when you've said what you wanted to say.

There is also an active role that the listener can take as well and it's this:

1. *Listen for ideas and thoughts.* And ask yourself if they make sense to you. If they don't, ask a question. "I'm not clear on this. Please go over that, again."

2. *Restate the ideas that are clear to you.* Voice them back to the speaker with something like, "So, what I hear you saying is . . ." Let him correct you if you've misunderstood him. If not, you've got it.

Conflict Resolution

Another big area in relationships is conflict resolution. When two or more people are having a problem, progress has a tendency to slow to a crawl. The first order of business is to determine who owns the problem. If you feel guilty, anxious, upset, feel slighted or defensive . . . in other words if you are the one hurting, then you own the problem. Now, you have to find a way out of it. And that way must start by communicating to others and coming up with a solution.

Dynamic Relationships

Remember, all relationships have the potential to be dynamic. What do I mean by dynamic? I mean alive, something that inspires or sparks your creativity. Something that tells you or shows you that you are making a contribution and your contribution matters.

Three traits that support dynamic, working relationships are:

1. *Trusting your feelings.*

2. *Openly communicating* those feelings in the context of your work.

3. *Being truthful.* If someone asks you for your opinion regarding something, tell them. If you try to hide it in order to spare their feelings, it will only surface in some other way down the line with possibly disastrous consequences.

Working Relationships

I've come up with some ideas that I consider essential characteristics of a good working relationship and here they are:

1. *Allow for individuality.* You're right to do the job your way as long as it's a way that promotes yourself and the company.

2. *Allow space to share ideas* and listen to the ideas of others without immediate criticism.

3. *Allow for openness* to explore and change.

4. Feel the freedom to ***ask honestly for what you want.***

5. *Cooperate rather than control.* You can only control your actions and reactions. Talk about what you want to be done and then allow others to cooperate with you in how it gets done.

Some final points to remember regarding relationships are: *The aware mind has power over the unaware mind.* Knowledge is power. When we have knowledge, we have awareness. When we have awareness, we have power. Be aware of what you say and do. Take responsibility for those two things. Be a clear and concise talker. Be an active, concerned listener who repeats the points he gets and asks questions about the points he doesn't get.

Be dynamic. Trust your feelings. Openly, communicate those feelings as they apply to the work and most important of all: tell the truth at all times. It's simpler, quicker and easier.

CHAPTER 2:
LISTEN BEHIND WHAT YOU HEAR

It seems to me that a lot of people today say they are understanding but don't convey the interest. They say things like, "I hear what you're saying." and then proceed to dismiss, discount, or ignore whatever you have just discussed with them. This may have to do with a lack of compassion more than anything else.

I became interested in this subject of compassion mainly because there seems to be a lot of gossip going on out there. There's a lot of jealousy and envy expressed in different ways toward our fellow workers and what I don't understand is why? Aren't we all working on the same team? Aren't we all working toward the same goal? And aren't we all supposed to be helping each other, cooperating with each other in reaching those goals?

In the dictionary I was surprised to find compassion defined as, "a feeling of deep sympathy and sorrow for another . . . to commiserate or pity." You know what? I don't agree. Certainly sympathy is one level of compassion but just sympathy or pity falls way short for me. It gave one other definition though, it said, "To show heart." And this I agree with.

So, I thought about this for a while and came up with this idea for compassion, see what you think. To me compassion is a way of treating ourselves and everyone and everything around us in a respectful and caring way. It is knowing that we are all on the same flight together and on the way we all need to talk, listen, share, support and help each other. That's what I believe true compassion is.

Now, lately I think a lot of us along our flight path have hit a few air pockets. We've either forgotten, or not learned just how to be compassionate toward our fellow worker.

Maybe I'm old-fashioned but I was always taught to treat others the way you want to be treated. Possibly that's what compassion is. In any event, it seems to be in short supply these days. And I think it's one characteristic that we need to spend more time developing.

What I've noticed lately is that there seems to be a group psychology at work here. Many times we tend to act differently in a group than we would individually. Crowds of people in a panic will stampede over other people, but remove them from the crowd situation and their behavior could be quite different—they wouldn't think of doing that. Where is the consistency here? Where is the compassion?

I believe that as human beings, we are all thinking, breathing, and creative individuals, and we are intuitive by nature. Now, as soon as I use the word intuition, I can hear a lot of you going, "Ah, intuition, sixth sense. What's he saying here? . . . psychic, occult? Look out!" Intuition simply means to be tutored from within, that's all. So, let's get this thing called intuition out of the closet and into the living room where we can take a good close look at it.

All creatures who roam our planet, including us humans, are intuitive. In the lower life forms, we call this faculty instinct. In man, it's a finer degree of knowing. We can't always explain how we know, we just know. Well, I believe that along with knowing what's going on for us inside, we also know how we want to be treated on the outside. Many times, though, through one excuse or another, usually coming from the committee in our brains, we tend to disregard this knowing sense and start acting-out in ways that go against our instinct. We are rude, disrespectful, or hostile, or blaming, or any number of things.

Now, don't get me wrong. I'm not saying that if you've done any of these things to your fellow worker, friend or relative that you have no compassion. We've all done them. What I am saying is that if there is a pattern, a consistency to this behavior, then maybe we do lack a little compassion. And maybe that accounts for repeatedly attracting certain situations to us. Situations that cause us more and more problems and more and more anxiety which give us more and more excuses to blame, explain and complain thus perpetuating a compassionless cycle in ourselves and in our environment.

We all have times when our moods are different. Times when we lack the energy, the effort or the desire to always act in the best way possible toward others. And I believe that knowing this; having that awareness that the other person is human just like us, allows them and us the space to be flexible, tolerant and compassionate.

Compassion is the understanding of those changes. What I'd like to do here is to build an awareness in all of us that the people we work with on a day to day basis have changes, emotions, loves, defeats, peaks and valleys and that this is something we can keep in mind when we approach those with whom we work. And that we cannot get away with treating them as if they were a machine.

Compassion is about giving and receiving. There's a time to give and a time to receive. And both are necessary if we are ever going to be whole and complete within ourselves. *You cannot be a whole and complete person if you only receive.* And you cannot be a whole and complete person if you only give. There has to be a balance.

───────── LIFE LINE ─────────

Allow people to give on their own level and
accept the privilege of their gift.

────────────  ────────────

If someone wants to give to you, let them. That's part of the balance. When you feel the time is right to give to another, do it. How do you know when to give and when to receive? Trust your instincts. Listen to your intuition. Also, consider this, receiving is probably the highest form of giving, you can't even have a giver unless you have a receiver. Allow people to give on their own level and accept the privilege of their gift.

This is what I mean by compassion on a day to day basis. Unlike the dictionary, I'm not suggesting sympathy but rather empathy. And there is a difference. Sympathy is entering into the feelings of another. It's the type of intimacy that we reserve for someone especially close to us. Empathy is identifying and sharing our feelings with another in an effort to understand them better.

So, how can we show more empathy to others? I have a few points that may help:

Ways to Show Empathy:

1. *Acknowledgment.* Acknowledging the other person's feelings without trying to dismiss or discount them. Rather than saying, "You shouldn't feel that way," it might be better to say something like, "You sound like you're angry about this." Acknowledging: telling the other person that their feelings, whatever they are, are okay to have.

2. *Be supportive.* And by supporting, I don't mean that you have to go in there and fix the situation for them, or make it better. By supporting, I mean that you convey to them that you are there for them. And that means listening, sharing, coming up with possible alternatives for them to choose from, and many times referring them to someone who can help them discover alternatives. Most importantly, though, it means doing all of the above without a judgment. It means that, although, you may not agree with how they have handled situations in the past, that you are there for them now, to listen and share and offer suggestions without speaking out, without attaching any rightness or wrongness to what they've done.

And if you feel your judgments are interfering with your capacity to have compassion, then *walk a mile in their moccasins.*

By compassion, I mean I want someone to be compassionate enough to say, "I care, I understand, I'm listening." Instead of saying that they're listening and then turning around and dumping all of their advice on you. "Gee, I'm sorry to hear about your mother, I lost my mother too and you just have to get over it and move on with your life." That's not compassion. That's discounting the other person's feelings and telling them what they should do. And whatever is right for you may not be right for someone else.

Compassion is allowing the other person to find their own peace, and their own way out of the situation without hearing all the "shoulds" and the "shouldn'ts". Compassion is not trying to take the pain or the problem away. It's hearing the problem and the pain and telling them that you are there to listen, support, encourage, and help if they need it. And that can be easy to do if you remember to *acknowledge* and *support.*

When we offer help to another, no matter what form it takes, we liberate ourselves from our own egos and see that we are all worthwhile, valuable people on the same flight together and that helps make the journey a little easier for us all.

———— LIFE LINE ————

The difference between listening and hearing
is that we hear with our ears,
but we listen with our minds.

Listening

Here's a story that illustrates the point that a lot of us hear but not many of us listen.

Three people are riding together on a bus. The first guy says, "Boy, it's sure windy, today." The second man, sitting next to him is not paying much attention and replies, "It's not Wednesday, it's Thursday." The third guy, turns to them both and adds, "I'm thirsty too. Let's all get off and get something to drink." When you aren't listening it can get pretty confusing, can't it?

The difference between listening and hearing is that we hear with our ears but we listen with our minds. To learn we must listen. Real learning comes from listening and it seems to me that in this super, high-tech age of sophisticated communication, many of us have quite simply forgotten just how to listen effectively to what's being said. Communication is a two-way street. If no one listens, there simply is no communication.

Many times someone who speaks at length about a subject can go on and on and on without really saying much of anything. We notice how his listeners begin tuning him out. One way to look at how to speak more effectively is to listen first!

So, what does it take to be a good listener? Let's take a look at some good listening skills:

To Be a Good Listener:

1. *Be 100% present, show interest.* Your body language can say a lot to a person talking to you. Show you care about what is being said by standing or sitting comfortably, but alertly, eyes focused on the person. This immediately shows that you have an open mind toward whatever is being said. Notice, I said *shows* you have an open mind. In a little bit, I'll talk about *having* an open mind.

2. *Take what you hear seriously and respond.* If you hear something you understand or agree with, say so. Quick feedback gives confidence to the speaker and propels the conversation. If you don't understand something or have a question, tactfully stop the speaker and ask for clarification. But do this as soon as the question comes up. This is another way of telling the speaker that you're listening to what he's saying.

3. *Actively listen.* It's not always true of all situations, but in general, the way you listen is important. A good idea would be to write down what you believe to be key words, phrases or points to remember. And then don't be afraid to go back over those points with the speaker at the end of the conversation in order to clarify your understanding.

4. *Relaxed concentration.* Listening requires the mental effort to concentrate. However, don't sit there with your hand to your head with such seriousness that you forget to relax a little. Just sit back, breath normally, and know that you'll hear everything you need to and if you don't, ask questions.

When I talk about concentrating when you're listening, I can't help but talk about the mind wandering. And it does. With everyone. And it's okay. In fact, the brain can listen 500 times faster than a speaker talks. So, naturally, there's a lot of down time in between sentences, phrases and even words. So, it's perfectly natural for your mind to drift a little when you're listening to someone. The point here is that you need to catch yourself when you're drifting too much.

You need to listen for key words and phrases and the only way you can do that is to ask questions in your own mind, "What is this person saying to me?" The speaker may make a statement and then launch in to a story about it. Now, you're listening and you're letting your mind wander because you understand the point of the story. If however, you don't understand the point, then you need to tell your mind, "Hey, wait a second, let's listen to this story. Maybe we can comprehend what she's trying to say."

5. *Have an open attitude.* I mentioned this briefly before, (about looking as if you have an open mind). Now you actually have to have one. And one way to do this is to first realize that nothing is carved in stone. Be open and receptive to any ideas presented by the speaker no matter how off-the-wall they may appear. Besides, even if the ideas presented are never used, they may give you ideas about something else that *can* be used. Having an open, receptive attitude in the beginning can help you see alternatives that you hadn't considered before. It also allows you to be more open and honest when you speak.

6. *Know why you want to listen.* This is really important, because none of us listens the same way to everything, and it's okay not to.

So, what are we listening for? Are we listening for enjoyment, understanding or evaluation? If you go to the movies, it's safe to say that you're listening for enjoyment. Understanding comes from listening to someone at a meeting or a lecture conveying information we need or want to learn.

LIFE LINE

Change happens when we listen for understanding. Growth happens when we incorporate that understanding into our daily lives.

Evaluation comes into play when we listen to several topics and see how we can incorporate them into our own lives, either at work or at home. It's how we judge what is being said and what points will be utilized in our belief system.

Change happens when we listen for understanding. Growth happens when we incorporate that understanding into our daily lives. Therefore, all growth starts first with effective listening.

Learn to listen and not just hear words. Learn to understand and not just nod your head. Learn to grow from where you are to where you would like to be.

CHAPTER 3:
TAKING VALUES TO HEART

Ethics? What do we mean when we use the term ethics? Many people are not clear on what the concept of ethics means. Well, they may not understand the word "ethics" but they do know what ethics feels like.

I believe most everyone has a sense of what feels right and what feels wrong, and we exercise that right/wrong feeling in every decision we make, every day.

In the Random House Dictionary we find that ethics is:

"a system of moral principles or rules of conduct or values for a group of people or individuals." Now, obviously, this can and does change greatly depending upon which part of the world you're living in. Many societies and religions still accept, and encourage, a man to take several wives. Others feel this is not ethical.

But when we bring it down to the basics, it comes to a simple matter of what is right and what is wrong. And of course, this easily becomes a matter of individual conscience in many areas.

There are legal ethics and moral ethics. Some cultures still practice animal sacrifices, over here it is considered legally and morally unethical.

But how does all this apply to me in my own day-to-day situations? What is right and what is wrong for each one of us? Tough question for most of us because many times we tend to look at the situation and put it on a scale of importance. Example: You go to the store and buy a loaf of bread. You hand the checker a five dollar bill and she gives you the incorrect change . . . in your favor! Do you tell her about it or do you keep it? Well, you say, a small issue. You may feel justified in keeping the money. After all, it was the checker's mistake! Some of you might, however, acknowledge the error and give the money back. But it seems like such a small thing. Many of us might not place a great deal of importance on rightness or wrongness of the choice made. In a larger situation, we might choose differently. Maybe. Maybe not.

I believe that *how* we choose in the small situations that face us will ultimately determine how we choose in the big ones later on.

Let's look at some common justifications that we may use sometimes:

1. *Everybody does it.* I don't know about you, but this seems to be a big one wherever I go. If Bob and Bill and Jane and Betty are doing it, why can't I?

The message that one clearly gets from this line of reasoning is that you are willing to push aside whatever you believe in your heart of hearts to be right or wrong and replace it with someone else's standards. Notice that you have shifted responsibility here. You are not owning your decision. You're placing it on whatever everybody else is doing. And it may not be the opinion of everybody else. Have you checked around to see?

Now, I'm not suggesting that you should have a different viewpoint than anyone else. I am suggesting that you take responsibility for whatever your viewpoint is and not simply decide to do, or not to do something based solely on "everyone else".

2. *They owe it to me.* I usually hear people speak of this when there is declining interest in the company they work for or in the job they're doing. What it really tells me is that there is a strong undercurrent of resentment going on with one or more people. A resentment is unexpressed anger that's been put on hold, so to speak, to be dealt with later and that later usually translates into behavior that means: "You didn't do this for me, so I'm going to do this to you to make up for it."

It's a great excuse, blaming someone else for your behavior. However, the person who really deserves the blame is you for not effectively dealing with the anger in the first place. And when you really get down to the bottom of it, anger is usually a secondary emotion anyway. If we were to respond to our first feeling you can bet we wouldn't lash out in anger. Anger most often stems from a lack of understanding.

3. *Role models.* What's the boss or supervisor doing? Is he saying one thing and doing another? Is he telling you how to do your job and not taking care of his very well? How did you observe your parents in situations around the house or other places? Did they always take responsibility for what they did or did they have excuses?

These are some of the more common examples of misdirected ethics that I've noticed over the years.

So, how do we overcome them? What's the appropriate way to choose effectively so that it's both a reflection of our own values as well as the company we work with? I believe we can feel ethics, and I use the "F.E.E.L." principle for determining ethical standards:

F. *Does it Feel right?* What is your inner feeling telling you about the situation? Are you comfortable or uncomfortable and why?

E. *Is it Equitable?* Is it a win/win situation, fair to both sides involved? Remember, if someone comes out totally losing, the resolution of that situation is too one-sided. Look for a way in which everyone gains something and work toward that gain.

E. *Is it Emotional?* This is different than, "How does it feel?" What I mean by emotional is: how much of your emotions in a given situation are you allowing to determine a course of action? If the situation is completely emotion-backed you may have a problem. Remember the balance. All things work in balance . . . right brain, left brain, heart as well as head, the intuition and the intellect, the non-linear and the linear. Everything seeks balance. Don't allow too much of one and not enough of the other.

L. *Is it Legal?* Am I abiding by the laws of the company, by the laws of the state, by the laws of the country? Am I governed by any law that I might be breaking? Take a look at this.

Every time you enter into a situation in which you believe your values are being challenged you can use this little test to check things out. Of course the bottom line behind all of this is: are we taking responsibility for the choices we make or are we passing the buck and saying, "Well, everybody does it," or "They owe it to me, so it's okay," or "That's what he says but that's not what he does, so I'll do it too."!

There is no right way to do a wrong thing. Take responsibility for what you do. Check your motives in whatever you say and do with the "F.E.E.L." test. Be aware. Stay aware. And stay open to change when you catch yourself making an ethical slip.

——————— LIFE LINE ———————

There is no right way to do a wrong thing.

And let's not just talk about change. Let's participate in it. Let's participate in it at home and work, physically, mentally and emotionally.

Some people don't know the difference between right and wrong. They don't know because of habit or perhaps some greater psychological problem, but the end result is that their feelings are buried. However, emotionally stable people do know the difference. Ernest Hemingway put the question of ethics very simply, and it has validity. He said, "What is moral is what you feel good after and what is immoral is what you feel bad after."

For me, integrity is something that I endeavor to live every day, in every decision that I make. And when I have a doubt about it, I check my feelings.

Wouldn't it be nice to leave the house open and the keys in the car, or not have to use keys for anything? The ideal situation would be that we never have to have any security systems at all! Ideally, that would be great. Unfortunately, there will always be starving people. There will always be people who will steal. There will always be people who are out of work. There will always be people fighting for money. And there will always be people who are wealthy, people with healthy relationships, happy lives, healthy lives, and growing lives. And you know, maybe that's part of the beauty of this planet. The beauty of our society. There will always be that mix. People are always going through transition.

We, as people, are the elite of the planet. We have been given a great gift. That's the gift of choice. And the choices we make today directly determine our future environment. They literally determine that! To do right or to do wrong.

So, what kind of choices do you want to make? What kind of choices do you want your friends, neighbors, and fellow workers to make? And are you willing to live with those choices in the long run? Are you willing to look at the choices you make every day with a new perspective? A more positive perspective? A more respectful perspective? The choice is yours.

Ethics & Values

Shared values are those qualities we establish between ourselves that are the framework for the decisions we make and the actions we take. When these qualities are indeed clear and shared, everyone and everything is working in sync toward the accomplishment of the goal.

When the values are in conflict, everyone is rationalizing and justifying, and when they aren't going behind someone's back, they are undermining the whole reason for working together in the first place—the goal.

Balanced values are working when everyone clearly understands the mission and the goal and all "row the boat" in the same direction they all have agreed upon. They not only cooperate with one another, but their communication is clearer and most importantly, the task is accomplished with a positive result.

——————— **LIFE LINE** ———————

"Every man takes care that his neighbor shall not cheat him. But a day comes when he begins to care that he does not cheat his neighbor."

–Ralph Waldo Emerson

———————— ✍ ————————

The word "values" comes from the Latin word "valere" meaning to be strong, and/or to be worth. For any thing, attitude, ideal, purpose, or goal to be of value, it must be the object of a preference or a judgment of importance.

The word "ethics" is from the Greek word "ethos," meaning custom or usage. A system of moral principles. The rules of conduct recognized in respect to a particular class of human actions or a particular group, culture, etc. Any object or quality desirable as a means or as an end in itself.

It seems to me that, in terms of today's standards, ethics has to do with our behavior and implementation of the values we hold true for ourselves and those with whom we associate.

Personal and Business Values

Everyone has degrees by which they operate. Situations are rarely black or white. Personal and organizational values may match, but if one side weighs too strongly, a complement value may be essential for project accomplishment. Example: urgency may keep us focused on accomplishing the mission, but it may also result in manipulation if not balanced with compassion. Loyalty may be weighed too heavily if not balanced with the perspective of truth. We see this in government and also have observed poorly balanced values in the corporate world.

The ideals, customs, beliefs, and standards of a person, society or organization toward which the people of the group have an affective regard will dictate the overriding culture. Values are rarely noticed and only occasionally discussed. They usually show up as the result of an action and then only if we choose to look at and take responsibility for them.

Values are a code of behavior upon which we determine how we treat others and how we want ourselves to be treated. It's interesting to note how much they all seem to overlap. Someone would not be considered loyal, without possessing honor. It would as well be difficult for someone to practice tolerance without also displaying integrity. Of the four, tolerance might seem to be the most difficult. If one had made a commitment to a friend, he or she would have to possess some degree of tolerance if the commitment concerned something that was not a part of a shared attitude, opinion, or practice. Another point: these values do not necessarily have anything to do with "right or wrong." They can work as effectively in the Mafia or a tribe of headhunters with their own code of ethics as they would in a community or an association.

When we talk about values and look at how they work in our lives, they seem to fall into three categories:

I. Individual responsibilities related to values.

II. Association or company responsibilities related to values.

III. Individual and association values related to social responsibilities.

The values we learn, develop, and use overlap and touch our lives much like overlapping circles. At the center, the area where the rings come together, is the area where our core beliefs lie.

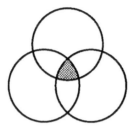

Core beliefs usually start in our childhood based on parents, and other significant teachers in our lives.

"Tell the truth."

"Do your own homework."

"Help others."

"Share your toys."

"Don't hit."

According to Parent/Teachers Richard and Linda Eyre, *"A true and universally acceptable 'value' is one that produces behavior that is beneficial both to the practitioner and to those on whom it is practiced. It is a principle that either accomplishes well-being or prevents harm or does both."*

Those individual values that we learned as children growing up tend to stay with us in one form or another for the rest of our lives. The only thing that will cause them to be directly changed is if we experience an overwhelming force in society that shows us the consequences of not having certain specific shared values. An example would be: killing is sanctioned in war, the extreme of values in conflict.

The next level of values that we typically experience comes when we work either for a company or an association.

For instance, if you work for a newspaper company selling a daily paper, the company will give you guidelines to follow to complete the various goals of your job, for instance: keep accurate records of the newspapers, and the money collected, make sure that they are delivered in an easy-to-spot place, and "Will you please get the

Sunday paper ready for Sunday delivery?" Timeliness is, of course, part of the equation.

These are rules and guidelines that express the values of accountability, honesty, loyalty, reliability, and a sense of urgency.

The next level of values that we experience comes when we either work through our church or an association that deals directly with the community in which we live. Most of us spend so much of our lives dealing with the first two areas that we barely have time to spend in the third, but the area of social responsibility is more important than one would think.

When Ben Cohen and Jerry Greenfield first designed their ice cream company they did so around two specific objectives: Jerry said, "If it's not fun, why do it?" Ben said, "Business has a responsibility to give back to the community."

From those two statements given at the first anniversary of their Ice Cream parlor, came a formal Mission Statement in 1988 that dedicated the firm "To the creation and demonstration of a new corporate concept of linked prosperity." It consisted of three interrelated parts:

A product mission: "To make, distribute, and sell the finest-quality all natural ice cream."

A social mission: "To operate the company in a way that actively recognizes the central role that business plays in the structure of society by initiating innovative ways to improve the quality of life."

An economic mission: "To operate the company on a sound financial basis."

They had exercised their mission not only within the company through picnics and profit sharing, but through the vendors they purchase from and the dealers they sell to.

They designed stationary printed on 100% non-deinked, post-consumer paper. And they founded their own social cause called One Percent for Peace. The group actively promoted the idea of redirecting 1 percent of the U.S. military budget to peaceful and humanitarian activities. Ben & Jerry's "Peace Pop" set aside some of its funds as well as its packaging to advance this cause.

Ultimately, all of these values ... *our* values, create a living, breathing sense of moral binding. In the final analysis, why we act, and how we act toward our family, friends, neighbors, business, and community reflects our core beliefs.

We all have to operate in a world larger than ourselves. Our values established in childhood, and later developed through the rules and policies and companies and associations and shaped by our responsibilities to the community, are greater than any corporate "bottom line." They are a direct reflection of ourselves and they do come back to haunt us, *if* we don't take the time to examine them and their importance to us, for they ultimately determine how we are treated in return—cause and effect.

At its inception, Ben & Jerry also decided to change the way their company measured success at the end of each year. They developed an alternative "two-part bottom line" that assesses the year by how much money is left over as well as by how much the company has helped the community.

And Ben & Jerry are only two examples of businesses and associations who chose to reposition themselves as a part in this growing idea of companies for social responsibility. Other organizations include such names as: Esprit de Corp. (clothing manufacturer), Celestial Seasonings (herbal tea), Sunrise Medical (wheelchair manufacturer), Newman's Own (food products), The Body Shop and Aveda Corp. (cosmetics.) These are just a few companies who see the need and stress the significance of strong values in business, because it not only strengthens the people involved by creating a greater sense of moral binding, but also leads to a level of trust among the people with whom they work.

When we all help, respect, are loyal to, take responsibility for, trust and are committed to a level of excellence and integrity, we cannot help but receive the same in return. The circle is complete.

With this understanding let's take a brief look at a few values. Most values seem to center around four ideals:

Honor: honesty, fairness, trustworthiness in one's beliefs and actions.

Loyalty: faithfulness to commitments, obligations, friends, family, or organization.

Tolerance: a fair, objective, and permissive attitude toward those whose opinions, practices, race, religion, nationality, etc. differ from one's own.

Integrity: adherence to moral and ethical principles. The state of being whole, entire or undiminished. Integrity is the thread that runs through all shared values showing a consistency of core beliefs.

How to Use the Value-Based Concept

Actions speak louder than words. People don't follow your finger, they follow your feet. I believe you should *tell* the world, but you have to *show* it first! It's so easy to escalate your virtues when talking, but in actuality, walking the talk is the test of a truly committed person. It is true, actions do speak louder than words. Thought determines what you want; action determines what you get, and how you are viewed by others.

Understanding right from wrong. With the kinds of events surrounding us today (political improprieties, international and corporate espionage and human rights infringements) sometimes the differences between right and wrong are not easily seen. We don't always know if our values are on-track or working toward the goals we established for ourselves and the group with which we work.

"It is so easy for most of us to live without considering whether our behavior is in harmony with our values that too often we see only in hindsight the implications of our actions." – Gregory Stock

Are you making decisions that are consistent with the values you have established and say you hold true to yourself? With this in mind let's take a look at a Values Checklist.

1. Are my values clear and consistent?

2. Are my values in consensus with others?

3. Are my values in harmony with my actions?

4. Am I able to adjust to change without compromising my values?

5. Does it feel right?

Remember, values are chosen, not assigned. We can always re-evaluate our values based on our actions and make adjustments.

CHAPTER 4:
THE ACCOUNTABILITY FACTOR

Whenever we speak of accountability, we're talking about responsibility: responsible, explainable, liable, and reliable to the job, how it's done, when it's completed and probably how well it's completed too.

What all these traits have in common is honesty. I don't feel you can really be accountable for anything unless you are first honest. You sure don't want to be accountable to someone for something if a lie is involved somewhere.

——————— **LIFE LINE** ———————

One lie can damage a hundred truths.

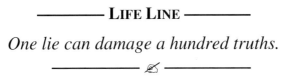

A familiar quote from the Bible states, "Know the truth, and the truth shall set you free." I like what Garfield the cat adds, "but first it will make you miserable." This is often so true. But in the long run, the truth is the best course of action. For one thing, it's a lot less complicated than a lie. First we must know the truth about something and accept it. No matter how serious something may seem to be, the truth never does as much damage as a lie. One lie can damage a hundred truths.

—————— LIFE LINE ——————

One of the most powerful tools that
any of us have is a track record.

Reliability

To begin is simple. If you say you're going to be somewhere, be there. If you say you're going to do something, you do it. Simply put: say what you mean and mean what you say. Soon you will create the habit of becoming dependable. That's something you can show people through your actions and through your words; that you walk like you talk.

And many times when we're new on the job, that's all we have to show people. Does he show up on time? Is she following through with what she said she was going to do? And then, if you do, the manager, co-worker, or boss begins to assign you an attitude of reliability. You can be relied on to do what you say. Actions speak louder than words. It's an old expression but it's true. So, take a look at your actions. Do they speak loudly? Could you depend on you, if you needed to?

Reliability leads to dependability. And with dependability you prove yourself responsible and in turn gain a great deal more trust with the people you work with.

One of the most powerful tools that anyone of us has is a track record. It's what we have that shows what we have done in the past. Most importantly, what have we said and what have we completed the way we said we would? Now, I can't ask this question without adding, "In most cases." Many times, circumstances are going to come up resulting in some unforeseen changes, and adjustments have to be made. But how do you respond to the changes? Do you notice what happens, do you take responsibility and develop a new plan of action to meet and overcome the unexpected? Or do you go around blaming and complaining?

Take a look at your reaction. Through our increasing awareness our minds become more powerful and we are able to more quickly see, accept and deal with the changes that occur. *Light overcomes darkness. The greater encompasses the lesser.* And so, *the aware mind has power over the unaware mind* and therefore has the ability to overcome the obstacles inherent in change.

The more aware we are of how we can work with our managers, co-workers, peers, neighbors, and friends, the more reliable, responsible and accountable we become.

There is one thing that doesn't show up on any balance sheet anywhere, but it does in our own hearts and minds. And that is this: when you are responsible . . . you feel good about yourself. Without responsibility to someone or something you cannot grow effectively, and if we cannot grow then we can very easily set ourselves up for self-defeating behavior: excuses, blaming, complaining, excessive judgments and eventually becoming irresponsible.

Now, there are always two sides to everything. What we call the upside and the downside. The upside to responsibility is that you receive all the strokes, the positives, the compliments for a job well done, for input well received and appreciated. The downside is the self-defeating behavior which leads to people not trusting you. They won't rely on you and therefore you won't get the promotion, the raise, the accolades and you won't get the support to continue doing anything. We all need some sort of support in whatever we're doing in any job.

But perhaps the most significant aspect of not being responsible . . . or accountable to the job at hand is the fact that you now become a "high-maintenance" person to the company. You have to be watched, checked over and checked on constantly and as a result, you become costly to carry on the payroll. You're not only not doing your job, but you will eventually drag others down as well. It happens. The high-maintenance person always drags others into the black hole of energy waste, causing others to pick up the slack. It's not only time consuming, but it's draining on the group.

How Accountable are You?

Okay, so how accountable are you? Let's find out. Let's just ask some simple questions:

First: *How do you react whenever you're given a new project?* This is interesting because your reaction to situations can usually tell you a lot. Do you feel overloaded or panicked? If you do, do you speak up about it and try to come up with alternatives, or do you simply complain quietly to others? It's important to remember: the accountable person is accountable to himself first. If you can't be accountable to your own needs, how can you possibly be accountable to the needs of others?

Second: *What's your track record?* Do you walk like you talk? Do you do what you say and say what you do? And how have you dealt with the changes that have come your way?

Third: *What's your CQ?* Your cooperation quotient? On a scale of one to five, five being best, how well do you cooperate with others?

Contrary to popular belief, most things do not get done by one person. If they did, we'd only need one person for every department. There's a flight crew for every scheduled commercial flight for one simple reason: the flight cannot rely on just one person. So, do you utilize others to help you, or do you take on the entire load yourself?

Fourth: *What's your reaction when others come to you for help?* Are you cooperative or do you just try to slide past it as quickly as possible.

Fifth: *What are other's attitudes towards you?* Do your co-workers, managers and friends come to you with questions looking for solutions? If they do, this is a clear indicator that you must be doing something to generate a feeling in them that you can be relied on, counted on to get things done or at the very least, you have some valuable input toward a possible solution.

———— LIFE LINE ————

Anything that takes us from where we are to where we want to be is growth.

———————— ✍ ————————

What are the rewards for being accountable? Well, I think they're obvious. For one thing you gain the respect of your peers and manager. On the more tangible side, you get the promotion, you get the raise. You move upward toward new responsibilities, newer challenges and this helps us grow as individuals, and as part of a team. Anything that takes us from where we are to where we want to be is growth.

On the other side of the sheet is: what happens when we are not accountable or responsible? We usually have less energy. We seem more confused, defensive, blaming, complaining and spend more time explaining than doing anything else. And the most tangible result of those kinds of things is the simple fact that we won't last long at the job.

If we continue to deny, or not own, our irresponsible behavior, the pattern will continue into every new job we encounter. Over and over again. I like the statement, "Wherever I go, there I am." and guess what? So does the problem.

Actually, it really takes more energy to be irresponsible than it does to be responsible. Being responsible reliable and accountable shows in many other ways. You become more fulfilled, happier, brighter, and quicker. People want to be around you. They want to work with you. It feels better to be a responsible person. You show others that you're cooperative, easy to be with and that what you do matters because you're showing everyone that it matters to you first. That's what really matters most of all in the long run. Like I said at the outset . . . if you can't be accountable to yourself, for your own happiness, fulfillment and sense of well-being, how can you possibly be accountable to anyone else?

CHAPTER 5:
ARE YOU TRUSTWORTHY?

In the overall scheme of things, trust would have to be the cornerstone of any relationship. *Any* relationship.

Trust accepts, believes, allows. Trust has faith. Trust enhances. Trust never tries to control or change but rather allows for change. In an atmosphere with healthy trust anything is possible. Without it, you can't have any solid, workable, or reliable relationship. Trust is essential. And today, trust is in short supply.

None of us is 100% trusting or trustworthy to someone else because we are dealing with different values. Yet, the more trusting we are, the more likely we are to be trusted by others.

Trust starts with you. If you don't trust yourself how can you trust anyone else? Now, I know what you're thinking. "What does he mean, trust myself? Of course I trust myself. It's those other people out there who I have to worry about!" Whenever I hear anyone talk like that I see them once again looking outside themselves for something that really needs to be looked for on the inside. In these times of double dealings, corporate espionage and a general lack of ethics in government, our confidence in our institutions has been slowly eroding, and our level of trust has gone down. But just because there are untrustworthy events coming to light does not mean you should go around not trusting people. What it does mean is that you should take extra care perhaps, to look at yourself in situations where your feelings of trust come up and see how you respond.

What is Trust?

Here are some questions you might ask yourself:

1. *Do I trust myself and my feelings?*
2. *Can I trust my feelings enough to act on them?*
3. *Am I willing to trust others a little bit at a time?*

What does trust feel like? Trust feels confident, dependable, loyal, honest, self-assured, *and safe*. I think safe is a key word here. Maybe it's feeling safe enough to express your feelings, ideas and thoughts openly and freely without having them discounted or criticized. And I believe that the safety we create with other people must first start with ourselves, feeling safe and comfortable with whatever's going on inside us at any moment and trusting that it'll be okay.

——————— **LIFE LINE** ———————

Trust is not gained overnight,
but it can be lost in an instant.

——————— ✍ ———————

When you're on a roller coaster, and you feel your stomach just drop away after you've headed straight down, you trust that your stomach is going to feel calm in a few seconds when the coaster levels out again, don't you? When you trust yourself you don't create static in the world around you. You have little or no chance of attracting negative circumstances to you. And those that do happen don't last very long and can remain relatively painless. When you are trusting of yourself you create an environment of confidence, security and stability. And you send out a message that says—in spite of immediate appearances, everything is going to work out. Everything is going to be safe.

Trust is not gained overnight. It very definitely comes over a period of time, bit by bit. In looking at different companies hiring practices, I notice many of them hire on recommendation or track record. They have trust established with a friend or worker; a belief that what they are told is usually true. A track record speaks for itself. What has the person done in the past? Is he always late or generally on time? Do they handle the tasks effectively or do they come back with excuses? A track record will help sort this out.

Trust can best be described as a firm belief in the honesty, reliability and ability of another, and the confident expectation to commit something to another's care. Trust is not always quickly or easily gained but it can be lost in an instant. And rebuilding trust can take a lot more time and focus than someone is willing to spend.

We are all creatures of habit. All habits are pieces of behavior built up little bit by little bit. If you want to change a habit, change your behavior. You are going to create an attitude of trust by your behavior. Are you fun to be around? If you are, you are creating a track record through your behavior of being fun to be around. And therefore, people can generally trust that you'll be fun. "So, who says I have to trust anyone? Hey, listen, I've been burned too many times. What could possibly happen if I don't trust?" Without trust what are you left with? Think about that for a moment.

What usually shows up when there is little or no trust is doubt, worry, anxiety, fear—all self-defeating behaviors. Without trust you get into jealousy and envy. Suddenly, you see others as having opportunities that you don't have or you think that they're doing things behind your back.

Not trusting is too high a price for me to pay.

Trust implies leadership because it translates into letting the other person do their job the way they said they would and seeing what happens. If they don't, you certainly have the option not to trust them to do that job again.

Notice too though, that when you send out trusting signals to others, you are telling them that you believe in them and in their abilities and that their efforts won't go unnoticed or unappreciated.

Developing Trust

Here are some ideas to think about regarding trust:

1. ***Be willing to turn it over.*** Remember, when you're flying in an airplane you don't have to be watching every part of the fuselage and engine to know and trust that you will get where you want to go.

2. ***Be willing to accept that what an individual says, she will do,*** and see what happens.

3. ***Keep your fingers out of it.*** You don't keep stopping your car to check under the hood to see if things are still running right. So, don't become too preoccupied with constantly checking up on how the work is progressing.

4. (Perhaps hardest but most important.) ***Be willing to take a risk.*** You have to risk trusting someone else and guess what? They have to risk trusting you. Just do it in stages and see what happens.

So, what's the payoff for all this? Peace of mind for one thing. And maybe the chance to discover how well you work with others as part of a team. A machine is made up of many parts and gears. And each trusts that the other will do their job at the right time. And when that trust is allowed to develop it only encourages more trust and support and safety, and low and behold, everyone's attitude begins to express that. We become more open, honest and fun to be with.

──────── **LIFE LINE** ────────

"There is a spark within each of us that can be fanned into flame."

—Brandies

──────── ✍ ────────

CHAPTER 6:
BURNOUT OR BURN UP

In this age of climbing the ladder of success, no word has received as much attention in the last several years as the word: *"burnout"!*

When someone is beginning to get so attached to their job and performance level to such a point that they seem to be either walking around in a daze, or so totally absorbed that the line between the job and the person totally disappears, we say that such a person is "burned out".

But what does this really mean? Well, quite simply, career burnout is a syndrome that affects most working people at one time or another. Stress, boredom and general dissatisfaction with the job we're doing all contribute to burnout. It's the unhappy feeling one gets when he or she no longer feels that they're making a difference in their work. It's a slow build-up of all the little frustrations, compromises and conflicts that take place over days, weeks, months and yes, even *years!* And it can translate into either not caring about the job anymore, extreme restlessness or both.

Burnout is a growing problem everywhere. A study by Opinion Research of Princeton, New Jersey clearly showed that one-third of 3,000 managers reported increased stress to perform at work. This is up sharply from recent years.

What's the problem, then? With all the new awareness toward job effectiveness training out there, why is the stress level going up instead of down? Well, one of the answers is the fact that in the last several years more and more management jobs have been consolidated or eliminated, subsequently increasing the work-load on the remaining positions. In short, people are having to do more and more work over a shorter period of time and are expected to get the same or better results. And what happens is that after awhile, the job begins to control the person instead of the other way around. It's not that these people are poor performers, it's just that they have been so burdened with work for such an extended period of time that they just don't have much energy or enthusiasm for the next assignment or project.

Perhaps the worst part of burnout is the people it affects. Usually, the best people. People who care about their jobs and put in the extra hours to make things work smoothly for others, people who genuinely strive to make things better for the company and the product or services it provides. These are the people burnout affects.

Burnout Symptoms

Here are some questions you might ask yourself concerning burnout:

1. Does the thought of going to work cause you to feel depressed, irritable or anxious?

2. Do you feel your mind wandering from the work at hand at any given time of day?

3. Do you feel a loss of effectiveness in the decisions you make?

4. Do you feel everyone is expecting more from you and you feel obligated to meet those expectations no matter what?

5. Do you feel a general loss of energy no matter how much sleep you get?

Take a close look at your answers. Although there is no precise medical definition for burnout, one of the most common aspects is a general wearing down or shift of our hopes and ideals. The enthusiasm and positive attitudes that we took into a job have slowly but surely evaporated into a malaise of indifference, anxiousness or irritation.

Conquering Burnout

So, what do we do about it? Here are some points to consider:

1. *Acceptance.* If burnout is something that you begin to suspect in yourself, don't condemn yourself for having it. No matter what feeling or condition that comes over us, the first and best step we can take toward any kind of recovery is to accept it. Trying to minimize, rationalize or deny it away will only make the situation persist and could very easily manifest into a serious health problem: heart attack, high blood pressure, alcohol, or drug abuse. Acceptance is the first step in any kind of recovery process.

2. *Ask for help.* Feeling burned-out is a condition that happens to all of us at one time or another. It has nothing to do with will power, lack of intelligence, motivation or desire. It's simply a mental, physical and emotional signal that our body's telling us to *take a break!* And sometimes, especially when the signals come from so many parts of us, it takes a step toward someone else, by calling out for someone who will understand us and trust us and help us get back on track. Someone who won't minimize, or dismiss what we're feeling.

Believe me, burnout is not something that's imagined. It's a very real condition.

3. *Take action.* Suffering career burnout does not necessarily mean having to change careers. It does mean that you need to stop and begin to take another look at just what your goals and expectations are and begin to explore ways they can be fulfilled that are most beneficial to you. This is a key word here . . . *you!* Not your husband, or wife, your mother, father, brother, daughter, son . . . but *you!!*

I'm not suggesting that you put all of these wonderful parts of your life completely out of your mind. I am suggesting that you begin by putting yourself and your well-being at the top of the list. You can't take care of your family unless you can first take care of yourself. A good example of this is when the flight attendant on an airplane is giving you instructions on what to do in case of an emergency. You are told that in the event of a loss of oxygen in the cabin, masks will drop from above your seat and that if you have a small child you must always put your mask on first, and then assist your child. The same principle applies here.

Take a look at your goals and ideals first and see which direction *you* want to go. In the long run, your family will probably support you.

As I said before, taking action on burnout doesn't always mean that you have to quit your job. It can start with simple things like a vacation, personal leave, exercise or just a mental health day-off. The point behind step number three is to do something to change the situation. The sooner the better.

4. *Take a look at your work and play habits.* Do you allow time in there for any thing spontaneous or are you the victim of a structured rut . . . doing the same thing the same way on the same day over and over. Break out of the structure. Change your routine. Explore ways of doing things differently. Experiment with a new sport or hobby, even if it's only for a day or a week. Move outside your normal self into a self that is having fun looking at something new, something different. Maybe it's something you always wanted to do but never took the time before. Make the time. This will give your head a big break and will do wonders for your attitude.

5. *Reflection—a quiet, pensive, introspective mental retreat.* All right, I know that some of you out there are saying, "I knew he was going to get around to this. I may be a little stressed on the job but I know I don't want to go up the side of some mountain and sit in the lotus position all day to find myself." And you know what? You don't have to. You can sit very comfortably at home or in your office, if you like. And reflection does not have to be static. It can be running, walking, exercising, breathing—anything but sleeping, talking or watching.

Reflection is mostly listening. Listening to what you say. Listening to yourself. Listening to that little voice inside us all. That's the voice. Yes, the one saying "What voice?" right now! It's not your brain. It's your heart. You ask "What's the difference?" Your brain says, "Put the key in the ignition, turn the engine on and let's go." Your heart says, "I want to drive to the park today and have fun."

Your heart tells you what you really want to do. Your brain tries to figure out the ways to do it. Your heart says, "I want to try hang-gliding and see if it's as much fun as it looks." Your brain says, "How can I figure out ways to hang-glide today? Do I know somebody? Can I get some lessons first?"

You listen to your brain 90% of the time, especially when you're working. Don't you think you should start giving your heart equal time? After all, you listen to your heart subconsciously. How about listening to your heart a little more consciously. That's what reflection allows you to do.

—————— **LIFE LINE** ——————

If it doesn't feel right in your heart, it's never going to feel right in your head.

After all is said and done, it's your heart that ultimately chooses what you do or do not do. If it doesn't feel right in your heart, it's never going to feel right in your head.

Reflection is a way of getting in touch with our hearts. It's where all our hopes, ideals, and dreams come from. Without it, all the rest is just a machine.

So, I don't care how you choose to do it: sitting, running, jumping, swimming, walking, but make plans to find out about reflection. Take time, sometime, each and every day to experience listening to your heart. A few moments will be fine. It's what makes all the other parts of us work in harmony. And believe me, when you're burned-out, you are definitely out of harmony with yourself and your environment. So do something about it now.

CHAPTER 7:
FAST & FURIOUS

As soon as I mention the word "efficiency" some people think: "How fast can he get the job done?" Not so. Efficiency is not a measure of how fast you can do something. It's a measure of how well someone operates with the least waste of time and effort. It's bringing both knowledge and experience to a job in such a way that demonstrates what you've learned and experienced from the past.

The shortest distance between two points is a straight line. The efficient person seeks out the straightest line from the problem to the solution. Perhaps the greatest myth surrounding this aspect is the level of work involved. Harder does not necessarily mean better. The efficient person works smarter not harder. Some people work hard every week and have very little to show for their effort at the end of that week. Other people put in fewer hours and earn ten, twenty, or a hundred times more. Why? I believe the difference is efficiency. To be efficient means to utilize your time, knowledge and experience in a better way than the next guy. A simple set of priorities would be a good beginning. People who are efficient are not necessarily smarter than the next person, but they are usually organized. Experience leads to knowledge. Knowledge creates awareness and the aware mind always overcomes the unaware mind towards finding a quicker, easier solution.

Did you notice one of the words I used there? *Creates!*

I believe that one of the most important keys to any kind of efficiency is creativity. It has to be. Someone has to look at something in a different way in order to cut down the time and effort it used to take to do the same thing.

Someone had to look at a simple tin or aluminum can and come up with a way of making it easier, simpler and faster to open without using a can opener. Creativity caused that to happen. Creativity causes us to find a different way to go to work in the morning to avoid the morning traffic. Creativity caused someone to develop a way for a computer to make telephone calls. And that creativity caused a major degree of efficiency to take place in what has become an ordinary, everyday, but highly necessary task.

——————— **LIFE LINE** ———————

Discover means to dis-cover or uncover what has always been there.

It's taking a situation and discovering a better way. A better way to accomplish our daily activities. A better way to accomplish the things we take for granted, and the things that slow us down. I love the word discover, it means to dis-cover, or *uncover* what has always been there so we can see and use it.

What can you bring to your job that can create more efficiency?

Sometimes, simple motivation can create efficiency. United Parcel Service has a chart in each of their offices with all their local routes worked out in a formula that says: if you have a certain number of packages, and travel a definite distance, then it should take you "X" number of hours to complete the route. Now, if you do the route in less time than the chart, they will pay you the same amount. You better believe that a driver is going to go out of his way to find a more efficient way to service his route.

What I'm trying to emphasize here is that there are ideas out there all over the place. This is an example of working smarter not harder. It's looking at something in a different way and becoming creative. Look at your pattern for the day.

How Efficient are You?

Let's take a little quiz called: How efficient am I?

1. *Am I doing everything I can to reach my goal?* Remember, smarter not harder. Is there a shorter distance between the start of my day and the end of it?

2. *Am I doing the same thing day in and day out without getting the results I want?* If you feel stuck, chances are, you are stuck and the only way to get unstuck is to first see it and accept it.

3. *Am I willing to look at something in a new way?* Your attitude is very important here because basically none of us really want to change. However, sooner or later changes do occur and people need to change with them.

Here we are back to growth, again. It is important to remember that change gives us the opportunity to do something new or do something in a new way, to learn, increase our knowledge and grow from where we are to where we want to be.

Remember what it was like when you took your first bite of pizza? It probably looked awful, but you tried it anyway and surprise. . . you loved it! Don't be afraid of something new. You might just like it.

4. *Is this going to help the company, today?* Are we making progress toward a solution here? Is what we are doing going to make a difference later on? And I don't care how small a difference as long as it makes a difference. As far as I'm concerned, there are no small differences. All of the small differences add up to big differences at the end of the year and those differences usually translate into a savings of time, money, energy or all three.

5. How often do you and your co-workers brainstorm? Brainstorming is just a group of people sitting around tossing ideas back and forth in an effort to come up with a solution to a problem. How often do you participate in something like that? Even if the result of a session is to find a better place to put a file cabinet that gets used a lot. It doesn't matter.

Wherever I go, I always encourage brainstorming. It clears away the cobwebs, and stimulates the thinking process. It's also a terrific tool to help create a new environment. No one knows the job better than the worker who works it. And by tapping the knowledge and experience of your fellow workers, you can adjust, add, subtract, create and improve your condition. Try it! It may break an old habit you've been wanting to get out of. We are all creatures of habit. But we don't want to be slaves to them. Learn to go into a brainstorming session without any judgments.

To recap quickly, here are five questions you can ask yourselves about your own efficiency:

1. Am I doing everything to reach my goal?

2. Am I doing the same thing without getting the results I want?

3. Am I willing to look at something in a new way?

4. Is this going to help the company, today?

5. When was the last time I participated in a brainstorming session with my fellow workers?

Okay, another expression we hear a lot is, "fresh eyes". He's looking at this with fresh eyes. So, what does that mean? Did he get an eye transplant last week, or something? No, it means taking a look at something without any judgments as to being right or wrong. Just observing something and seeing how it works. Someone with fresh eyes can often see something that others cannot because of their judgments.

A simple story illustrates this: A truck is driving along and reaches a tunnel. The driver gets stuck at the entrance because he overestimated the clearance and as a result, the top of the truck is jammed into the top of the tunnel. Now, this has traffic stopped in both directions. Everyone is climbing out of their cars and trucks to figure out a way to free the truck. Backing up doesn't work because he's too far into the tunnel and the engine doesn't have enough power. Pushing him out doesn't work for the same reason and a combination of both fails as well. Now, along comes a little girl and sees the whole problem. She maybe spends all of a minute sizing things up when she simply asks the driver, "Why don't you let some air out of the tires?" No one had thought of such a simple solution.

That's what having fresh eyes does. It allows us to let go of the traditional ways and take a completely different approach.

Now, the rewards and benefits for becoming more efficient, I think, are rather obvious. If you're a U.P.S. driver, you get to go home earlier with the same rate of pay. If you're doing the same work for people and constantly coming up with newer, fresher, better, easier ways to get the job done, more people are going to want to work with you. You gain more experience, more knowledge, more awareness which in turn leads to the raise and promotion. The corporate world is constantly looking for creative and enthusiastic people, people who are willing to take the reins and provide direction—and they are willing to richly reward them for their efforts.

Creating Efficiency

Some ideas to think about concerning efficiency are:

1. *Plan your work and work your plan.* Take time to look at what you do and put it in writing. Actually see it in front of you. It won't be long before you will revise, adjust, and change the routine for the better.

2. *Take think breaks.* Take two to five minutes every few hours to close your eyes and imagine the goal in front of you, the task that you've set out for yourself today. And visualize yourself completing that task. You may just see an easier, simpler way of achieving it. The best ideas are usually the simplest ones.

3. *Do the right things instead of doing things right.* This may not make sense to you at first but think about it. Sometimes, it's important to look at the overview, rather than what's directly in front of us. If you concentrate too closely on putting one foot directly and cleanly in front of the other, you may just miss the fact that you are walking directly and cleanly off the cliff just out of range. You have to get the big picture.

What I'm saying here is that you can be focused on your job but don't be so focused on the details that you miss other opportunities for change, a change that may make the challenges easier for you. And a lot of changes happen from the mistakes we make.

We all want to be able to have a role in making something work; whether it's a car, delivering a package or designing a flower arrangement. And if we can do that "something" in such a way to enhance our self-expression, then we feel better. We not only feel better about the job, we feel better about ourselves. This feeling leads us to the next success, the next creative insight, the next change, the next raise, the next promotion. The feelings only get better and better as we build our personal confidence level.

CHAPTER 8:
ATTITUDE (NOT APTITUDE) EQUALS ALTITUDE

In talking about relationships with others and ourselves, one trait that shows up in any relationship is a person's attitude. What's your attitude, toward work, and toward others?

It's like the attitude you present in the morning. Do you say, "Good morning, God." Or do you say, "Good God, it's morning?"

An attitude is a manner, a disposition or a feeling about ourselves. And it's very revealing. Your attitude is pretty much going to determine your day. Is your attitude showing? What kind of feelings are you carrying around today? Can you look at a situation as an opportunity or do you only see a problem?

Problems to Projects

If we can learn how to turn a problem into a project, we can then change our attitude. Once we have a project, we can come up with a solution. Coming up with a solution challenges us. And I firmly believe that every challenge can give us an opportunity to expand ourselves to learn and to grow.

A football team can't reach the goal in the end zone if they're constantly stuck at the same position down field. Expanding and growing is what keeps us moving toward our goal both personally and professionally.

Once again, we're getting back to thinking. Because thinking controls so much of what we do and say, our thinking has a direct bearing on what our attitude, our outlook towards ourselves and others will be.

William James, considered to be the father of American psychology, once said, "To change becomes increasingly difficult and requires purposeful effort to counteract the system all ready set up." Now, a lot of people interpret that as meaning you can't teach an old dog new tricks. But he didn't say that. He said that it becomes increasingly difficult, not impossible.

So, we have to be aware of what we're doing. We have to want to change. And we can do that if we want to. If you can change your thinking, you can change your attitude. What kind of attitude do you have? Look at your thinking. What goals do you want to achieve? Look at your thinking. Your attitude is a direct reflection of your thoughts and if they're negative, how does that affect conditions surrounding your goals? It sure can't help them any.

Learn to generate a positive feeling within yourself to match the positive goal that you've set for yourself. And learn to carry that feeling with you throughout the day. Try this: Some evening take a note pad and write a feeling about a goal you wish to achieve. Keep it simple. The simpler the better. Once you have that written down, recall an experience that caused you to have that feeling. Now, as you're remembering the experience, feel that feeling. Then, go to bed. Wake up the next morning and look at your feeling and recreate it for yourself. Now, start your day. But before you leave for work make sure you take your piece of paper with your feeling written on it. Carry that piece of paper in a pocket with you and whenever you notice yourself getting down and feeling different from your feeling, get the paper out to remind yourself. And don't forget to recreate the experience from your memory to help you get that feeling back. The important thing to do is to hold onto that feeling for just a day. Do it. I guarantee that whatever comes up for you during that day, the way you approach it will be different. Instead of looking at how bad things are or what the problems are, look at how good things are. What do you have now, that you didn't have before?

Be grateful that we have the ability to know our own worth. Learn to look at a situation and ask yourself, "What contribution can I make to solve this problem?" instead of, "Great Scott, look at the problem we have here!"

Whenever we talk about prosperity in business, we talk about having a million-dollar attitude. You take a Rockefeller's money away from him today and tomorrow he'll go out and make a million dollars. Why? It's not only the money that brings success, it's the attitude. When you are constantly looking for the solution you will find one. You won't allow yourself to stay stuck in a problem. It's a consciousness.

Give everyone one on the planet a hundred thousand dollars and by the end of the day some will be rich and others will be poor again. Why? Attitude and our consciousness. And maybe a few will have some losing lottery tickets, but mostly it will be due to the lack of a good attitude, and a scarcity consciousness.

──────── **LIFE LINE** ────────

Richness has not as much to do with money as it does with attitude.

It's believing you have a million dollars in the checking account and not really having it. It's facing any kind of situation and looking at the simple fact that your positive, problem-less oriented approach will produce a solution to any situation.

Richness has not as much to do with money as it does with attitude. With feeling. Joseph Murphy said, "When you feel prosperous, money will come to you in avalanches of abundance." And feeling is the key behind our attitude. It all starts with a feeling.

You can't always surround yourself with positive people but you can choose to surround yourself with positive feelings. The choice is always yours.

When you feel confident, you talk, think and act confidently. When you feel love, you will express it. When you feel happy, healthy, wealthy and wise, you will project that, and it will come back to you.

Ideas About Attitude

Here are some ideas to remember about attitude:

1. *Look at any situation as an opportunity, not as a problem.*

2. *Create a positive attitude for yourself for the day.* Write it on a piece of paper, the night before, and carry it around with you the next day to remind yourself.

3. *Speak positively*. Say what you want, not what you don't want. Also, when entering into a conversation, if those involved are taking the trend of the talk into a tail spin, spiraling down to nowhere with gossip, rumors, and hear-say, it's up to you to either ***Lift it or Leave it***. Remember, most people follow, but leaders initiate.

4. *Surround yourself with as many positive feelings as possible.* If you remember nothing else, remember this: We function on feeling. So, check out your feelings. Are you feeling down when you'd rather feel up? Do something about it. Do you blame it on a circumstance or the people around you—or do you own it?

Remember, if you can own your own feelings, you can then do something to change them. When it comes to feelings, there are no victims . . . only volunteers.

EPILOGUE:
PEOPLE MAKE IT HAPPEN

For thousands of years no one flew airplanes. Why? Because no one understood the principles of aerodynamics. Yet today we take flying nearly for granted. Marconi was committed to an insane asylum for suggesting that voices could be transmitted through the air without wires. Today we send not only voices, but pictures as well. Even as recently as less than one hundred years ago, homes were lighted by either candles or gas lights. It took Thomas Edison to develop the electric light bulb and proclaim, "I'm going to make these things so cheap that only the rich will be able to afford candles."

The mind of man is a beautiful thing. It seems that nearly anything that is conceivable is ultimately possible; all that needs to be done is to discover the principle by which it works. Space travel, advanced medicine, nuclear energy, and computers are all recent developments of technology which began as someone's idea—someone's thought. When rightly used, they are beautiful tools which assist man in his physical world.

It is easy to see why a person living in a world of physical convenience would begin to adapt to the technological way of life. It is easy to see how people become complacent and comfortable with the idea of having things done "for them." Albert Schweitzer was once asked what is wrong with people today, and he replied, "People just don't think."

Yet man's mind is an amazing tool. If man is left to his own devices, he will discover, develop and create. But the average person in our society finds that, if he allows it, most of his thinking is done for him. Consequently, many people fall into the trap of either blaming others, "It's their fault," or defeating themselves, "I can't do it."

I believe that something absolutely phenomenal is locked up within each one of us—something so great and so powerful that we have not seen the likes of it before. As Walt Whitman put it, "You are not all contained between your hat and your boots."

I believe that it is possible for each of us to release this energy, either in part or in total, and direct it into any specific area of our lives that we choose. The problem is that many people do not know how to release this energy. What is even worse, most people don't even know they possess it. Plato said that the ignorant don't know they're ignorant. A law cannot be effectively applied until its presence is realized.

My personal experience is that there is a law of life which can be relied upon as surely as the law of acrodynamics. I believe that our awareness that this "law of laws" exists is our springboard to a fuller and richer life, and that by our understanding and application of these laws and concepts presented in these writings, we have the right to fly as far and as high as our dreams can take us.

SECTION II:

THE
SERVICE
EDGE

*Money is simply an indicator of
how much service you provide.
To increase the money flow in your life
you must increase the service you offer.*

CHAPTER 9:
CUSTOMERS' BILL OF RIGHTS

Would you accept a thank-you letter from someone who mailed it with a note that said, "I have been one of your customers for many years and really appreciate all the positive support you have offered. It's really good to work with people who have my interests at heart." You ask, "Why wouldn't I accept it?" Strange as it sounds, the letter was written by someone who referred to themselves as a customer. Now, you may not refer to the people you serve as customers, but as passengers, guests, members, clients, or some other term specific to your business. Even if you don't use the word "customer" in your business you'd still accept the letter, wouldn't you?

In this book, ideas will be presented that are invaluable for people who are serving people. Whether you call the people you serve, guests, members, clients, or customers, the fact remains that good service will be rewarded with repeat business and loyalty. Let's move beyond words to embody the principles of providing service for the people with whom we conduct business. Our world is moving so fast today that it's a bit difficult to keep up with it—let alone understand it. We've put men and machinery on the moon and nearby planets. We've got submarines that will dive to the ocean floor. Our nuclear physicists and biologists are probing the inner-most particles of matter. Our computers can solve some of the most complex problems of life in seconds; universal equations, DNA comparisons, etc. And yet we are still running around with health problems, management breakdowns, communication challenges, and personal dissatisfactions—in short, people problems. It's interesting to think about what business use to be. Few of us remember the "good old days," when merchants knew their customers' names and companies provided quality merchandise and iron-clad guarantees, but that way of doing business was standard practice at one time.

As the population grew, the neighborhood businesses were lost to large corporations and franchises. Businesspeople no longer knew their customers. Sure we had more selection and faster service, but it seems we lost something too. What got lost in the process was the personalized service that made us feel special. For a while growth was so rapid that it didn't seem to matter if any attention was paid to the customer. There were plenty of customers to go around, so if you lost one, you could get another. It was certainly a short-sighted view. Before long no industry had the only game in town. There were many businesses providing the same products and services; an airline is an airline is an airline; one burger is as good as another. At that point, something new had to be done to keep your customers loyal. After all, your loss was your competitor's gain. And the competition remains fierce!

It wasn't all that long ago that most every business had become increasingly aware of the importance of service for customers. Companies that were losing ground, running toward the red instead of into profit, began to notice that there were some companies that continued to increase their market share despite the economy or the competition. One of the qualities that was universal with all the successful companies was attention, and commitment to customer service. What customers want today is not so different from what they have always wanted, and that is service—*customers want to be treated as individuals.* To have meaning and significance and to be made to feel that their opinions are the reason the company exists.

——————— LIFE LINE ———————

"The real purpose of business is to
create and keep a customer.
Without customers there is no profit,
and eventually, no business."

As the impact of customer service became more apparent, industries that never concerned themselves with pleasing customers began taking a look at the value of *each* individual customer. No longer is customer service the private domain of restaurants and clubs. Now financial institutions, hospitals, and manufacturers are realizing that without customers, not only will the bottom line not improve, but it will cease to exist. As Theodore Levitt, professor of Business Administration at Harvard, states in his book *The Marketing Imagination,* "The real purpose of business is to create and keep a customer. Without customers there is no profit, and eventually, no business."

In a world that is increasingly competitive in goods, the only edge we may be able to maintain is in the quality of service. The customer will buy only once from you, unless you can distinguish yourself from everyone else in the market through your service level. You may not have the opportunity to "sell" that customer again. The real purpose of business must ultimately be aimed at creating a loyal customer base.

When we talk about customer service, several companies probably come to mind. There are service leaders in all fields, department stores, high tech, food chains, and overnight mail service. Many are recognized as companies who put the customer first. A research firm conducted a service rating on various companies based upon their customer's perceptions of their service quality. The companies that rated highest with their customers on service charged about 9% more for their goods and grew *twice* as fast as the others. The service oriented companies had a 12% return on sales, while the others had a mere 1%. Numbers like that are hard to dispute, particularly when the ratings come from the actual customers of the businesses. Is there anyone who wouldn't like to charge more for their product *and* increase sales?

The Value of Customers

And while we're discussing the profitability of customer service, let me suggest another way to view your customers. Have you ever considered the customer as an appreciating asset? Think about the potential new business that each client could provide. Any business contains this potential, clothing, airlines, cleaners, restaurants. We're talking about a networking referral system here. For instance, if you operate a cleaning service and one of your clients refers your service to a restaurant, suddenly all those uniforms, table cloths and napkins turn into dollars. Look at this example:

My friend Tay Taylor ran a restaurant for many years. Suppose just one of his customers entertained his clients at Tay's restaurant regularly. Let's call him Mr. Big. What if Mr. Big, spent $500 a month for entertainment. That's $6,000 a year, $60,000 in ten years. Now, Tay and his people treat this guy really great, and as a result, Mr. Big encourages just one of his friends to consider entertaining his clients there also. Mr. Big is now worth $120,000, considering his own business and the customer he referred.

What if just one person per month that Mr. Big entertained, decided that Tay's is perfect for his own business entertaining? 12 months equals 12 clients worth $6000 a year. Well it boggles the mind. Anyone have a calculator? Now factor in that each one of your waiters can serve 5 tables each night (a conservative estimate) and that waiter is responsible for $600,000 potential business each night! When you look at customer service from that point of view it gives a whole new perspective on training, compensation and employee responsibility.

When you think about it, everyone is a customer! You and I are customers at various times during each day. We all respond pretty much the same way when we get bad service, or run into an offensive salesperson . . . *we don't go back!* And when you don't go back, how many people do you tell? Probably a lot more than if you had good service. As a matter of fact, a Washington D.C. consulting firm, Technical Assistance Science Foundation, has done extensive research in the area of complaints. Their findings indicate that customers who are dissatisfied tell at least 10 people.

────── **LIFE LINE** ──────

It is 6 times more expensive to acquire a new customer than to retain a current one.

When you are considering a purchase, whether it's a new car or refrigerator for your home or a complete computer system for your company, knowing that a friend or associate was dissatisfied will weigh heavily when you are making a purchasing decision. Can your business thrive, or survive, under that kind of negative input? Not likely. When you think of the bottom line, keep in mind that it is 6 times more expensive to acquire a new customer than it is to retain a current one.

So, as a business, it is always in your best interest to provide good customer service. Simply put, a good customer service standard is to treat your customers as you would like to be treated.

Customers' Bill of Rights

Let's consider what I'd like to call the Customers' Bill of Rights. It would probably include of some of the following items:

CUSTOMERS' BILL OF RIGHTS:

To be treated with respect.
To be told the truth about products
   and manufacturers' guarantees.
To pay a fair price.
To have knowledgeable sales people.
To have merchandise meet acceptable
   standards of quality.
To be listened to.

> To be assured that problems will be
> considered by decision makers.

I saw this poster prominently displayed in an office. It's called "What is a Customer?"

> A customer is the most important person ever in this office . . . in person or by mail. A Customer is not dependent on us . . . we are dependent on him. A Customer is not an interruption of our work . . . he is the purpose of it. We are not doing a favor by serving him . . . he is doing us a favor by giving us the opportunity to do so. A Customer is not someone to argue or match wits with. Nobody ever won an argument with a Customer. A Customer is a person who brings us his wants. It is our job to handle them efficiently for him and profitably for ourselves.

─────── **LIFE LINE** ───────

The courtesy you use within
the company will be reflected
outward to the customers.

Are these items a part of your company policy? Do all employees know that the customer is the focus of your business? As a manager or staff member, do you treat others in the corporation with the respect and acknowledgment you want for the customer? You see it is contagious, the courtesy you use within the company will be reflected outward to the customers.

Creating the customer service edge will impact your business dramatically. There are many techniques that can be used to increase your ability to meet the needs of your customers. The purpose of this book is to elevate individual sensitivity to yourself and others. As leadership deals largely with "soft" skills, this sensitivity is an integral part of high-performance leadership. Applying the tools needed to improve the interaction with customers every day is a part of that elevation awareness. Awareness of yourself and your communication skills, as well as your customers will provide the stepping stones for building a strong and loyal customer base.

CHAPTER 10:
FIRST IMPRESSIONS

Let's begin at the beginning . . . your customer has just entered the picture. Once you've greeted your customer and are beginning a dialogue about your product or service by finding out the customer's needs first, the clock is ticking. You have only 4 minutes to make an impression. A study done at UCLA indicated that in that 4 minutes 7% of the impression comes from the words said, 38% of your impression is made by intonation or intent, and 55% of the impression is the result of body language.

Since 55% of your impression is made with body language, your customer may respond to you before you have a chance to dazzle him with your product knowledge. His first response will be to your body language; and it will be on a subliminal level. If you don't think this is true, let's try a little test. How would you feel about someone who conveys a bored, arrogant, and preoccupied nonverbal attitude?

Gestures like yawning, impatience, and an attitude of, "I've got better things to do with my time." Often I ask the question, "Would I buy a used car from this person?" We pick up the signals of body language from childhood and they remain with us on a subliminal level throughout our lives.

We speak with more than just our words, we speak with our bodies. Our bodies communicate how we feel about other people on a non-verbal level, but most importantly, how we feel about ourselves. These messages are conveyed in our business transactions, as well as while dining with our friends. Even the most simple of situations, sitting in the waiting room to see the client, the doctor, or the employer can tell a story that is most revealing.

———— **LIFE LINE** ————

To fully understand the personality
of a person, we must read
body signals in clusters.

———————— ✍ ————————

Let's take a look at some annoying habits, habits that convey individual anxieties, inner conflict or apprehension. You may have wondered why some people crack their knuckles. Cracking the knuckles may indicate inner conflict, or a need to "get on with it" so to speak. It shows impatience. Picking at the cuticle often reflects a need to be recognized or acknowledged; it also is a way of expressing concern. For instance, a person worried about finances may pick at his cuticle. A young child often sucks his thumb when needing reassurance. An adult, placing the fingers over the mouth displays a lack of assurance, and hides the conversation. It may also mean astonishment. Biting one's fingernails may indicate worry as well as sagging self-esteem and a need for approval.

By observing and understanding these patterns we can supply others with the assurance they need, thereby encouraging them to become more receptive and cooperative. A woman who attended one of my seminars approached me with a problem. She said, "I've been to psychologists, therapists, I've been to doctor after doctor and no one seems to be able to give any positive solution for my nail biting."

She had bitten her nails right down to the quick. It was unsightly. I said to her, "You may find this hard to believe, but you have got to keep your fingers out of your mouth." She said, "No one ever explained it to me that way before." We both laughed. Later in the conversation her need for attention and love in her marriage was expressed. She also had low self-esteem because she felt she was overweight.

Of course, this is an isolated case. You can't take one incident or gesture and expect to uncover the complex nature of an individual. To fully understand the personality of a person, we must read body signals in clusters—and it doesn't hurt to get to know them a little bit either. There are a number of reasons why people respond as they do.

Body Language

There are some basic kinds of body language that we are all familiar with: crossed arms sometimes indicating hostility. People often equate folded arms as a sign of resistance, defensiveness or defiance. This is not necessarily so. When the arms are folded loosely and positioned low on the body the person may just be relaxing, tired, cold or bored.

More than not, however, when you see this crossed and closed-in position there is an element of reservation. You must then look for some other confirming signals that will tell the whole story. Failing to recognize the early signals of disagreement generally causes a build-up of tension. Fidgeting indicates uneasiness. Hands on hips demonstrates a power position. There are a number of others that may be a bit surprising, but can provide you with clues about your customer's feelings. When you become more aware of the subtleties, you will be able to consciously adjust your own body language.

Happiness can be indicated not only by smiling, but enlarged pupils or free, unrestrained movement. Disagreement is clear when a frown appears, but also by constricted pupils, flared nostrils or a rigid body. When you reach agreement, you may see nodding, winking or continued serene eye contact.

Is your customer interested in what you're saying? Watch for stillness of body and even breathing. Have you lost her? Her eyes will be vacant or looking away; her shoulders may be hunched or her fingers may be drumming. Your own interest in the customer will come through subliminally when you exhibit some of those same signs.

If a decision is in progress, your customer may look toward the ceiling, blinking rapidly or turn away and look at nothing at all. When the decision is made, she may take a deep breath followed by a sign of relaxation.

A word of caution; don't over-read body language. Remember crossing your arms is natural when you're cold. When resistant, a person's fists may be clenched, his posture rigid or tense, the face may be strained, and he may also avoid eye contact. Just be aware of the potential meanings. Also, consider your own body language. What does your customer see when he looks at you? Are you smiling or preoccupied with a task at hand? Are you interested in meeting him, in finding out what he wants, or are you thinking about what you'll say next? Is your customer an opportunity for you or just another interruption in your already stress-filled day? Do you look away, appearing bored or distracted? Do you approach your customer with an open handed, smiling gesture, or are your fists clenched and your smile forced? Do you press too close or demand more eye contact than your customer is comfortable with? A quick point here, who breaks eye contact first, the leader, or the follower? A leader will generally break eye contact first. Why? Leaders are either consciously or subconsciously used to putting people in their comfort zone.

Remember, the customer will be reading your body language, even if only subliminally. If you've ever had an encounter that seemed to start out on the wrong foot from the beginning, it may have been from the body language signals you each picked up subliminally. Have you ever said to yourself, "You know, he said all the right things, but I just don't feel good about the deal." Could be his body language was sending you information that contradicted his words. Know your own body language and use it wisely. It can be a valuable tool in closing a sale or solving a problem.

Effective Speaking

Your body language has made its statement and, of course, will continue to influence the interaction, but now you have the opportunity to speak to the customer. 38% of your impression will be the result of the tone and inflection of your voice. Let's test your reactions. Speak the words, "How may I help you" in monotone, now, say *"How may I help you?"* with inflection and enthusiasm. You see, the words never changed, but your response to them may have. Have you ever been surprised at a reaction to the words you've said?

I know a firm that answers the phone, "It's a great day." Often the receptionist speaks these words so fast that they are indistinguishable, and do not at all convey what her employer intended them to. The literal meaning may not have elicited the response you received. Often we are completely unaware of how we sound. Our tone of voice will give us away every time, unless we learn how to control it.

Here are some techniques that will help you modulate and control your voice for more effective communication:

First, be sure that you **speak clearly.** Whenever a customer has to strain to hear or understand you, he is uncomfortable. In addition, slurred, lazy speech will give the indication that you are indifferent or bored or *both!*

─────── LIFE LINE ───────

Act enthusiastic and you will be enthusiastic.

───────── ✍ ─────────

Avoid a monotone. You'll certainly bore your customer to distraction, and again, it gives an impression that you are bored as well.

Think of someone **telling a story** about something that was very exciting to them. The pitch, volume and speed of their speaking varies depending on what they are relating. Infuse your voice with some of that zest. You may be surprised how enlivening your speech will actually enliven and rejuvenate your attitudes. Let your customer catch some of your enthusiasm about you and your product from your voice. Remember, when you act enthusiastic, you will be enthusiastic.

Keep in mind that some speech patterns can be distracting or irritating. If you have colloquial language patterns and accents, you may want to modify them when you are dealing with customers from other areas. Of course, if you are speaking to someone who exhibits the same patterns, it can reinforce your communication. "Y'all come back now," will get an entirely different reaction in Houston than in New York City.

Pay attention to your vocabulary. Keep it professional and use words in the right context. It will make an overall impression on the customer. He will make judgments about you simply by the words you choose. Again, it depends on your customer. If you are discussing high-tech with a techie, you'll need to use all the exact terminology or it may be assumed that your product knowledge is limited, whether it is or not. But use that same high-tech vocabulary with me and you might as well be speaking Greek. When we discuss complaints, we'll talk further about the actual choice of words for a desired effect.

If you have access to a tape recorder, record your voice. You'll find you sound different to others than you sound to yourself. See if your voice is well modulated, not too high or low. And listen for the "uhs" and "you knows" that fill up spots where you are searching for a word or idea. Those little fillers can become, uh, you know, uh, a little, you know, distracting.

———— LIFE LINE ————

Customer Service
Rule #1: The customer is always right.
If the customer is wrong:
Rule #2: Refer to rule number 1.

———— ✍ ————

Although only 7% of the impression is made by *what* you say, customers still look to you for product knowledge, whether it's how the special of the day is prepared or how many gigabytes of memory or storage are in the personal computer. Job training is critical in this area. Learn all you can about your product or service and if a customer comes up with a question you are unprepared for, know where to find the information. There are some customers who will want all the details, others will want only the final result, but don't miss out on any of them simply because you didn't do your homework. Remember how irritated you become when you can't get information from a sales person, or you find out that what you received was misinformation? Put yourself in their shoes and respond accordingly. Remember the two rules of Customer Service: Rule number 1: The customer is always right. If the customer is wrong: Rule number 2. Refer to rule number 1.

CHAPTER 11:
THE CONFIDENCE LEVEL

Since you create the first impression for the customer, let's talk a little about you. The way you look, the words you say and the way you say them are all reflections of who you are and how you feel about yourself.

Abe Lincoln had a good way of putting it. Two men approach him to seek his opinion. One man was tall with long legs, and one man was short with very short legs. They said, "Mr. Lincoln, how long should a man's legs be?" Mr. Lincoln thought, and then said, "Well, I suppose a man's legs should be," he stopped abruptly, looking at the tall man's legs, and then glancing at the short man's legs, and carefully continued, "I suppose a man's legs should be just long enough to reach from his body to the ground."

Do you feel confident and self-assured or are you always expecting people to find out that you're really incompetent? Do you feel you look your best or are you feeling uncomfortable about your body: too fat, too thin, too short, too tall, and so on? Are your clothes clean and pressed, or did you just throw something on after you gave it the sniff test?

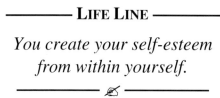

──────── LIFE LINE ────────
You create your self-esteem
from within yourself.

Self-Image

If you don't feel good about *you*, then you won't be able to really listen and respond to the customer. Furthermore, the customer may see or feel something in your attitude that dissuades her from wanting to approach you for the sale. In a difficult situation with a dissatisfied customer, you cannot change what the customer feels, but you can change how you respond to her. If your self-image is low, your response may inflame the situation rather than resolve it. So, since you can't change the customer, let's talk about what you can change, and that's you.

You create your self-esteem from within yourself. Self-esteem comes from the self. There are probably some heads shaking out there. You're saying that your self-esteem is low because you didn't go to an Ivy League school, or your spouse is always nagging you about your faults, or your parents didn't provide the loving support you should have had. Well, the truth of the matter is you—and only you—are in charge of your self-esteem. Self-image is the way you see yourself in your mind. Self-esteem is the way you feel about yourself. And both of these equal your self-worth.

The mind is incredible. It can create and reinforce every aspect of your life from your physical well-being to your attitudes about yourself and others. What has your mind been telling you? Chances are, if your self-esteem is low, it has been telling you all the negative and none of the positive. Did you ever have a conversation with yourself like this: "Boy, you sure are dumb. How in the world could you say such a stupid thing to the boss? He's never going to promote you now. And furthermore, you have no will power. The first little bit of stress and it's right for the chocolate chip cookies. You're so fat that your husband/wife is going to be out the door if you don't shape up. No one in their right mind could love someone as stupid as you!"? Can you imagine your confidence level as a salesperson if that's the conversation going on in your head?

Have you ever wondered why some people seem to excel, and others remain status quo. Do you think it has something to do with the way we think? Or do you believe that success is a hit, or miss proposition?

I actually believe that many people just don't think. Now, don't get the wrong idea here, I'm not saying that some people are more capable of thinking than others, because I don't believe that. I am saying that it appears that some people just don't think. When you look at it, there is no corner on the market for success. Success is available to all of us, and yet only a few soar beyond, to areas of which others only dream.

——————— LIFE LINE ———————

If we do what we have always done,
we will get what we have always gotten.

——————— ✎ ———————

Change

I too, have fallen into the non-thinking category many times by taking the same old path because it was easy, or familiar. When you stop to think about it, *if we do what we have always done, we will get what we have always gotten. To do the same things over, and over, and over, expecting to get different results is a good definition of insanity.* To reach excellence in anything, we have to be willing to make some changes.

———— LIFE LINE ————

"Men are often interested in improving their
circumstances, but they are
unwilling to improve themselves.
They, therefore, remain bound."
–James Allen

The curious thing about this mind of ours, however, is that it can only hold one thought at a time. And it can't distinguish between something real and something imagined. So if you focus on positive, supportive conversations, you will soon see the reflections of those thoughts in the world around you. The way you dress will change, because when you feel good about yourself, you will automatically take better care of yourself.

We have to be able to stimulate our minds with ideas of an uplifting, constructive nature, ideas that will move us into positive directions so we can reach out and capture our dreams.

My friend Cavett Robert said, "Please Lord, don't let me die before I'm dead." Often people want change in their lives, but they are unwilling to initiate the change. James Allen stated that, "Men are often interested in improving their circumstances, but they are unwilling to improve themselves. They, therefore, remain bound." Isn't it strange that in one year it is not uncommon for a person to spend upwards of $1000 on the outside of their head, and often not a nickel on the inside?

We must be able to capture an image in our minds which is consistent with our desires and objectives. But many people are not willing to move in new directions, they stay locked in their old ways of thinking—even though they are not getting the results they desire.

—————— Life Line ——————

If you are looking for a change in your life, and in your customer response, that change will have to begin with you.

Often people wonder why they are not progressing in their business, or in their personal lives. It may be because they are harboring what I call "non-survival" attitudes and ideas, ideas that are not conducive to progress and productivity. These can be carry-over habit patterns from the past, and when we allow such outdated ideas to clutter our present moment, we give them all the power they need to express themselves in a very real way, right here, right now.

It boils down to this, if you are looking for a change in your life, and in your customer response, that change will have to begin with you.

Your Internal Dialogue

Here are some positive conversations you can have with yourself:

1. *Tell yourself the truth about your best moments.* We've all done things we've been proud of. Don't sell yourself short by attributing your success to someone else or brush it aside with "Oh, it was nothing." I'm not suggesting you let your ego run wild, but give yourself credit where credit is due. Accept acknowledgment gracefully with a "Thank you." If you've accomplished a difficult task, acknowledge its difficulty and your contribution to its completion. Learn to accept and acknowledge your successes. Also realize that mistakes are a part of life and we can learn from them. Use them as stepping stones or guideposts, as athletes do in tennis, skiing, or golf. We cannot totally avoid mistakes but, if we learn from them, we will surely increase our odds for future success, and understanding failure is clearly an important key to success.

2. *Imagine yourself accomplishing the things you desire* and responding in the ways you choose. The old saying "What you see is what you get," can also be "What you see is what you become." Experimental and clinical psychologists have proven that the mind cannot distinguish the difference between a physical visual impression and one imagined.

An experiment was conducted at the University of Wisconsin with three groups of people. Each was asked to make baskets on the basketball court, and each was given 20 minutes to do so. They were then scored. The first group was asked to make baskets each day for 20 minutes and return in one week to be scored again. The second group was asked not to practice and return in one week to be scored. The third group was asked to mentally imagine making baskets for 20 minutes a day and return in one week to be scored again. One week later the groups returned. The first group, who practiced, improved 24%. The second group who didn't practice, didn't improve. The third group, who practiced mentally making baskets for 20 minutes a day, improved 23%.

Whatever images your mind is projecting about you will be reflected in the physical world. Since you can control what images your mind projects and since your mind cannot distinguish between the real physical world and imagination, utilize this powerful resource to put yourself in the picture the way you want to be. Keep the goal clearly focused and soon your life will be a reflection of the image. Remember, your mind can hold only one image at a time, so why not make it positive.

3. *Be compassionate.* Accept others *and* yourself for who you are. It is often easier to accept others for what they are in spite of their weakness than it is to accept ourselves. We know that we cannot change others. They are acting and responding according to their own experience and awareness. Our task is to make our interaction with them as positive and productive as possible. What we can change is ourselves. Acknowledge your strengths and weaknesses. There is nothing to be gained by concentrating on your weak points. Once you've acknowledged them, you have the tools at your disposal to change them. Obviously it will take time and there will be some bumps along the way. When you hit one of those air pockets called a mistake, take a deep breath and forgive yourself. Take a moment to learn from it and re-evaluate your goal. Think of an example of a positive experience and applaud that strength. Let the negative experience go once you've determined why it happened the way it did. Now get on with the positive, forward movement of your life. Applaud your strengths and address your weaknesses.

——————— LIFE LINE ———————

When you feel confident about yourself
it will be expressed in everything
about you in the outer world.

——————— ✍ ———————

4. *Be active in life.* Fill your days with activities that give you pleasure and challenge. Participate in the multitude of opportunities that surround you. There is much to be experienced in the world. When we are an active participant—learning, growing and giving, our minds do not have time to worry and reinforce negative images. If you are visualizing your golf swing, you can't be thinking about a situation that did not go well at work. If you are learning something new, you will be busy concentrating on that and feel the special excitement that comes from mental growth. If you are giving of yourself to the community or your loved ones, you will be focused on an activity outside yourself and benefit from the special pleasure that comes from helping someone else. An active life will keep you growing and let you bring something special to every interaction you have.

When you feel confident about yourself it will be expressed in everything about you in the outer world. Your customer will respond to the confidence you project and you, in turn, will be able to respond in a positive way to the customer; listening to his needs to reach a mutually agreeable solution.

Let's recap what we've covered so far.

First: Everyone is a customer. Satisfied customers become your best sales people because they tell other potential customers about you.

Second: How you speak is critical. A customer's impressions of you is 7% what you say, 38% the inflections of your voice, and 55% body language.

Third: You reflect your self-esteem. Your body language, speech and appearance are a reflection of your self-esteem. You are in charge of how you feel about yourself.

Fourth: The mind can create and reinforce either a positive or a negative self-image. When your self-esteem is good, you can be open to listening and responding to your customers' needs.

To relearn and re-pattern your habits and your thinking can be quite a task indeed and it does take continued desire and expectation of seeing results. However, the universe always says yes. It will support you wherever you are, but to reap the rewards of the satisfied customer, you must direct your energies toward all that is positive and productive.

CHAPTER 12:
WHO ARE YOUR CUSTOMERS?

How can you deal more effectively with customers? Some people seem to have a natural gift for this, and others need coaching. There are some techniques that can help you in determining what your customer is looking for in an interaction and how you can adjust your own personality style to meet those needs. Carl Jung, father of Jungian Psychology, defined 6 basic behavioral styles and proposed that we all respond to each other within the context of those styles. These basic behavior styles can be co-mingled, but there is usually an identifiable type of behavior. In recognizing these types in ourselves and identifying them in our customers, we can adjust our own behavior to provide them with the kind of information they require in a manner they will be receptive to. Remember, your customers will remain who they are, but through knowledge and practice you can choose how you will respond to them.

For our purposes here, we'll identify Jung's behavioral types in a more contemporary context and simplify the six types to two based upon their decision-making style, and then we'll briefly cover the six styles.

——————— LIFE LINE ———————

Your customers will remain who they are, but through knowledge and practice you can choose how you will respond to them.

———————— ✍ ————————

Decision Makers

Quick Decision Makers: Within this category there are some variations in style and behavior, but in general these are the people who prefer to be given the bottom line. They are interested in the big picture and do not want to be bogged down by details. Their speech patterns are rapid. Some may be more inclined than others to spend time in social conversation. This distinction is easy to make within a minute or so based on the direction of the conversation. The quick decision makers who are sociable will be highly sociable, people oriented and very descriptive in their language.

Slow Decision Makers: The most immediate difference you will notice from Quick Decision Makers is the speed of their speech. These people will be more controlled in their vocabulary and slower in their speech. Facts are the key in any kind of presentation. They will want all the details and are interested in how things work. The traditional values will apply and change is something to be avoided. Rules and regulations are to be followed and all questions are to be thoroughly answered.

The first three of the six types fall into the quick decision-maker category.

Six Types

Direct: They are in a hurry. They want information and results quickly and are not interested in a lengthy discussion of the pros and cons. They appreciate a direct approach with the big picture in mind. They are ambitious and dynamic. Impatient with slow or detailed activities, the leader wants to get going toward the goal. They'll have a direct style of communication, unwilling to engage in social banter like a Sociable type or to argue opposing views like an Autonomous style. They will be resourceful in solutions to problems. Look for classic corporate attire.

Sociable: They are also in a hurry and will make a quick decision; but they want recognition more than results. They are more willing to chat; and like emotion and drama. They will be highly communicative and sociable using language filled with images. These are the folks who want people around them. They thrive on interaction and respond to the human drama of life. They are always willing to help others but are bored by details. They'll be fashionably dressed and enjoy material status symbols.

Autonomous: They are quick decision makers; and they want action. They will appreciate creativity and balk at restriction. Likely to avoid the surface sociability, they will move forward with their own ideas and solutions. They are looking for excitement. They enjoy the big picture, love a challenge and are not interested in details. Freedom is important and they find opposing views stimulating. New ideas and even risks are part of their pleasures. They create their own fashion, despite the current trends or corporate culture.

The second three types fall into the slow and deliberate category.

Cautious: They are slow decision makers. They want to ask questions, and have them all answered. They will be more relaxed and have a long attention span. They want to be appreciated and not pressured. They will be controlled in speech and understated in dress. Most likely their job will be one of a very specialized nature. Family oriented, tradition is important and change is difficult. They will be looking for facts and security in their decision making.

Prudent: They are also slow decision makers; and demand precision and details. They dislike change and need constant reassurance. They believe that rules and regulations are meant to be followed and questions need to be answered. They want a good value for their dollar. Everything has a place in their world and should stay there.

Controlled: They will be slow decision makers and like time to think things over. They will appreciate a clear presentation and seek security and peace. They look for appreciation. Sometimes considered shy, they prefer to distance themselves from the superficial or emotional. Facts and how things work are important to them. An independent worker, they enjoy working with ideas but have no time for chit chat.

Type Interaction

As an example of the types within the categories, suppose they have gone into a clothing store. The sales might go something like this. Mr. Direct will ask for the sale or solution immediately: "Do you have this size in blue? Yes? Put it on my charge account." Ms. Sociable may be in just as big a hurry, but will stop long enough to ask you how you think they look in the item. Mrs. Autonomous may decide quickly and her choice will be strictly her own, despite fashion, putting various items together to create her own fashion statement. Ms. Cautions will most certainly try each item separately. Mr. Prudent may ask about washing instructions and solicit your opinion of each color. And Mr. Controlled probably won't buy today; but will be back to reconsider.

Imagine an interchange between a sales person and potential customer, who are very different personality types:

Ms. Direct: So, Mr. Cautions, you see that upon completion, you will have the best widgets west of the Pecos. Now, may I have your signature here?

Mr. Cautious: Well, Ms. Direct, I'd like a complete cost breakdown by day, and a guaranteed completion date, plus a three-tiered presentation on potential earnings verses expenses. I'd like those widgets to be exactly the same as my Dad used; and, I'm not so sure about the future of widgets anyway.

What do you think the chances are of this sale being made? If Ms. Direct wants to convince Mr. Controlled to accept her widget proposal, she will need to slow down, collect all the details and present them to Mr. Controlled in his terms. Otherwise Mr. Controlled will make the judgment that she really doesn't know what she's doing, and is trying to pressure him into a deal he's very uncomfortable with.

If the situation were reversed, Mr. Controlled would need to speed up his presentation, show the finished widget proposal, and put all details in printed presentation to be reviewed later. Of course, the presentation would be filed unopened, or reviewed by someone other than Ms. Direct.

You can see where the difficulties would come with a quick decision maker, who is interested in a quick solution, handling the complaints of a slow decision maker, who wants the whys and wherefores before he feels satisfied! Or vice versa!

When you determine what type of behavior is most often exhibited by you, then you will understand how to temper it when dealing with someone who may be entirely opposite.

Everyone has style. By being aware of your own style, and the styles of others, you'll be able to soften a difficult situation with a dissatisfied customer by finding a satisfying resolution—and you may even close an important sale.

CHAPTER 13:
GAMES AND STRATEGIES

Eric Berne in his book *Games People Play,* explained how we all find ourselves acting out different roles within our relationships. On a very basic level, your customers will play "games" with you. These games are most likely subconscious, and when you learn to distinguish them, you will find it easier to reach the solutions you desire, while making your customer feel like a winner.

Customer Games & Strategies

The Bargain Shopper: Without a doubt this customer believes that he can get it for less down the street, or at least he can make you believe he can and you'll come down on your price. In this case, service is less important to him than price. Chances are you won't be in a position to start a bidding war over the price, so you'll need to find a way to convince this customer that he is really better off with your product, even if it is more expensive. You may want to give him the benefits of your product versus the price. Point out that the price is only one aspect of the purchase. If he buys a more reliable product now, he'll save a bundle on repairs. Make him feel like he's getting a bargain from you that only a really smart shopper would be able to see.

Poor Pitiful Me: This customer seems to expect to be mistreated. Nothing ever works out for him, including his purchase of your product. Low self-esteem is at the bottom of this attitude, so find a way to be encouraging and supportive. If the product requires repair, let him know that you realize the importance of the product to him and that you especially value his business. Let him know that you are seeking a solution and value his input. Combat his negative view with the positive aspects of the product and reassure him that he's making the right decision.

How Dare You: Working on the premise that the best defense is a good offense, this customer will bluster about his pride and dignity being attacked. What he's really saying is that he needs and wants to feel special. So make him feel special. If he is complaining about service, let him know that you will handle his complaint personally, because you especially value his business. If repairs are in order, arrange rush service for him. Perhaps he's looking for an exchange of goods. Offer him an upgrade of a newer or larger version.

The Salesperson Promised: You'll never know for sure what another salesperson said. This customer wants to play one against the other to get what he wants. He's put you in the difficult position of agreeing that the salesperson was wrong or saying that the truth may have been stretched. The best position is firmly in the middle. You can agree that the customer has a right to be upset by conflicting information, but stand firm with the policy. You may want to suggest a miscommunication or suggest that perhaps the salesperson didn't specifically point out the policy in the sales material.

The more you know and understand about your customer, the easier it will become to provide superior service. One added benefit for you is less stress. As your customer service skills increase, each encounter will be smoother and more productive. Your self-esteem and your confidence in your ability to do your job will continue to increase. You'll have a three-way win going: the customers will be better served; the company will benefit overall by increased customer satisfaction; and you will feel more confident and less stressed in your job.

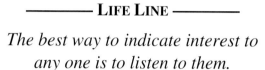

──────── LIFE LINE ────────

*The best way to indicate interest to
any one is to listen to them.*

────────── ✍ ──────────

What is Your Customer I.Q.?

What is your I.Q.? I'm not asking about your intelligence here. I know you are all bright individuals. What I'm asking is; what is your Interest Quotient? How interested are you in your customer?

The best way to indicate interest to any one is to listen to them. I mean really listen, actively—not passively. Do we really hear and understand what the other person is saying? Don't spend the time he is talking thinking of what you're going to say next. Listen with your eyes, ears and mind. Watch his body language. Is he saying one thing and showing another? Hear his words, and observe what kind of person he may be. Is he a leader, talking quickly and looking for results? Or is he cautious, wanting a full explanation and reassurance? What are his words, exactly, and what do they mean? Do you understand what he is trying to communicate, or are you jumping ahead to assume what he means? This is all a part of concerned listening.

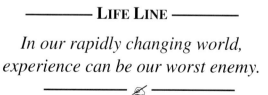

──────── LIFE LINE ────────

*In our rapidly changing world,
experience can be our worst enemy.*

────────── ✍ ──────────

Whether we are aware of them or not, there are some major barriers to listening. They may be cultural. As the world becomes smaller, we are becoming more keenly aware that different cultures have different customs and styles of communication. If we breach the etiquette, the ability to listen will surely be impaired. Another barrier to listening is certainly that of language. When someone is trying to communicate in a language they are not familiar with, it takes a special effort and patience to listen and understand each other. There are attitudinal barriers to communication that may be influenced by education, social standing, economics or sex. When we bring prejudices to communication, we close out the opportunity for understanding. A vast difference in age or values can impair your listening, because you may make judgments about what is being said based upon your own experience. In our rapidly changing world, experience can be our worst enemy.

Listening is the key factor in overcoming barriers: Listen before you speak. Once you've heard the words, repeat them to ensure that you understand what the other person was trying to communicate. Incorporate what you can observe about the other person in your understanding of the words and then choose your words and responses based upon thought—not emotion.

We all have some pet peeves about other's listening styles. Are there people you know who constantly interrupt, or put words in your mouth? Someone who never smiles or looks at you in a conversation? Is it possible that you know someone who ignores your part of the conversation, or asks questions after you finish speaking that indicate they weren't listening? Once we become aware of listening habits, our own and others, we can focus on enhancing our listening skills. If you tend to interrupt, consciously listen until the other person is finished. If you tend to wander away mentally, concentrate on looking at the other person and absorbing every word. That will also keep you from asking questions that were already answered in the conversation. Be interested in the customer and what his needs are. If you can't discern what he wants, you can't provide it!

Listening Languages

It has also been discovered that we tend to have three basic listening languages: *Visual, Auditory and Feeling.* If you listen carefully to the conversation, you will note key words that indicate what kind of listening language the customer has.

Mr. Visual: He returns his car to the dealership for service. "Would you just *look* at this paint? It's already *showing* signs of wear. I can't *imagine* how a car that costs this much could fade this quickly. It is *clear* to me, that if you want to *see* repeat business, you'll *focus* on better quality."

Ms. Auditory: "This paint is already fading. Someone is going to *hear* about this. The salesman *told* me that it was very good quality. It *sounds* to me like you better start *tuning in* to the quality of your product."

Mr. Feelings: "I don't *understand* how a car this expensive could have trouble with paint already. You better *get a handle* on your quality control. I *sense* a real lack of *caring* on the part of your sales people when they sell these cars with bad paint."

——————— LIFE LINE ———————

Communication is most effective when both parties have similar speaking styles.

Because these communication patterns are so ingrained in each of us, we have the tendency to filter out responses that are contrary to our own personal style. Research has determined that *communication is most effective when both parties are matching or mirroring these styles.* Once you determine how your customer communicates verbally, you can adjust your choice of words to match his, and your effectiveness will increase.

As you observe your customers and yourself along these guidelines, you will be able to adjust the way you respond to your customers so that they are most at ease. After all, that's what customer service is all about: making your customer comfortable and happy to do business with you.

Observation of the personality traits and listening styles can be extremely helpful in improving your communication with your customers. As you practice and increase your powers of observation, you can identify and then mirror your customers.

Listening Skills

Here are some techniques to use to improve your listening skills today:

1. First and foremost, *concentrate on listening.* Be aware of all the ways to listen: listen to body language, words, styles and tone. Put your body in an active state and let your body language indicate intense interest.

2. *Search for areas of interest.* Sometimes it seems difficult to find common ground. But if you ask questions and get the customer talking, you will find he has something to offer. Keep looking for opportunities.

3. *Hold the finish.* Wait until you've heard it all before you comment. Don't judge what the customer is saying until he is finished. As a matter of fact, don't judge what he has to say at all. Remember your goal here is to get to the heart of matter. If you are thinking about what you have to say, you'll miss what he's trying to tell you.

4. *Focus on the conversation at hand.* Resist distractions, whatever their cause. If you concentrate on all the ways of listening, you won't have time to be distracted!

5. *Keep your mind open for the options.* Be flexible in your approach, using all your creative powers to gather the most information. While the facts are important, don't let them tie you down. Include them with all the other observations you are making.

You might want to make a reminder for yourself, with just the key words: *concentrate, search, hold, focus, options* to jog your memory while you're on the phone or meeting with a customer.

Types, Games, & Listening Skills

First: There are six basic behavioral types: Direct, Sociable, Autonomous, Cautious, Prudent, and Controlled.

Second: By identifying ourselves and then our customers, we can tailor our responses to meet the needs of our customers.

Third: Listening is a skill that can be improved with practice.

Fourth: When we can provide information to someone in the manner they find most compatible with their own personality and listening styles, we increase the possibilities for making the sale or solving the problems. Remember, we have been given two ears and one mouth. Sometimes we get that mixed-up.

CHAPTER 14:
TELEPHONE TALK

So much of our business is conducted by telephone, and yet, it is still a refreshing surprise to talk with someone who has good telephone etiquette.

Frustrated in Frankfurt

Don't you find it frustrating when:

–It is impossible to tell what the company name is because the receptionist mumbles it or says it so fast you can't understand what is being said.

–You have been put on hold before you can even let the person know who or what you want.

–You have been transferred to five different departments, telling your story each time before you reach the correct person.

–The phone rings ten times and *then* you're put on hold?

Needless to say, whenever any of these things happen, the customer perception of service drops dramatically. Once again, it is that first impression that is lasting.

If you have ever worked on a busy switchboard, you also know that answering the calls and responding to the callers is no easy task. And yet, if that first contact is a pleasant one, the customer will remember the company in a positive way regardless of what follows. Since that first contact is so very important, let's look at some ways to make it more pleasant and productive for both the caller and the one who answers.

A standard rule of thumb for answering calls is to *pick up by the third ring*. Most customers will not be offended with that amount of time, and it gives you adequate time to politely put another customer on hold.

Whether your primary job includes answering the telephone or it is an extension of many other duties, be prepared. *Always have a pencil and paper ready* or easily accessible, so that when the call comes through you won't be rustling around on your desk trying to find something to write the message on. While you're looking, the customer is waiting. And what if they are calling long distance and giving you valuable information that you can only half listen to while you look for the pencil?

Identify yourself or your company. Be sure that you speak clearly, so the caller can understand. Admittedly it is very difficult to continually answer with a company name, particularly if it is long and complicated, but remember, it is the first thing the customer hears. If you are answering for yourself or an individual, give the appropriate name and department along with a greeting, "Good afternoon, Wiley's Wood Works, this is Hilda." Or, "Good morning, Willie Wiley's office, how may I help you?"

———— LIFE LINE ————

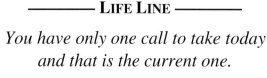

*You have only one call to take today
and that is the current one.*

Whatever is happening around you, when you answer that phone your voice should sound like you are glad to get the call. As far as customer service is concerned, you have only one call to take today and that is the current one. Put some enthusiasm in your voice. Avoid that monotone. During my sales calls, I've heard a good many people answer the telephone. And I know that the same number of calls are coming in at each location, but somehow when just one person is able to answer with enthusiasm, it makes my whole day. I've consciously worked on using an enthusiastic tone when I answer my own business calls and one of the things I've discovered, is that my own attitude takes a turn for the bright side as I put energy in my voice and a smile on my face. Try it. It's a nice side benefit for you while you make the customer feel more at ease.

In any busy office, it is necessary to put customers on hold. Most of us are understanding when it happens to us, as long as we aren't on hold for very long and it is done with common courtesy. *Ask the customer's permission* before you put them on hold and give a reason for the delay. "I have another call coming in. May I put you on hold?" Then wait for the reply just in case the customer is calling on a cell phone with a low battery and it's an emergency.

If you need to transfer the call, *explain why and give direct dialing instructions* if possible, in the event the call is not completed. We all like to be informed. The more information we have about any situation, the less likely we are to become frustrated.

——————— LIFE LINE ———————

To build the relationship with your
clients, you need personal contact.

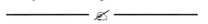

Although the information is important, it also makes a difference how the information is given. People respond to people. Impersonalness can be the ultimate affront. People generally don't want information from computers, even if they are, in fact, more efficient and up-to-date than the information they can get from people. (There are some good phone-mail systems available but be sure to check them out thoroughly.) Pacific Gas and Electric learned this as a result of their diligent efforts to provide their customers with the very best. During a particularly bad storm season that knocked out power throughout northern California, PG&E set up a recorded message that was kept up-to-date with information about affected areas and estimated repairs. Sounds pretty thoughtful. But what they got for their trouble was complaints. So PG&E went back to real people answering real people and got rave reviews. Humans want human contact. It is reassuring, especially in emergencies or when we have a problem, to actually speak to another person. We are less concerned with the specific facts than we are with the desire to connect with another person. You can't program concern or reassurance into a recorded message. To build the relationship with your clients, you need personal contact.

Complaint Department

Let's talk about the complaint department. Earlier we talked about ways of dealing with customers when we had time to see them, speak to them, and listen to them. In those situations, we had the opportunity to create a new satisfied customer. But there is another customer opportunity that is often misunderstood—that's the *dis*satisfied customer. Let's take a walk over to the Complaint Department.

When that topic comes up, people get one of two responses depending on whether they are the complainer or the complainee. If you are doing the complaining, you probably expect to confront a disinterested salesperson who, 1) won't solve your problem, and, 2) will make it as difficult as possible for you to make your complaint. "No, Mr. Jones, I don't have the authority to do anything about it. Fill out these forms in triplicate and we'll get back to you—maybe."

If you are receiving the complaint, you expect to hear, "You are the most incompetent person I've ever seen. Your product is junk. I demand satisfaction or else." With that kind of expectation, neither side of the complaint counter can benefit. But when you re-consider what a complaint can be, you will see it is the best source for generating customer loyalty that you can find.

In a study done by Technical Assistance Research Programs, a Washington D.C. consulting firm, they determined that complaints offer tremendous profit opportunities. They found that if a customer makes a complaint about a major problem, involving $100 or more, he is twice as likely to become a loyal customer even if the problem is not solved. Solve the problem and the return rate is 6 times as great. If you can solve the problem quickly, your customer is 9 times more likely to become a long term loyal customer. Remembering that getting a new customer costs 6 times as much as keeping one, this rate of return can greatly impact the bottom line.

If you're not hearing from your customers, you're in big trouble. "Why," you ask? "They must be happy if I'm not hearing any complaints." Unfortunately, just the opposite may be true. You see there are reasons why people don't complain. Sometimes they feel it is not worth the effort. Others don't know how or where to complain and worst of all, they feel no action will be taken because the company doesn't care enough. With that kind of attitude, your customers will buy from someone else, and you'll never know what's wrong, and you may never see them again.

Let's face it, you can't please all the people all the time. Your dissatisfied customers will either complain to you or switch brands altogether. Worst of all, the customer who changes brands will tell ten or twelve people how dissatisfied he was with your product. As a matter of fact, *13% of the disgruntled clients tell 20 others.* With the potential of that kind of bad press, it's certainly better to encourage your clients to complain! So make it easy for them! Don't wait for those letters to come in. When did you last write a letter of complaint? Consider establishing a toll free number and make it convenient for the customer.

It's a numbers game:

Dissatisfied Customer =
Loss of sales and 10-12 bad referrals.

Listen to Complaint =
2 times as likely to become a
loyal customer and 5 good references.

Provide Solution =
6 times as likely to become a loyal
customer with more than 5 good references.

Quick Response =
9 times as likely to become a loyal customer.

Your added bonus? It's actually more economical to handle complaints by phone than by mail! In fact, Proctor and Gamble found it *40% less expensive to deal with complaints by phone than by letter.*

When people complain, it's because the product didn't live up to the advertised expectations, implied or real. What you can learn from complaints is what isn't working, either in your product or your advertising. A wonderful example is Polaroid. With their early instant print camera, they received numerous complaints that the camera stopped working after a period of time. Well, the answer was simple enough, the batteries needed to be replaced. What Polaroid discovered through the complaints is that the customers didn't realize that the camera even needed batteries. Polaroid could have simply written the problem off to "ignorant" consumers. Instead they gave the information to their product development team, who created the SX=70 film packs with built in batteries. Every time you change film, you change batteries. Of course we're all digital now, but the example is still valid.

In order for your company to reap the benefits of complaints, you have to make it as easy as possible for your customers to reach you. Not only might it good to install a toll-free number, but you have to make it easy for your clients to find you. One major vinyl floor covering company came up with a brilliant solution. They found that their customers were not reading the cleaning instructions included with their floors and were actually damaging the floors with improper cleaning, causing many complaints. To make it easy for the customers to call, they printed their toll-free number on the flooring and the buyers had to call to find out how to remove the phone number. When they called, they got complete care instructions, that way the vinyl floor covering would provide the kind of long wear and beauty for which they were designed.

──────── Life Line ────────

Service is the vehicle that will take you
successfully through the 21ˢᵗ century.

──────── ✍ ────────

Service oriented companies take a very positive position on
complaints. In fact they view complaints as a golden opportunity. A
top corporate executive stated: "A live customer on the line with a
complaint. Wow! What an opportunity! What an opportunity to
service him, and make him into a lifelong friend." In an expanding,
extremely competitive market, some companies continue to enjoy an
exemplary reputation for service. One of the ways they maintain that
edge is to continually remind the customer how hard they are working
at customer service. They make themselves visible to their clients and
use personal follow-through when the repairs are complete. What the
customer perceives is that he can count on the company. The side
benefit to this follow-up is that sales opportunities are created when
they learn that the problem may have been the result of the incorrect
item. Now you have the opportunity to reevaluate the situation to
avoid future problems. The bottom line is service. Service is the
vehicle that will take you successfully through the 21st century.

Chapter 15:
Handling Difficult People

What do you think about encouraging customer complaints? This idea could be terrific, but it will not be successful if you don't provide the support and training for the line staff who will be answering all the calls. Handling a complaint in a professional manner is a difficult task and requires training and support. Let's look at a few key ideas that will increase your effectiveness when dealing with a dissatisfied customer.

By being prepared for the angry and abusive customer, you increase your chances of reaching a mutually agreeable solution to the problem. The customer will be satisfied and turned into a loyal, repeat buyer and you will have a good feeling about your abilities and contribution to the solution.

Understanding & Resolving a Problem

The caller is angry and accusatory. Remembering that you can't change the customer, you have the opportunity to decide what your response will be. You know that the tone of your voice is 38% of the impression you will make. And your body language? Well, it will influence the tone of your voice and your responses even if the customer can't see you! So adjust your body posture; uncross your arms; sit up straight; and don't let your eyes wander, the disinterest will come across in the sound of your voice. All this will be "heard" by the caller, but even more important, adjusting your posture, will adjust your mental attitude to handle the call in a professional manner.

1. *Get ready to start writing.* The concentration of writing down the facts will help you stay out of the emotions of the caller. Get their name and write it down. It will also provide the back-up for the conversation, when you begin to sort out just what the customer wants. If Polaroid had not kept track of the kind of complaints they were receiving, they would not have learned about the batteries. Worst case: should the complaint go to legal action, you will be able to document who, what, when, and where and perhaps avoid the difficulties of going to court.

2. *Avoid the emotions.* Do not allow yourself to be pulled into the customer's anger. He is not really mad at you, but at the situation of a product or service that did not live up to his expectations. With your self-esteem in tact, you'll be able to listen to his words without taking any of them personally. It's not easy, but you can do it!

3. *Listen To Me!* That's really what the customer is saying when he calls. All his anger has built up. He's fuming and ready to explode because he feels hurt, frustrated, let down, mistreated. So listen intently. Listen to the words, without making judgments. The customer is so accustomed to being ignored, and you can sometimes diffuse the whole situation simply by actively listening. Let the customer know you are listening by saying: "Uh-huh," or "I see," or "Yes."

4. *Encourage them:* "Tell me more," or "I'm with you," or "I understand." Don't interrupt. Let the caller tell you his story, while you concentrate on understanding what he's saying and getting it down on paper. You will need all the information you can get to find a good solution to the problem. In the meantime, the customer is letting go of all the built up emotions, so that a rational discussion can follow. Your goal with every call is to solve a problem and prevent it from happening again.

Now it's time to move the conversation from the emotional to the rational so that a solution can be reached. Begin building a rapport with the customer by using his name (remember, you wrote it down as soon as he called). Let the customer know that your goal is to solve the problem. He is accustomed to getting the old "brush-off" now, so reassure him you are committed to a solution. Let him know you took notes by referring to them. This will re-affirm that you really were listening. Now ask him some questions for clarification. Your tone of voice here is extremely important. The questions are not to cast judgment or imply that his complaints are not valid. You may even want to say something like, "Just so I'm clear about this point . . . " Emphasize that you are looking for a clear understanding of what happened.

5. *Create the solution.* You've convinced the customer that you are indeed on his side, so now's the time to ask him what he would like done about the problem. I know this sounds a bit risky. You're expecting he wants $10,000 in damages and 51% of the company's stock, but most often, the customer is not thinking quite so big. You may find he only wants an apology or to let someone know what happened, or what about using your ingenuity to mutually discover a solution?

Let me give you an example: Recently I stayed at a fine hotel in Baltimore. Unfortunately, my bags went to Pittsburgh. Because of some minor delays due to weather, I arrived late for an early morning presentation. My bags would not be arriving until mid-morning—well after my presentation time. The gift shop was closed. I called the night manager for assistance with acquiring a toothbrush, toothpaste and razor. His response was, "We have no arrangements for that, I'm sorry." I said that was unfortunate, especially because of the four diamond rating of your hotel and suggested that he try the hotel next door, which I knew offered emergency kits for guests in this particular predicament. He said, "Well, I suppose I could send the bellman over to see if they would oblige." I said I would really appreciate that.

My question is, why did I have to come up with the solution to what must be a regular situation for guests in distress?

If the solution calls for an action, such as sending out a repairman, you may not be able to accommodate the solution immediately. In this instance, you may have to sell your solution, and word choice is critical. There is a world of difference between: "I can't do anything but send out a serviceman, and he can't be there before Wednesday," compared with "I'll be glad to dispatch our service specialist. I will make sure that repair is scheduled for Wednesday, if that's a convenient time for you."

You may have to go further and show him what the value of the solution is. For instance, repair is better than replacement; parts are guaranteed; he'll be able to maintain his work schedule; new machines might take weeks for delivery.

Once you've reached a solution, you can close the conversation by reiterating what you have agreed to do. Review what actions will be taken by you, and by the customer if required. Continue to reinforce the sense that you are on his "team". "Let's be clear about what *we'll* do next . . ." Ask again if the customer is in agreement.

So often we hear people say things like, "We've never done it that way before," or "That's not possible," or "I'll try." Eliminate these statements from your vocabulary. This type of verbiage is not acceptable to a customer, and in most cases they will resent the statements.

———— LIFE LINE ————

It is better in the long run to under-promise and over-deliver.

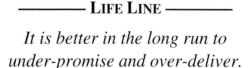

6. *Now . . . Do It!* Whatever you have agreed to do must be followed through with, and completed on time. If you require the assistance or cooperation of others, be sure that you get their commitment for completion and the appropriate priorities established. Let this part of the program slide and you've lost your credibility with the customer and wasted your time and his. Remember—it really comes down to treating your customer the way you'd like to be treated if you were in his position. Put it all in writing to the customer. This will reassure the customer that you are serious about his complaint and your commitment. Furthermore, you will have one more opportunity to mend the relationship and create a loyal customer.

7. The *attention to follow-through* can't be stressed too much. The result of promising more than you can deliver will create the perception in the customer that you have failed to keep your promises. It is better in the long run to under- promise and over-deliver. Let me give you an example of what I mean. If you promise to get back to a customer at noon and end up calling at 3:00 p.m., the customer will perceive that you didn't deliver. It won't matter that the quality of your product or service is superior, because the only thing the customer will remember is that you didn't do what you said you'd do. Customers would prefer that you say you'll get back to them at the end of the day in the first place, rather than expect to hear from you at noon and not get a call until 3:00 p.m.

An interesting side-note about perceptions comes from the health care industry. They discovered that patients who were told exactly what to expect in terms of post-operative pain, recovered one-third faster than those who didn't know what to expect. The panic caused by not knowing what to expect actually delayed the healing process. When you have an angry customer, he's suffering emotional pain. Let him know what to expect (and produce it), and he'll be on the road to recovery.

Here's a short list to help you focus on your actions when you deal with a dissatisfied customer.

Action Plan for Complaints:

1. Make it easy to complain.

2. Be prepared when the customer calls.

3. Listen! Listen! Listen!

4. Write down what the customer says for better understanding and as a future reference.

5. Ask the customer how he wants the problem resolved.

6. Create and sell the solution, if necessary, choosing your words carefully to remain positive and supportive.

7. Follow through!

Just to be sure I've been clear about complaints, let me reiterate:

1. The complaints you receive from customers represent Golden Opportunities to create a loyal client base.

2. No news is *not* good news. It is very bad news indeed, because most customers would rather change than complain.

3. Make it easy to complain with toll-free numbers that people are able to find.

4. The staff receiving the complaints must be prepared to respond in a professional and organized manner.

5. Follow-through on the information received from customers is critical to maintaining a service edge.

——————— **LIFE LINE** ———————

The complaints you receive from customers represent Golden Opportunities to create a loyal client base.

You'll be your own best judge. Just ask yourself this question, "Am I providing the quality of service that I feel represents our company in the best possible manner?"

CHAPTER 16:
IS THERE A BETTER WAY?

——— LIFE LINE ———

Customer service doesn't just happen.

It isn't serendipity that brings people committed to customer service to the same company. One of the things that service leaders have in common is an obsession with the customer. Customer service doesn't just happen. This customer orientation is exhibited throughout the company, not just in the sales force or the ad department. There is back-up support in manufacturing, maintenance, shipping, accounting, in fact, in every area of the organization. Without the complete support of every department, complete service quality cannot be achieved. If you want your customers to believe in your commitment to service, you have to have a shipping department that will bring people in on Sunday to meet an emergency deadline. The accounting department must be willing to examine customer questions regarding their statements and respond in exactly the amount of time they commit to—remember, if you say you'll get back to them by 3:00 p.m., be sure you do.

How to Make Fresh Fish Fresher

One of the very difficult things about customer service is that your customers' perceptions of your service or product quality may come from the most unexpected sources. There is a wonderful story about a retail food store where a woman complained about the fish not being fresh. Since the man who purchased the fish daily for the market was there, he responded that the fish was absolutely fresh, straight from the fish market or the pier every day. He would guarantee that it was fresh. The lady responded, "But it's packaged. It's in a plastic supermarket package!" In her mind fresh fish was the kind you bought right off the ice. If you had taken the time to package it, it could not possibly be fresh. There's no arguing about it with the customer. Once a customer perceives something to be true, it must be acknowledged and responded to as absolute. The market responded by setting up a fish bar directly across from the packaged fish for customers who felt like the lady. What they found out was that their packaged fish sales did not decrease, in fact, they doubled their total fish sales.

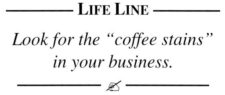

——— LIFE LINE ———

Look for the "coffee stains"
in your business.

Another example comes from the airline industry. A passenger found coffee stains on the flip down trays, and automatically assumed that the engine maintenance was just as careless. You never know where your customers will form a perception of your company. This underscores the need to be aware of every minute detail within your operation and to listen carefully to your customers. If you pay close attention, you'll get a clue or two about what they perceive about you. Look for the "coffee stains" in your business.

When talking about customer service, it's helpful to take an overview of how your product fits in the market place. A professor at Harvard has created what he calls the Total Product Concept. This model defines products by four categories: generic, expected, augmented and potential. Let's use a department store as an example. On the generic level, the store provides a building and clothing. At the expected level, they provide standard shopping hours and fashionable clothing styles. The differences begin to show at the augmented level, where they invest more in staffing, selection, a specialized buying based on individual store locations. Their reputation would be created at the potential level. This is the level where you experience the best possible world. The policy of "return anything," the ability of sales people to implement decisions on the spot, a pianist in every store and flowers in the dressing rooms brings the stores far beyond the expected level for a department store and establishes the customer perception of exceptional service. Do you know a place like that?

In this environment, exceptional service becomes the norm. Unfortunately, too often business focuses inward on the generic level, paying attention to technical performance or month end figures, rather than on the customer. Think about how your customer will perceive your product. What are the things on the augmented level and the potential level that will give you an edge in the marketplace and keep your customers coming back?

We've spent a good deal of time talking about customers and how critical it is to meet their needs. Yet there is another significant aspect to customer service.

The service edge is carefully developed and enhanced by a corporate commitment not only to it's customers but to its employees. A key ingredient in this commitment is effective employee training. Employees who are well trained have confidence to produce superior products and provide superior service, thereby minimizing repair service or customer dissatisfaction.

What Gives a Company the Service Edge?

One company that has been using extensive training to provide a significant edge in the marketplace is McDonald's. The training for each work station is intensive and progressive. For example: there is an eight point process required of each employee at each work station.

1. They read about the specifics of the work station.

2. They watch an audio-visual on the work station.

3. They acquire additional personal instruction from a trainer.

4. They are assigned to a buddy/mentor who actually works the station. In this process, accuracy is stressed more than speed and the mentor makes the objectives of the station very clear.

5. They take a written and oral exam about the work station.

6. They work the station alone, under observation with ongoing feedback and progress review.

7. They receive a performance evaluation in regard to specific standards and objectives of the station.

8. They move to the next work station and repeat the process.

It may seem outlandish to provide such detailed training to make a milk shake, but when there are 12 customers in line and 3 fast food outlets within 2 blocks, the speed and consistency of preparing that shake will impact the bottom line. In businesses where you have only minutes to respond to customers, each second takes on more significance.

In providing this kind of training, McDonald's assures that the customer will receive the same kind of service at each facility. In addition, each employee will be well trained for more than one job and will be able to perform each task thoroughly and efficiently. An employee is given the information and support necessary to bring him up to the standards, then it's time to increase his speed. The mentor system allows the new employee to learn the "tricks of the trade" from someone who actually does the job and the bonus is the spirit of teamwork created among the staff.

Other industries are following McDonald's lead, including hotels and departments stores. Here is a six point sales/service standard that has been developed for the employees of one retail organization:

Sales/Service Standard

1. Recognize the customer within 30 seconds by smiling, making eye contact and a verbal greeting.

2. Talk to every customer within 3 minutes.

3. Ask questions to identify customer needs and make suggestions.

4. Offer product advice and additional merchandise.

5. Conclude by asking if the sale may be put on the company charge account.

6. Smile, say "Thank you," and invite the customer back.

Whether you are a part of top management or an employee, who faces customers every day, the time you take to evaluate the details of your job to make yourself more productive will return tremendous benefits to you and the customer. Look carefully at your position and how you interact with customers. Consider how you can establish your own customer service standard. You may want to talk with your peers in similar jobs and determine how your departments interact in the customer service chain and work out ways to improve communication between yourselves. Certainly as you improve your abilities to do your own jobs, customer service will improve.

Recap: The Customer Service Edge

Customers are not just a part of your business, they are your business. Without them, it won't matter if your product is infallible. In an impersonal world, sales and repeat sales will be determined by the personal relationships built between the business and the customer.

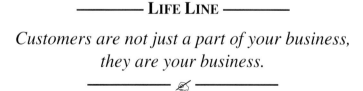

——————— LIFE LINE ———————

Customers are not just a part of your business,
they are your business.

Building the relationships takes time, energy and focus from the top of the organization down, from the sales people to the plant workers. It takes a long time to make a customer. It's an attitude that the customer is always right, even if he's wrong. It's a little like the comment by the cartoon strip character, Pogo, "We have met the enemy and he is us." We are all customers. We all have perceptions of every business we come in contact with. When we stop to think about what we want as customers and begin to provide it for our own customers, then we can create the service edge we need.

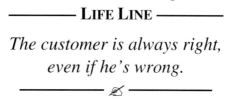

─────── **LIFE LINE** ───────

The customer is always right,
even if he's wrong.

─────────── ✍ ───────────

It's the awareness of the uniqueness of each customer that makes it possible to address his specific needs. The way to discover who your customer really is, is listen, listen, listen. Listen with all the techniques available: body language, voice tone, character type, style of communication. When you have distilled what he wants, then find a way to provide it. If he wants "fresh fish" find a way to make your fresh fish fresher.

Encourage your customers to talk to you. If you don't know what's not working, how can you fix it? Get that toll-free number, establish a survey for your customers, hold a forum where they can express their concerns or simply call them up and ask them! Dissatisfied customers can become your very best salespeople if you just give them a chance to talk with you. If you act on their input, you'll not only have a loyal customer, but one who will sing your praises to their associates. It sure beats cold calls!

Take good care of the customers who do complain. The solution to the problem may be as simple as an apology or as complicated as changing technology, but the result will be well worth the effort. Follow through on your promises. Make it clear both verbally and in writing, exactly what you can do. Remember, it is better to under-promise and over-deliver than to miss the mark on a promise. Keep your patient healthy by telling him exactly what will happen.

Make employee service a part of customer service. Support employees with training to make their jobs easier and more rewarding. Let everyone know that each job is critical in the customer service chain. The sales staff may be able to get the order, but if production can't supply the product, maintenance can't repair it, or accounting can't bill properly, not only will the sale be lost, but the customer will be sure to tell his friends. Did you ever notice how the most unhappy customer just happens to play golf with the chairman of the board of your company? When customer service is the focus throughout the company, your customers can sing your praises on the golf course.

Evaluate everything. It's important to know where you are in every aspect of the service cycle. Look at your service. Does it provide and project product value? Do employee training programs provide what you currently need to meet the service standard? How is your coffee stain ratio? Look around and listen. Be prepared to ask some direct questions and make some changes. View every aspect of your business through the customer's eyes and then redefine these aspects continually based on customer perception.

Now, *live it with passion and total dedication.* Customer service is not a "To Do List." Implementing the techniques and ideas we have discussed here will not entirely assure your success. Dedication to the customer as your primary focus is a continuing way of life for any company that wishes to maintain the edge. "Do unto others," is a familiar phrase, but absolutely true when providing customer service. Give the quality of service *you* would like to receive to your customers, and you will see the benefits in every aspect of your business—and your life.

Epilogue:
The Service Edge

When you are too busy to give your customers top quality service you have just created one of the most dreaded monsters in the business world, and that is the *lack* of business. Why would someone want to return to give you their business if you do not have their interests at heart? The most successful professionals I know are those who put super-service first on their list. The least successful business people are the ones who are creatures of habit; resistant to change and who provide service to their customers when it fits into their schedule.

Your attitude will make the difference in the service you provide, and you control your attitude.

You might have asked yourself why some people have such junky lives. Usually it's because they do not know a better way. They choose junky thoughts and for the present they are satisfied with the pay-off—sympathy, self-pity, and other non-survival attitudes and reactions. It's like going to a movie; you make the choice, you pay your money, and you go in and see it. The film may be humorous or it may be a horror film. You know that you can get up and leave anytime you choose, because it's only a movie. Why would you sit there if you didn't enjoy it? For no reason at all. Still, we sit through life, flashing illusions on our minds that we do not enjoy all the time because we have not had the awareness, self-discipline, or understanding to do things differently. There is only one reality, and that is yours in this present moment. You choose your life; no one else can live it. No one else can even see it as you do, for no one else can get in your head to look out from within. We too often attempt to beat up the screen when things aren't going right; we blame outside circumstances and point fingers at them. Well, life is just like the movie in the theater. If you don't like what's on the screen the only way to change it is to run a different film in the projector. Your mental projector can do that for you.

In customer service, attitude is the prime ingredient. The bottom line is that "like attracts like." If you treat the unreasonable customer the same way you treat the reasonable one, it's amazing how often you can turn a frown into a smile.

SECTION III

THE

SALES

LEADER

*Sales Secret:
Find out what they want—
then help them get it.*

CHAPTER 17:
THE ART OF WORD MAGIC

If you have never thought of yourself as a salesperson and you are not particularly fond of selling—this chapter will surprise you, it is an important chapter for you to read. On the other hand, if you are "in sales" and you want to continue to expand your knowledge, your skill, and your income—this chapter is imperative!

We've heard it said that nothing happens until someone sells something. It would seem then, that selling, or the ability to acquire the skills of selling would be a most sought after commodity. Strange though, that when we look at successful people, people in any field, and we observe their patterns, traits, and results, we call them either smart or lucky. Then, when we design a plan to tie together all the elements of success—of which successful people exemplify—we call it manipulation.

Well, take heed my friends, call it what you will, but it makes sense to me that if anything can be accomplished at all, there must be a better way to accomplish it. This certainly holds true with the art of selling. Books have been written and programs offered to share the specifics of selling; softening the atmosphere, effective questioning, overcoming objections and how to close the sale. I'll cover these areas, but with a new element. You see, my belief is (and the conviction only grows) that people buy you, not your product or service. You may have the best product or service in the world, but if your customer does not perceive you as confident, reliable, trustworthy (and all the attributes of one with whom he or she wishes to work with) then the sale will most likely not be made.

What can you do to build in an element of security to ensure that your prospective client will look to you for positive support in handling their account and filling their needs on a regular basis?

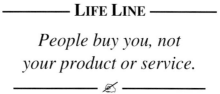

———— LIFE LINE ————

People buy you, not
your product or service.

Right at the top we come back to the age old topic of self-esteem. How do you feel about yourself? What do you think of yourself as a salesperson? How can you change the image you have of yourself to shift from one who sells to one who excels? Simple, but not easy.

I don't want you to get the idea that all you have to do is to change a few words, put on a different necktie, or memorize the four reasons people don't buy (which are: no need, no confidence, no money, or no hurry), we'll talk about those later. There are a few more aspects that enter into the picture. I mean, really, if it were so easy to be a success, then everyone would be successful, everyone would be rich, everyone would be totally in love, and everyone would be healthy. But they're not. Ask yourself then, why? Basically I believe that successful people form habits of doing things that unsuccessful people will not do. Also, many people are unwilling to give up their present life-style, even for a better one. Now that may surprise you but it's a known fact that once habit patterns are established it takes an unusual individual to forge ahead into new and uncertain paths, and even risk failure, all for a glimpse of possible success. Are you such a person? You may say *"yes"* emphatically, and yet your character, your fiber, and the proof of your words will be displayed in the results you achieve.

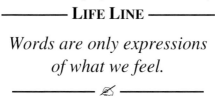

——————— LIFE LINE ———————

Words are only expressions
of what we feel.

It doesn't matter what stage of development you are currently in. You could be the top salesperson in your company, or a newcomer, bringing a unique twist of freshness and enthusiasm into the business. There is no one who cannot gain significantly by utilizing a new idea, applying a useful strategy, or opening their mind to possibilities.

I look at it this way. When a flower is growing it's alive. A flower that is not growing is dying. As long as we are thinking, moving, challenging, and pushing toward greater areas of expression, toward more, toward better, we are growing. When we stop our quest for advancement, when we close our minds to new ways and new ideas, we begin to die a little. And bit by bit the deterioration process sets in. What you need then is a good kick in your . . . *complacency.*

Word Magic

So where to begin? I can't think of better place than with the words we use to describe our everyday experiences and situations. I call it word magic. You too, will see the magic in this word restructuring process, and you will marvel at the magic when you see situations melt before your very eyes from irritation to satisfaction, from indifference to compassion, from "I wouldn't touch that with a ten foot pole!" to "Where do I sign?"

———— LIFE LINE ————

We talk to ourselves all the time, the problem is
that we believe what we say.

———————— ✍ ————————

Here's how it works. We attach feelings to words. When you think about it, words are only expressions of what we feel. In themselves they have no meaning. Yet just the mere utterance of a sound can evoke anger, or inspire confidence. Which would you prefer in your sales presentation? By the way, this works for the way *you* respond to the words you think and speak as well as the way *others* respond to them.

Psychologist David McClelland stated that we talk to ourselves all the time, the problem is that we believe what we say. After all, look who said it—you did. There is scientifically proven to be a microscopic movement of the larynx whenever we think. We are always talking to ourselves. I was presenting this idea at a seminar a while back, and at the break a man came up to me and said he had been sitting in the back thinking to himself that *'if this guy for one minute thinks I'm sitting back here . . . talking to myself'*, when he realized that's exactly what he was doing. We all do it, and we will continue to do so. So let's take advantage of the process and use it for our benefit. Let's restructure the negative statements into more positive phrases for health, success and happiness. Einstein said that the difference between the right word and the wrong word is like the difference between a lightning bug and a lightning bolt. Your customer wants to experience positive action when he deals with you so why not give it to him. Here are some suggestions to give you a feel for what I mean:

Instead of saying what you can't do, say what you can do. In other words don't say, "I don't want to misinform you or give you any wrong information," turn this around by saying "I want to make sure I give you accurate information, let me check this out and I'll get right back to you." In any event you are going to have to supply the person with the information, so why not do it in a positive manner?

When your client asks you for a delivery date don't say, "We can't have that to you until Tuesday." Say with enthusiasm, *"You're in luck, we can have that for you on Tuesday."* This creates a whole different feeling, almost as if he is getting special treatment.

Instead of asking your client, "How much do you have to spend on this?" ask her, "How much have you set aside for this investment?" One says you don't think the client plans very well, the other says you think they plan very well.

How about substituting, "I'm calling to see if you received the delivery," with, "I'm calling to make sure your delivery has arrived." A simple shift of words can make a significant change in meaning from being meek or curious to efficient follow-up and appropriate customer service.

Don't think so much of what you want to say, rather think of what the prospect wants to hear. When talking about selling, consider restructuring your sentence to convey the feeling of having an opportunity to purchase. An example would be: "I'd like to sell you the automobile." Contrast that with, "Let's find a way to put this together so you can purchase the automobile." People like to purchase, but they don't like to be sold anything. Think about this also: when you have a cost, you are putting money out, when you invest, you spend money to receive a greater return. You add value to your product or service by substituting the words: "investment", "monthly investment", or "initial investment", for the words: "down payment", "monthly payment", or "deposit". And for goodness sake get, "I'll be honest with you," out of your statements. Think of what you are saying. You have just said that your prior comments may not have been truthful. Be forthright and clear with your communication, and there will be no reason to doubt your truthfulness.

──────── **LIFE LINE** ────────

Enliven your speech with
adjectives that sparkle.

Another habit we've gotten ourselves into is the term "I can't." Now this is really not acceptable in the vocabulary of a successful salesperson. Replace it with either "I will," or "I won't," or "I don't want to," or "I don't choose to," or "I'll get to it later." But don't tell people, "I can't." All you are really saying is, "I won't." Use your creative mind and find another way. No one wants to be told what you will not do for them.

Here's another one that we hear all the time. "I haven't had time." No, you haven't taken the time. Be truthful, people respect that.

And what do you think about people who say this: "Could you spell your name for me?" What an insult. It implies that the person is of such low intelligence that he doesn't know how to spell his own name. Why not simply say, "Please spell your name for me."?

And how about enlivening your speech with some adjectives that sparkle. Instead of using the mundane and trite words like good and nice, put your thinking cap on and say what you really want to say. Consider more descriptive words such as: attractive, wonderful, exciting, splendid, or fantastic. There are a thousand more to fit your particular situation.

──────── **LIFE LINE** ────────

When you know the magic, you will always have
a place in the kingdom.
—Walt Disney

Finally, use statements that lift *your* spirits, build confidence in you, and support *your* sales efforts such as:

"My comments and ideas are valuable to others."

"I make a difference."

"I enjoy providing a service for other people."

"I am surrounded by people who support me."

"I express the traits of a successful person."

Walt Disney put it this way, he said, "When you know the magic, you will always have a place in the kingdom." There are those people who learn, and we all do to some extent. We learn from our experiences, from our accomplishments and from our set-backs. But then, there are those people who seem to glide more smoothly through life because they have been diligent in their efforts to consistently apply what they have learned. AND, there are those people who know the magic. Creating magic with words is part of the success experience, it can be fun and extremely profitable. See what you can do to adapt this idea into your world.

Chapter 18:
Know Yourself,
Know Your Product

Francis Bacon said that knowledge is power. Whether you are a novice to your trade or a veteran who has experienced the gamut, this one bit of truth will provide you with a pillar of strength.

Let's say that you are a new realtor. You have passed your exam and have a basic handle on the business. But, you have not sold any real property and are somewhat unfamiliar with the territory. Here's where knowledge-is-power comes into play.

Select a building that is for sale, a home, an apartment complex, an office building, it doesn't much matter. Now, begin to gather all the information about this piece of property. Who were the previous owners, when was it built, what is the current maintenance condition, the taxes, the zoning restrictions, city planning for that area, easements, water rights, and population projections. Also explore the financing opportunities and look for creative alternatives. You may want to go to the extent of gathering some remodeling estimates to have them as suggestions for potential buyers. In other words, take a real interest in that property.

──────── LIFE LINE ────────

If you are just selling the product then
you have missed the magic.

──────── ✍ ────────

Now you may be new on the job, you may never have sold much of anything before, but I'll bet you that you will be one of the most qualified sales people to turn that property. Knowledge is power. This example can be applied by any person in any business, whatever you are selling. The veteran salesperson has acquired much of her knowledge through training and years of experience, and product knowledge is a natural by-product of dealing with an industry or item for a period of time. Still, one cannot be too smart when it comes to second-guessing the competition, creating a network of information, and gathering support from the people around you to gain an edge in your market.

Knowledge, Gain, Benefit

By now you may be getting the erroneous idea that all you need is product knowledge. Well, yes and no. Yes, because you have to know what it is that you are selling, and no, because if you are just selling the product then you will have missed the magic. We must sell the benefits of the product. A prospect would not want to know the forging process of the kitchen knife as much as she would the benefits of consistently being able to slice tomatoes tissue-paper thin. A potential client is not as interested in how the money changes hands in the mutual fund as she is in the dividends it pays. Your customer's focus is not as strongly directed toward the installation process of the wallpaper as she is in the feeling that will be created when she entertains her friends and clients. *Sell the benefits.*

To discover the multitude of benefits for your service or product let's look at the facts. That is, what is *known,* what will be *gained,* and how will the customer *benefit.* An example of this is to define your product or service. Let's say that you are in the hospitality industry, a hotel for instance. You *know* that you have a property that accommodates people for their sleeping, meeting and convention needs. A *gain* is that your client's people will be able to make more efficient use of their time by being in one location. The *benefit* of being in one location is to have more time to share together to accomplish the objectives of the meeting.

Another example would be to use an automobile as the product. Let's say it's a sports car. You obviously *know* that it is sporty in appearance. You could *gain* recognition and popularity, and one *benefit* could be new friends by expanding your social circle. Air conditioning for the car is another *known.* Because of this you *gain* comfort and coolness, and arriving to your destination fresh and relaxed is a *benefit.* You may know that the car has automatic door locks. You would *gain* added convenience, and some of the *benefits* would be safety and saving time.

Selling the benefits will create value in your product or service. You move into a unique category of salesmanship when you move from *selling* to *providing an opportunity* to fulfill your customer's dreams and desires. People will more often purchase what they want, rather than what they actually need.

When you sell the benefits, your customer will respond to you, your product or your service more favorably, for you are speaking directly to their feeling nature.

─────── LIFE LINE ───────

If you assume their needs, you may
lock yourself out of the sale.

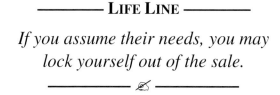

Involve the Customer

Let's talk about getting your customer involved. Getting people involved in the sales process will create a memorable experience.

Whether we become involved in driving to the party, cooking the dinner, building the fence, or in the sales transaction, we tend to remember the experience better when we are part of the process. So get your people involved. Have them look at something, hold something, or help you. Put the item in their hands, have them touch it, feel it, listen to it, smell it. Whatever you are offering, give the person a chance to experience ownership. To get them involved both physically and mentally you can lock them into a statement with comments like, "Sure is a beautiful outfit, isn't it?" or "I can imagine what your friends will say, can't you?" By making statements like these you elicit involved response. The person must bring their attention into focus on the subject at hand and communicate with you.

Be careful not to overuse these phrases. They can become trite and noticeable. Also, be careful not to use this technique before you discover the needs of your prospect, and you begin to get a positive position response. *If you assume their needs, you may lock yourself out of the sale.* For instance, you could easily assume that your prospect would want the extra power in the automobile engine for passing on a two lane road. Your statement might be, "You would want an automobile that will give the power to comfortably pass another on an uphill climb, wouldn't you?" The person's response might be, "No. This will be our second car and we'll just be doing city driving so it might be better if we continue looking for something that will suit our needs better." Don't assume they will agree to something just because it sounds logical to you. Find out the customer's needs and get those facts first.

Another way of getting your customer involved is to talk about them, not about you. Cavett Robert stated that people don't care how much you know, until they know how much you care. It sure is tempting to share how you received the awards on your wall, your experiences in Singapore, or how well your children are doing in school. Instead, probe them for information that will give you insight into their reasons for using your services or product.

Involve people by using their names. The sweetest sound anyone can hear is the sound of their own name. Use it, but don't abuse it. Listen to the pronunciation of the name. If you get it wrong, you may create a distance that will destroy the personal quality you are striving for.

One good method for getting the name right is to repeat it several times mentally, Ask for the spelling, and write it down. Comment on it if it's unusual, and mentally associate it with something that rhymes with it. A tip that I have found useful if their name did momentarily slip my mind is to ask, "What is your full name again?" By asking that question you are implying that you do know their first name, but you would like them to refresh you on their last name. They will most likely give you their first and last name at that time. Also, when meeting someone, it's helpful to greet them by saying, "It's good to see you." That way, if you have met them before you have covered all the bases. If you have met them before and you say, "It is so nice to meet you," you might insult them because they feel that you think they were not important enough to remember in the first place.

One fine technique for getting people involved is by asking them questions, it is by far one of the easiest ways to gain valuable information about your prospect. Simple questions like:

"What type of service have you received before?"

"How do you plan to use this product?"

"Share with me, if you will, just how you want your people to feel at the convention."

"Where have you traveled before and what was your experience?"

These are simple questions that get people talking about themselves and their experiences. Invaluable information will be shared, so listen closely to their comments. We call this type of questioning open-ended. Usually these questions begin with who, what, where, when, and how. Resist questions beginning with "why", at least initially, often they can sponsor defensiveness. I'll expand on this later.

──────── LIFE LINE ────────

For any life to be great it must be
focused, dedicated, and disciplined.
– Harry Emerson Fosdick

──────── ✍ ────────

Listening

My final comment on getting your customer or prospect involved in the sales process has to do with raising your I.Q. Don't get me wrong, I'm not saying that you have a low intelligence quotient, as I indicated earlier I'm referring to the fact that most people have a low Interest Quotient. Basically they don't really take an interest in the other person. Therefore I want you to tune in to me now. I am going to present to you one of the most powerful concepts in communication, a concept that is used by very few people. But then, very few people are truly successful, are they? I call this the concept of being *100% present.* In theory it sounds so simple, *all you have to do is to pay attention.* But understand me when I say, *most people don't pay attention. Focus in with your eyes and ears on what the other person is saying.* Don't think of what you'll be saying next—*focus on them.* When you are 100% present, you convey a courtesy, an interest and a power to your client that will be respected and responded to.

──────── LIFE LINE ────────

If you truly desire to excel,
being 100% present is essential.

──────── ✍ ────────

I admit that it's difficult to focus our minds sometimes. Harry Emerson Fosdick said that for any life to be great it must be focused, dedicated, and disciplined. I've probably lost several of you already. You've been home with the kids, thinking about dinner, even wondering about tomorrow—it's natural. But people know when they have your full attention, and they know when your mind has left your body. If you truly desire to excel, and maintain top sales performance, being 100% present is essential. You will find the benefits and the rewards will be worth your investment, so make this item a top priority on your list.

CHAPTER 19:
QUESTIONS—USE AND ABUSE

The art of questioning is fascinating. Are you aware of the control you possess when you master the art of skillful questioning? Do you realize that you can literally lead someone into the sale when you understand the dynamics of the questioning process? And did you know that by questioning your client you can discover valuable information to overcome potential objections before they even arise?

——————— LIFE LINE ———————

The most important secret in salesmanship
is finding out what people want
and helping them get it.

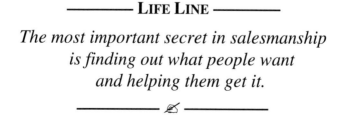

Questions can literally make or break your sales presentation and, of course, they can be the critical key to closing the sale. But asking the right question, with the right timing, in the right way, takes practice, patience and persistence.

Yes, questions can get your prospect to share their needs, wants and desires. You can discover an overwhelming amount of information about people simply by asking the right questions. Let's take a look at some of the different types of questions that we as salespeople can ask to get answers that will fill your clients' needs, put money in your pocket and YOU on the sales charts. The most important secret in salesmanship is finding out what people want and helping them get it.

Open-Ended Questions

We talked a little about open-ended questions before. These are the type that get the client talking. When you get the person talking you have an opportunity to make many discoveries about their likes and dislikes, feelings and attitudes. You can also gain insight into the basic make-up of the individual, because when they are thinking on their feet, they will tend to be less controlled with their body language—we'll touch on that later.

An example of open-ended questions would be:

"What kind of feeling do you want to create in this room?"

"How would these ideas benefit your business?"

"When would you like Susan to begin leading the project?"

This type of questioning cannot be answered with a simple "yes" or "no" and can get people thinking favorably about your product or service, it will give them a feeling of involvement because they have an opportunity to participate in the sales process.

Closed-Ended Questions

Closed-ended questions are excellent tools as are open-ended questions. They are especially effective when you need to gain specific information. Also, using positive closed-ended questions during your sales presentation will elicit agreement through the process. Some examples of positive feedback closed-ended questions are:

"Wouldn't it be terrific if we could get this installed soon?"

"Won't it be a relief to have all your accounting problems resolved?"

"Doesn't it make sense to investigate this now, before crisis management sets in?"

"Isn't it about time for you to really treat yourself right?"

You can see that this type of questioning must be handled skillfully, and when you do, you will help your client see the benefits of your service. Be watchful, however, not to overuse these, as they can begin to sound contrived.

Closed-ended questions can be useful in getting a decision by giving people a choice. When someone orders a hamburger and you ask, "Would you like anything else?" the answer may be, "No," because there are too many things to think about. But if you ask "Would you like fries and a soft drink?" you'll probably get a "Yes" response on one or both. When you offer too many choices the decision to not buy is usually chosen. When you limit the selection to two or three items, you have increased the odds to purchase.

Dangerous Questions

Watch for the D.Q.'s, dangerous questions. What could be dangerous about asking questions you say?

1. To begin with **when you put your client on the spot, or begin an assumed close too early, you have just dug yourself in—deep.** You can develop a sense about a person, even if you have only talked with them for a few moments. If he has his arms tightly folded high on his chest, if he is resistant to your encouraging comments, if his eyes dart from point to point noticeably not giving you his attention, if the physical space between you begins to widen, you can be pretty sure that you will have a challenge handling this one.

You can begin to build a supportive atmosphere by asking for his opinions—and listening to them. Also, *your* body language is important here, for when there is tension in the air, muscles begin to tense and movements become abrupt and strained. So relax and give the person the benefit of the doubt.

2. A dangerous approach is when you lose control by asking *a question that could lead the person off on a tangent.* You may end up totally departing from the subject at hand, resulting in possibly having to go back to ground zero, and losing precious time. Talkative people are sometimes the worst offenders. When you ask them what time it is, they will tell you how to make a watch. If you ask them about their travels, they will give you a verbal trip to Southeast Asia.

What to do? Hold gently to the lead of the conversation and keep guiding the person back to the subject. Example: "As you were talking, your comment reminded me of something that could really be a major factor in your decision today," or "You know, you really have a point there, and when you think about it, the same thing pretty much holds true for this item we are discussing here today." Then bring them right back to the subject of the sale.

3. *There is danger in telling vs. discovering.* When you are only telling them the facts (one after another, ta dum, ta dum, ta dum) you lose them. When you tell them they will doubt you, when they discover it they believe it. So why not draw out their feelings about your product, *and* get them to confirm their belief in it as well? Here are some simple suggestions:

"You would certainly want quality and reliability as part of your guarantee, wouldn't you?" Who wouldn't agree with that?

"You mentioned 'state of the art', this is important to you, isn't it?" If he mentioned it earlier you know he is interested in it, so he has to agree with you.

"Service is a factor in many peoples' decision, as I suspect it is in yours, am I right?" Well, he's not going to say, "No, I'll just buy it and take my chances."

I think you get the idea. By following this line of questioning you are implying benefits and your customer is agreeing with you. You also build rapport by letting the client discover, and share the benefits of your product for himself.

4. *On occasion you can frighten people if you don't specify the reason for your question.* If you are a stranger and you ask a person questions like:

"What were your earnings last year?"

"What time does your husband come home?"

"Where do your children go to school?"

"What are your plans for the evening?"

This type of questioning can be threatening if not prefaced with your reason for asking, especially if you are not well acquainted with the individual. Their mind will begin to work overtime on why you are asking them these questions. *(Is he with the I.R.S.? Does he want to come over to our home before my husband returns? Will he intercept my children on their return from school? If I leave tonight should I be concerned that someone will break in?)*

These thoughts are taken to the extreme, of course. But just be aware when you are asking ulterior motive questions.

A friend of mine once asked an attractive young lady what she was doing on Saturday night. Her mind ran through all the scenarios of him asking her out for the evening. Wondering what her reply should be, and wanting to accept a date with him she said, "Saturday night? I have no plans for Saturday night." He said, "Great, my uncle is in town. Would you be able to watch my three year old son while we go to the ball game?"

Avoiding the D.Q.'s

Here are some basic rules to help you avoid getting yourself in over your head with dangerous questions:

1. Stay away from religion, politics, and racial issues.

2. Structure your question to accent the positive points.

3. Focus on the solution, not the problems.

4. Use questions that lead your prospect to action.

5. Plan some of your questions ahead of the presentation. There are always three types of presentations: The one you plan to give, the one you give, and the one you wish you had given. Planning will give *you* the edge.

While we're at it, let's nip this one in the bud right now. How about this question: "May I help you?" Bad, bad, bad! You are 99% sure to get the response, "No, I'm just looking." Switch it around, be creative. Greet them with a simple, "Good afternoon, let me know when you have a question. I'll also be glad to help locate your size quickly. Take your time and call me when you need me." Now you've got their attention—you're not just another salesperson.

Also, give them a choice. When you confront them with:

"May I help you?"

"May I take your order for the shipment?"

"May I activate the insurance policy?"

The overwhelming reply will be "NO!" And folks, that's not acceptable around here.

Instead, give them a choice in a round-about way:

"Are you looking for blues, or greens?"

"Would delivery of the shipment be better for you early in the week, or toward the end of the week?"

"Is a yearly premium adequate for you, or would you prefer quarterly and monthly options?"

Just remember, whenever you give them a chance to say no, they will.

Hot Potato

Here's a technique I've labeled the Hot Potato. We all know what you want to do when you're holding a hot potato . . . you want to get rid of it. The Hot Potato technique works the same way—you pass the question back to the other person.

A friend of mine has an obsession for shoes. She cannot pass the shoe department without at least a brief visit. I have seen the poor salesman running back and forth fetching shoe after shoe. She will shop till *he* drops. If the salesman would just pick-up on the hot potato idea he could save himself a lot of anxiety. Here's how it works. "Do you have this shoe in navy?" "If I can locate it in navy would you like it?" Now tell me, why should he run back to the stock room for the fifth time if she's not going to buy it anyway?

Your client asks, "Does the computer have a good graphics board?" Now you could certainly respond with a simple yes or no. But that's not too clever, is it? Why not say, "Is graphics important to you for the work you will be doing?" If he agrees it's important, he'll be the proud new owner of a computer with a high-quality graphics board, because you'll find a way to make it part of the package, won't you?

Here's another example of skillful questioning. You may have found yourself in a similar situation. With the Hot Potato you answer a question with a question. My friend returned home to find that his wife had purchased a new dress. He said, "But honey, another new dress?" She said, "Yes dear, you want me to look as good as Barbara did the other night, don't you?" Now if he says no, he has bought himself a whole new set of problems, and if he says yes he has just bought a pair of shoes, and a handbag to match.

Now for some final thoughts on skillful questioning.

1. Don't put your customer on the spot by asking questions he doesn't know the answers to. Make your questions simple.

2. Ask, and then listen. That's why you asked the question in the first place. Listen for her beliefs, needs, desires and potential objections.

3. Treat personal or confidential questions with respect. Also, keep them to yourself.

4. Direct the customers' statements to areas that will reinforce their positive feelings.

5. When in doubt, don't assume—*ask*.

One of the best ways to reach out to people, to show interest, and to insure positive response is to ask questions. Questions can help you guide people toward the best possible outcome for all concerned. When you are skilled at asking questions, you can make just about anything happen.

CHAPTER 20:
VISUAL LISTENING

Seldom does anyone buy because of logic alone, most often the emotions become involved. That being the case, why not involve as many of the senses as possible, you would certainly enhance your chances of getting to a "yes" quicker, wouldn't you? Let's take a look at some of the aspects that come into play regarding the emotional purchase.

What is your appearance? This can be taken two ways. How do you feel you look, and how do others perceive you.

I'm not going to get into a long dissertation here on dressing, but this area does deserve a simple commentary. I believe that when you are confident in what you have to sell, and have a sincere belief in yourself and your product, you can march into the corporate office in cut-offs and sandals and make the sale. Problem—in today's world you may not get into the corporate office in cut-offs and sandals. We are talking about a game here, and as in any field, there are guidelines to follow.

The Clothing Game

1. Respect your client. You can show respect for your client by dressing for the situation. When you go to a formal dance do you wear a sport shirt and tennis shoes? Of course not. If the president invited you and your wife to dinner, would you go in shorts? Probably not. When you are working on your automobile on the weekend, do you wear a suit and tie?—No comment. The same holds true in the sales arena, dress for the feeling and atmosphere you wish to create, and *you* probably know best what that is. Look into the mirror and ask yourself, "Would you buy a used car from that person?" "Are you dressed for a picnic, or to make the sale?"

2. Dress for the job you want, not for the job you have. How many of you have heard that statement before? It's old, but true. If it looks like a duck, sounds like a duck and walks like a duck, it's a duck. If you look successful, sound successful and move forward with confidence, you will increase your probability of success.

3. Dress up, not down. Whenever you have a question as to what to wear, dress up, not down. In other words you will most likely be safer to go to a little extra trouble to look better than to wonder or worry if you are dressed properly. And when you take the extra time to create a positive image, it says you care.

4. Use common sense. You don't have to spend a fortune on clothes. Invest in classics and basics. Be well groomed, neat and clean. Take pride in yourself because others will respond to you in direct proportion to the way you feel about yourself.

5. Unless you are in a fashion, entertainment or artistic industry, standardize your clothes. Dress to look sharp but not flamboyant, you'll be more likely to create a non-threatening atmosphere for your client. And for goodness sake, *get those sunglasses off when you are talking*. People want to see your eyes. The eyes are the windows to the soul. Eye contact will convey confidence and trust. Don't hide behind your shades, let people in to experience your enthusiasm.

Body Signals

You recall that we talked about body language earlier. The same concepts apply here, but now let's highlight some of those points and take it a bit further.

- Although eye contact is good to show interest and convey trust and confidence, prolonged eye contact is not natural. The question often arises as to who will mostly likely break eye contact first, the leader or the follower? Very often the leader will. It is quite normal for a leader to initiate, and a leader is most often aware of an individual's comfort zone. When considering eye contact, take into account that the speaker will not tend to connect nearly as much as the listener because when you speak, your eyes may shift with your thoughts.

- Observing body positioning and movements must be acknowledged to some degree if you plan on building a comfortable climate for your client. Showing your receptivity to him by facing him, and being aware of his interest, or disinterest can be valuable. For instance, if he tends to face toward the exit, if his feet are pointed toward the door, if he glances at his watch, if his eye contact is minimal, you might be wise to schedule another appointment, or do something dynamic to capture his interest because it's a sure bet that you don't have it now.

- Another indication of disinterest, impatience, or boredom is the tapping of fingers or feet, deep sighs, partial yawn or a general laid-back position. Be careful here not to read any body signal by itself. These signals must be read in clusters. For instance, when combined with tapping fingers and a laid back posture, a deep sigh can mean boredom, but when the clients body shows signs of interest by leaning forward in his chair, or stepping into the conversation, and his eyes go from upward quick shifting movements to more of a steady gaze toward you, and then he breathes a deep sigh, he has just made his decision.

- Now, how do you know if his decision is directed in favor of your product or service? Again, by reading the cluster of signals. A very reliable sign is steepling the fingers, this displays confidence. When the general trend of body positioning is positive, and then the fingers are steepled, he is most likely displaying confidence in favor of purchasing. On the other hand, if body positioning trends are more negative, and *then* he steeples his fingers, he may be confident that he is going to continue looking around.

- Hand to mouth gestures are something that you, as a salesperson, must be very aware of. These gestures generally convey uncertainty, lack of confidence, withholding of information, or reluctance to speak. While making a sales presentation, a good rule of thumb is to keep your hands away from your face. Watch for hand to mouth gestures in your client as well. His hand may go to his mouth when he says something he doesn't mean, when he is uncomfortable with what he says, and when he is not too sure he believes what *you* are telling him.

And before we leave the subject (for the second time) of reading people's silent signals I'd like to say a final word about pacing.

- By pacing I mean following the movement patterns of your client. Research indicates that when people are in agreement they will tend to mirror one another's movements and positions. So one aspect of creating receptivity in your client is to pace, or mimic her movements, speed of movements, and body positioning. Experiment with this idea, in fact, observe yourself in a conversation with a friend, or someone with whom you are in agreement. You'll find that you will, more often than not, adapt the same body positions.

   Pacing also means to be aware of your prospects enthusiasm. You can't come out of chute number one with over-zealous, over-powering enthusiasm for your product if your prospect is laid back, soft spoken, and reserved. Pattern your emotions to complement your prospect, not to offend him.

SCOPE

Now, here are five pay-off conversation starters. I call it my SCOPE technique. The only time you communicate with words alone is when you are writing a letter. But the moment you can be seen or heard by another person, your voice inflections and body movements also become part of your communication. Your voice can say more than your words. The following are five positive-results statements to open a conversation. Deliver these five opening statements with sincerity, interest, and enthusiasm. Notice these are all open-ended questions and are designed to be answered with more than a simple yes or no. These examples are directed toward retail cosmetic sales, but can be adapted for any situation.

<u>S</u>*ample:* "Here, let me give you a sample of the product." (walking over to the client) "Try this, you'll love it!" (wait for a brief moment, then ask) "How does it feel?" This gets the person involved and immediately focuses the attention on the product.

<u>C</u>*ompliment:* "That's an attractive blouse you're wearing. Where did you get that?" Without question, this comment must be sincere. You can comment on anything that you sincerely find interesting about the person's attire, personal grooming, children, speech accent, or any number of areas that may present themselves at the moment but, *sincerity is the absolute key here!*

<u>O</u>*bserve:* By observing a person's tan you could say, "I see you have a tan. How often are you outdoors?" This question will also determine if the person is using tanning cream, if so, it opens the door to share the benefits of a tanning product. You may also observe that he or she is wearing a membership pin, a class ring, or a bracelet. The main point here is that you are focusing your attention on your client with alert observation, and for the purpose of gaining a response with an open-ended question.

<u>P</u>*roduct:* "I see you are looking at the ABC cosmetic line. How have you used this type of skin care product before?" The words "this

type" are important so the client does not think you are just referring to the ABC line and respond only with "I haven't used ABC."

_En_dorse: "I noticed you looking at the ABC line. I use their products myself and they are outstanding! What are you currently using?" Here you are personally endorsing the product line and you are opening the door with a sincere desire to share your experience about the line with the client. This type of an approach says, "I'm interested in you—let's talk."

Have some fun with this idea. People are people, and in most cases they will respond favorably to your interest and comments. When you think about it, we all have somewhat the same desires, the same needs and the same wants. In fact, you might look at it this way, we've known each other all of our lives—we just haven't met before.

Chapter 21:
Insights and Oversights

Did you know that your behavior is reflected in the world around you?

Take a look at your environment. You can consider a person's automobile, home and office as a good indicator of the attitudes and behaviors of that individual. A cluttered physical environment can be an indicator of a cluttered mental environment. In contrast, to the *clean* desk. I always say a clean desk is a sign of a sick mind. Seriously though, as with everything, we look for balance.

How many times do you suppose you have lost a sale because of some silly thing you may have done that violates the traditions of someone else? All of us have at one time or another, and probably more than you ever realized.

When entering a person's home or office, watch where you place your hand bag, or briefcase. Whatever you do, don't set it on top of the person's desk, or on a fine piece of furniture. This reminds me of an incident that occurred in our home. An interior designer made a personal call to give us an estimate. When she walked into our master bedroom she proceeded to place her briefcase on our quilted bedspread. Then, she sat down on the bed, instead of using the sofa or chair. The briefcase left dirt stains on the bedspread, and I really didn't appreciate that. Of course, she probably really didn't appreciate *not* getting the contract. And unfortunately, she may never even know why.

Now take Herb. Herb tunes our piano. We have a grand piano in our living room. I guess you might say that Herb came with the piano, because two complimentary tunings were included with the purchase.

Herb arrived shortly after the piano was delivered to our home. It had been raining that morning. He took one look at our white living room carpet and proceeded to take his shoes off. I said, "That's very considerate of you, but you really don't have to do that." Herb said, "I know, but I would prefer to." Not only was he considerate of our home, but he did an excellent job tuning the piano. Herb now writes his own ticket, he tells us when he thinks our piano needs tuning and he schedules an appointment. It's out of my hands, and I think it's great.

You see, the personal behavior we display and the statements we make are seldom separated from the individual who makes them. The potential client perceives the individual, his statements and behavior as one, and judges the entire situation from all the available evidence.

————— LIFE LINE —————

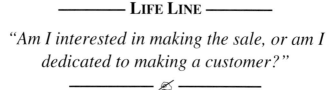

"Am I interested in making the sale, or am I dedicated to making a customer?"

Nothing seems to build confidence in a client more than a genuine unselfishness on the part of the salesperson. When you have the buyer's interest at heart you can capture their confidence at once. Ask yourself this question, "Am I interested in making the sale, or am I dedicated to making a customer?" Your behavior will be a significant factor in the end result. When you sincerely care about the customer's needs, and see them satisfied by your product or service, or through someone else, you will begin to establish a reputation that is priceless. A simple method to accomplish this attitude is to take a reverse posture. If the situation were reversed, how would you like the salesperson to treat you?

Ethics

Let's talk about ethics in sales. Webster's defines ethics as, "Moral principles, quality, or practice; the morals of individual action or practice." Every profession has a code of ethics, and that includes the profession of sales. Take the ten test. Here are ten questions that offer a guideline to determine right from wrong:

1. "Is this a sound judgment that will stand the test of time?"
2. "Would I do this to my best friend?"
3. "Will this be a benefit or detriment to society?"
4. "Will anyone be hurt emotionally or physically by this action?"
5. "Am I willing to have this done to me?"
6. "What will be the reaction of my friends if they find out?"
7. "Will I be ashamed to share my actions with others?"
8. "If I owned the company, would I do it?"
9. "If it were posted on the sales bulletin board, would I do it?"
10. "Would it be good if everyone did this?"

Guilt is a feeling that I rely on to guide me in my actions. A person who feels guilty of some unethical act usually knows it. I have seen salespeople push ethical considerations aside, and revert to the code of the jungle in an attempt to close the sale. But, there is a sense of right and wrong within a person. Yes, people do purchase on emotion. And this emotion is strongly influenced by the areas we have already covered: Appearance, Body Language, Behavior and Ethics. Today we are dealing with a sophisticated public. The sales arena has no real place for the charlatan. By continually sharpening our skills through education, training and experience, the success that we have so long strived for, will be our natural result.

Objections →Opportunities

All right, now how about objections, obstacles or opportunities? Let's take a look. You can use word magic on this and turn all your objections into opportunities. Sound too good to be true? Well, when you do, you will discover one of the most powerful and satisfying techniques in sales. In many cases, when a prospect poses an objection, he is asking for your professional opinion, and he wants *you* to put his mind at ease.

We talked earlier of the four reasons people don't buy, and those are: no confidence, no need, no money, or no hurry. By handling these issues skillfully you'll be on your way to creating another satisfied customer. Let's consider some ideas for each of these.

No Confidence: If your customer seems to display a lack of confidence in you, your product or your company, then build confidence. "How?" you say. Well, testimonials, photographs, references, success stories, guarantees, and demonstrations. There are a number of avenues open to us here. Bringing the boss, sales manager, even the company CEO into the picture to support your claims, can be a valuable asset in creating credibility. A display of team interest and effort in satisfying the customer will weigh heavily in your favor.

No Need: Create one. We don't usually buy what we need anyway. We buy what we want. Whether for business or personal use, creating the desire to purchase is a trait of sales excellence. Share the benefits that will be gained by using your product or service, and when possible, demonstrate the results. Get the person involved and observe the psychological shift in thinking from observer, to owner. They say you can lead a horse to water, but you can't make him drink. But you can give him enough salt to make him want to drink.

No Money: This is one of the most common reasons people put off buying anything. And yet, price is rarely an objection when value has been created. When a person is directed to look upon his purchase as an investment, an investment of value, one that will derive long-term benefits for him, his company and his family, you have moved beyond the price objection. In this instance a cost break-down is often effective. One example would be the sale of a copy machine. The total cost may be upwards of $1,500, yet if you look at the daily cost over the lifetime of the copier, you are considering only a nominal amount. When you consider the cost of an insurance policy you can look at it in terms of money saved in tax advantaged dollars creating the feeling of, "Why didn't I do this earlier?" When cost is measured with value, order and priorities begin to evolve.

No Hurry: Offer discounts or specials. End-of-the-month, or end-of-the-year specials. Find a way to create the need for your customer to buy *now!* Quantity purchase, limited stock, rising prices in sight, these are just some of the reasons that can offer valuable savings if action is taking immediately. Throw in the delivery charge, waive the installation charge, offer a complimentary gift, or even provide additional support for a period of time. A sale delayed is a sale not made. Possibly you have been dealing with the wrong person and you may need to get to the decision maker. Everyone benefits by taking action now.

Objection Insights

Consider this, everyone has two reasons for doing anything; the one they give, and the real reason. Your mission, should you choose to accept it, is to define the real objection. How do you know that the objection is real, or just a ploy to put you off? Here are some tips:

1. *When did the objection occur?* If you get the brush-off early in your presentation, without having had the opportunity to share the benefits as to why your potential client needs your service, then most likely it's a ploy to get you out and on your way. But, if you have been given the opportunity to make a valid presentation, and there was a good ear to listen to you, and then the prospect says, "We really don't need any," you can bet that there is a hidden agenda—a deeper meaning.

2. *Is your communication clear?* Lack of clear communication can cause problems because the situation becomes convoluted—the prospect doesn't know what you expect of him. If he's thinking one thing, and you're thinking another, he may have a real, but unnecessary, objection. And remember, people buy for their reasons, not yours. Make sure you know what their reasons are.

3. *Don't over-sell.* I have seen people who just can't stop selling. They do a great job of making the sale, so great that they keep on selling—until the prospect finally decides not to buy. Overselling will actually create objections. Recognize buying signals and act on them by knowing when to stop.

4. *Look behind what you see and hear.* If the person gives you a jovial slap on the back, gets up and shows you to the door, and says, "Give me a call in a few months." She probably means it. If, however, her response is more like, "Well, uh, I'm not really too sure, maybe I'll be in a better position in a few months." you can be sure that she wants you to give her one good reason to buy now.

5. *Head 'em off at the pass.* Prepare yourself for objections that you know will arise. You know your product, you know your service. And you know what people often object to. Why not develop planned statements that counter the objection even before they arise? Example: "Some people have expressed concern about the lack of privacy in the front yard. So we have sketched out some ideas on building an atrium—look at this beautiful sanctuary that could be created." When you bring the issue up first you put the customer at ease, and you show that you have already put some thought into the situation.

If the customer should object first, respond with enthusiasm, "Well, I guess great minds run along the same track. I had the same thought and here's what I came up with."

In the right situation, another enthusiastic response to an objection might be, "Yes, and isn't it great? Here's what we thought we could do with that."

Don't let objections block your success—learn how to handle them. They can be some of the best opportunities in helping you to close the sale.

CHAPTER 22:
EVERYBODY WINS

To satisfy objections and help keep the customer, it may be necessary to negotiate. Each of us negotiates something everyday. When treated correctly, all negotiations large and small, from military agreements to "lights out" for your children are handled through a process that requires effective communication. The skilled negotiator always maintains the edge in designing a favorable final outcome—for all concerned.

There is a simple thread of similarity in all successful negotiations and these patterns can be recreated, the principles will work for anyone. Although no two negotiations are ever alike, there are standards in human behavior, body signals and speech to guide us. It stands to reason that there are many ways to reach a decision—some better, some worse. By gaining an awareness of the strategies of effective negotiating (and implementing the tools properly) you will reduce anxiety, build confidence, and command respect.

——————— LIFE LINE ———————

The skilled negotiator always maintains the edge in designing a favorable outcome—for all concerned.

———————  ———————

Negotiating Made Easier

In real estate there is an asking price and a selling price. When you buy an automobile you generally receive a discount from the sticker price. You can negotiate for quantity purchases, additional time, hotel rates, and travel packages. Here are a some thoughts that will make your negotiations easier:

Realize that virtually everything is negotiable. With that knowledge, whether you are the seller or the buyer, do your best to avoid making the first move to negotiate. Usually this weakens your position. In both buying and selling assume the attitude that you want it, but not "that much." This labels you with an attitude of being willing to say *"no"* thereby it strengthens your position. Obviously, if no action is taken by the other person to negotiate, you may have to initiate the process if the transaction is going to occur.

Never reveal your top or bottom line first, and never accept the first offer. When you do accept, only accept with considerations. "Ok, if we can agree on a figure of $25,000 we'll want you to provide the extra support packages as well." Don't ask, "Will you throw in the extra support packages?" State what you expect to happen, if it's not acceptable, do you suppose they'll tell you? You bet. Also, by doing this you avoid negotiating on one issue only. When you have numerous considerations, you create options, benefits, and give-aways. This type of situation allows you to build a major issue out of a minor point, taking the pressure off the major point of the negotiation.

One other reason not to accept the first offer is that it always leaves the other person feeling like he could have gotten it for less. To this day a friend of mine feels that way. He offered $375,000 for a home. The realtor said the sellers would never accept that, it's too low, but she was obligated to submit the offer. The realtor returned and said, "I've got good news, they accepted." This left my friend feeling like a poor negotiator, for he felt that if he had offered an even lower figure, they may have accepted that also. Now, all the realtor would have had to do to get both parties feeling good about the situation would be to say this, "I have good news for you. I presented the offer to the sellers, and of course, they won't accept $375,000, but they will consider $377,000 if we can wrap this up immediately." The realtor could have always come down to the $375K figure if she really needed to. This way my friend would have felt as if he had negotiated down to the rock bottom price.

Never assume that you know all the facts, there is always a hidden agenda. Speaking of that, what's your hidden agenda? Whatever it is, *keep it to yourself.* Give as little information as possible. It's always tempting to relinquish unsolicited information. Example: "When do you need the shipment?" "We need it by Friday, because our people want to begin working with it on Monday." What you have just said is that you don't really need it until Monday. You don't need to qualify what you say. State firmly and confidently that you need the shipment on Friday.

Another example: "We only have $10,000 budgeted for this project, since there are other divisions that need our financial support as well." What you have just said is that there is more money, but you're not willing to appropriate it. What the person on the other end hears is that you have the money, but you are not yet willing to part with it. Make your statement like this, "We have a maximum of $10,000 for this project. What can you do for us?"

Once the negotiation is complete, *always declare the other party the winner* with statements like: "Boy, you sure drive a hard bargain." or "It's been great working with you on this, your company must really value your negotiating ability." or "You sure know how to maneuver your way through a negotiation, I respect that." These comments say you have taken time to look at the other person's skills and abilities and have considered their position.

Remember, we are dealing with people, and everyone likes to feel like they made a good deal. You will do well for yourself if you acknowledge the other person's importance and leave all doors open for future negotiations. You may find this easier to do when you realize that, "The best things in life, aren't things."

Chapter 23:
Close the Sale or
Close the Door

For as many years as I have been presenting sales programs, the topic that has been requested most often is closing. Why do you suppose this is? I think that many people have an erroneous concept of the sales close. I believe they fear it, they dread it, and therefore they avoid it. And there's the paradox. Because you avoid it, you dread it and you fear it. People often fear rejection; they haven't learned to read closing signals properly; they often take hesitation as reluctance and become flustered; they don't know how to build agreements throughout the entire presentation; they don't handle objections well, and they regard the close as a separate part of the sales presentation.

Contrary to popular belief, closing is simple and fun. It is what makes selling pay off. To put into action all the time and effort in preparation, presentation and persuasion, and then not to close doesn't make much sense. My philosophy is simply this, if you don't ask for the order, you have a built in *no*. So why not ask? And as long as you're asking, let's ask in a way that gives you the best possible opportunity to insure the sale. Your prospect wants to buy, and if you don't ask for the order, he'll continue looking for a salesperson who will. You don't have to wait for your client to close the sale for you.

The sales process is a win-win situation, not a win-lose confrontation. Through your professionalism, you are assisting the prospect to fulfill a specific need. You are there to make it an easy, smooth and pleasurable transaction.

In many of my sales programs I stress building the close right into the presentation. By doing this you very often eliminate the need to use any of the standard closing strategies. To me, building the close into the presentation means making sure that you cover many of the areas that we've already discussed. To make it easy, remember to C.L.O.S.E. the sale:

C is for Communication. Communication is a two way exchange of information that is designed to produce a particular response.

L is for Listening and Leadership. You can lead the conversation through effective listening. I like to speak of *Concerned Listening,* in other words, putting back into words what you hear someone feeling.

O stands for Observation. Observe behind what you see. As we have discovered, many insights can be gained in selling by observing a person's body signals and general environment.

S is for Speaking. Anyone in sales is a speaker. What you say and how you say it can make all the difference in the world. Remember the quote, "The difference between the right word and the wrong word is like the difference between a lightning bug and a lightning bolt."

E is for Enjoyment and Enthusiasm. If you are not enjoying yourself in the process, if you don't feel and express enthusiasm for your work, it will show. Again, people don't buy your product, they buy you, and if you're not sold why should they bother?

What happens when you've made your presentation and you still don't have the sale? You may want to consider one of the closing techniques that we'll discuss in the next chapter. Some will feel good to you, and others . well, others may feel uncomfortable.

So many sales people fail to close the sale for fear that the customer may reject them by saying, "No." The fact is that by not asking for the order, you have a built-in "no". So why not ask? When you think about it, the customer doesn't really feel the value of the product if there is no attempt to close the sale. It's as if the person is left hanging with no real direction. Closing the sale is commendable, respectable, and responsible. People are asking you for your professional opinion and they are relying upon you to offer them guidance and direction to fulfill their needs. There is no one close that will work for all situations. You will have to evaluate the situation and determine which type of close will be most effective.

But first I'm going to offer some guidelines here. Please keep in mind that each person will deliver the close in his or her own individual style, but that style will not develop until you feel perfectly comfortable with the words. And how is that accomplished? Through practice. Some people will make a dozen sales while another person will make ten times that amount in the same time period. Why? Comfort and confidence, which comes from practice. Here are some thoughts to consider when using closing statements:

1. *To fail, wing it! To succeed, rehearse it!* These closing statements must virtually flow from your lips like honey. They should be second nature, natural and effortless. This type of professionalism only comes through practice.

2. *Deliver the close in a natural and relaxed manner.* Observe yourself in a mirror as you deliver the closing statement. Listen to yourself on a tape recorder. Notice that when you are relaxed, your voice will be softer and easier to listen to. You will not sound harried or pushy, but confident and concerned for your customer.

3. *A sale now is certain, a sale planned for later is doomed.* When the customer walks away he or she may never return. The tendency to delay a decision until later is common practice for many. When you run into this type of person use these four points to help the decision process: a.) Tell him why your idea is a good one. b.) Show him how he can benefit from it. c.) Automatically assume that he will go along with your idea. d.) Assure him that he has made the right decision.

4. *Have enough closes to outnumber the objections.* A skilled salesperson will discover numerous ways to close the sale. If an objection arises, another close is used. Applying a variety of closing techniques during a presentation can be beneficial in helping the customer make the decision to take action now.

5. *Use the order form to make notes.* A simple way to begin the close is to open the discussion by listing the customers name on your order form. If the question, "What are you doing?" comes up, just say that you are taking a few notes to help you organize your thoughts.

6. *Whenever you ask a closing question, be silent.* The first person who speaks weakens or loses her position. This can be difficult, but it is well worth the wait.

Closing the sale can be fun if you approach it that way. Just as in anything however, there is a knack that can be developed, and fine-tuned by your persistence. We never really stop learning new ways to sharpen our skills. The ideas offered here will only be as valuable as you make them. In the final analysis you will be the one who makes the difference.

Here we go. The moment of truth. You presentation is just about finished. You feel good, confident and secure in yourself and your product—but they haven't said "Yes" yet. I have to say it again: There are many ways to reach an end; some are better than others. Here are seven closing techniques that I have personally found very helpful. Some blend, one into the other. Let's take a closer look, they are quite easy to apply.

Seven Closing Techniques

1. *The Forecast Close.* Closing begins the minute the salesperson and the prospect meet. I have found that one way to assist the close is to forecast, presume right from the start, that the prospect is going to buy. Speak in terms of ownership. Statements like: "When this is delivered, you'll find that the office efficiency will greatly increase." "Would you be more pleased with the textured or smooth surface?"

"How will you use this with your family?" In other words, get the person thinking in the direction of ownership. Pose questions that create a need for one to think of how they will use your product or service.

The effectiveness of this technique lies in your absolute conviction and expectancy. You know the sale will be made once you get all the details together. The only question is when. Let's take a retail store example next. You have shown her the garments and have narrowed them down to one that looks great. You feel it is time to close and you think the presumptive (forecast) technique will be the easiest, most natural and perhaps the surest way for you to close, so you say this: "Let me see—you will want this garment by the weekend. This is Tuesday. We can manage that if we get the tailor on it right away." You don't have to ask her to buy, she will confirm her intent in her response. You could have varied your closing words by asking her, "How soon must you have this dress?" Presume that you have the sale and proceed confidently.

One reason this technique is so valuable is that it is so usable. You create no threat, apply no pressure and are not offensive. You quietly lead the prospect to a decision.

I have mentioned that you should be on the lookout for closing signals. What are they? Well, when the customer asks a post-sale question, like, "How will I be able to fit all my clothes into the closet you are building for us?" or "What happens if I end up with too many of these in our inventory?" A post sale question is any comment or question by the prospect that indicates ownership.

Another closing signal is when the customer is paying very close attention. This can be displayed in many ways. Steady eye contact, leaning forward, sitting on the edge of the chair, verbal sounds that indicate readiness to buy, and verbal agreement to your comments. Two additional ways that customers convey buying signals are: making a commitment statement such as, "Yes, this does seem to fit our needs," and raising a sincere objection. When the objection is out in the open you have an opportunity to close, because when you have handled the objection you have a clear path to the sale.

2. The Course-Deviation Close. This type of close is a natural follow-through once all the facts are presented, and it really looks like you have properly matched your customer with your product or service. Basically you deviate from the major issue with an incidental question. Here's a simple example: "By the way, do you prefer the blue or the green?" He answers, "I prefer the blue," which is the same as saying, "I'll take the blue." Now, if he isn't ready to buy he will tell you, either by requesting more information, or by asking for other options. Notice the phrase, "By the way . . ." This creates an incidental topic of interest, something that is minor to the actual item being purchased, but significant in that, by getting agreement or confirmation on the minor item, the major item will naturally be part of the package. Example: "Boy, I can remember our last trip to Paris, we sure enjoyed the gourmet restaurants and the quaint hotels—by the way, will you be wanting tickets to the opera, and a tour of the Louvre?"

We have a few items in play here. Your comment about the major item or issue at hand must be positive. It's meant to reinforce the benefits that will be received once the sale is made. The incidental item comment is only added to get closure on the sale. It really doesn't matter at this point whether they want to go to the opera and the Louvre, but when they decide, they just bought the package to Europe. Now, for a most important bit of phrasing, "By the way." When you say, "By the way," leave no pause between your initial statement and your incidental statement. If you give your client a chance to answer or comment on the initial statement, you have lost the power of the Course-Deviation Close.

3. The Go/No-Go Close. To stop this close, your customer must take some physical action. One of the secrets of all great salespeople is that they do something, and say something in closing their sales. Actions speak louder than words. The premise of this close is to start doing something from which the customer will have to stop you in order to avoid buying. Action steps like: filling out the order form, making the initial order placement phone call, scheduling the shipment date, initialing the preliminary start up. Do something that causes the customer to take action if the sale is to be stopped.

Here's another way to incorporate the Go/No-Go close into your presentation. When you feel the prospect has digested the information and should be ready to close, simply say, "Please excuse me for just a moment? I'd like to call my office to tell them how you want this contract handled." When the prospect says, "Certainly," he has just given you his order in his answer to your question.

Most salespeople seem to be as much afraid of the order form as the buyers themselves. You might want to get used to filling out the form as you go through the presentation, using it as a note-taking device. If the customer asks what you are doing, you can respond by saying, "I'm just keeping my thoughts organized on this form so I am clear on what we've discussed."

4. The Miss-the-Flight Close. People are rarely moved to act immediately on offers of financial gain, satisfaction, and enjoyment, but when faced with the possibility of loss—get out of their way. The Miss-the-Flight Close is based on a person's desire to avoid loss, no matter what the cost. Briefly, it points out that if the buyer fails to take action he stands to lose something because of an imminent event or action. We've all been faced with this situation. The sale will end on Saturday. The former customer will come back to get the last automobile on the show room floor. The insurance premium will be X number of dollars more in two days on your birthday. The message is—buy so you don't lose. And it makes sense. One example could be: "Now I can't promise that this stock will be the same tomorrow as it is today. In fact, the current trend indicates that you will stand to lose a substantial amount by postponing your decision to invest."

With the Miss-the-Flight Close, you speak in terms of what will be lost, rather than what will be gained. You are relying on a basic emotion—the fear of losing.

5. The Warm and Sunny Close. Have you ever shopped at a clothing store where you felt like you were getting a real deal on some fine outfits? Well, you may be. I have noticed a technique that successful salespeople use to accomplish this, and put the customer in his comfort zone. Let's say you go in to buy a suit. You have your selection narrowed down to a couple of suits which look really good on you. Either would serve the purpose well, and you're debating on which suit to buy. The sales person tells the story about his regular client who, just last week, came down from Alaska to order his yearly stock of suits, ties, shoes, and shirts. "Why he bought seven suits, matching ties, shirts, and shoes. We ship orders like that to him every year." So there you are, with your two meager suits. "Oh well, I'll buy them both." And no doubt you'll probably end up with some ties too—and you will feel good about it. Why? Because you are not making an enormous investment, you're just buying two suits and a couple of ties. The contrast between the large purchase and yours is significant, creating a feeling of savings.

Think about it, you can apply this same idea to just about any situation. The salesperson says, "Did you know that the Mirage Country Club just ordered 30,000 flats of petunias." The customer thinks, "My ten flats sounds like a real deal now, maybe I should buy twelve." The salesperson says, "My last customer is putting 1100 cases of these into his stores on a trial basis." As the customer you think, "Maybe I should increase my order to twenty-five cases." The insurance salesperson shares his three million dollar policy experience with a client. The client immediately thinks that his $200,000 policy isn't too much after all.

In a way, this could sound very intimidating, but it would be correct to say that this type of close presents the facts of relative quantities, making the lesser amount more appealing.

6. The 180 Close. Why the name 180? Because this may be your last chance to turn your prospect in the opposite direction to save the sale. When the customer says, "I'll think it over." "Let me get back to you on this." "I have your material, let me think about it." "I'll sleep on it." or a thousand other put-off statements, and you feel that they may be reluctant to purchase, you can respond by saying:

"I can understand why you would like to do that. I have felt that way before myself. But, you probably wouldn't want to think it over unless you were interested, would you?" The customer will probably say, "No."

"Well, maybe I can help you now by clarifying some of your questions. Please do me a favor and share your concerns with me. It's not the quality of the product is it?" The customer will say, "No."

"You're not concerned with . . ." Here you add comments that confirm how good your product is—how does it feel, the benefits that would be experienced, etc.

"Could it be the initial investment that is concerning you?" The Customer may say, "Yes." Now you have the opportunity to use a variety of suggestions, negotiation techniques and value-building confidences, for instance: offer a gift certificate or other incentives with the purchase; use a daily basis price breakdown such as: using this cream only comes to about ten cents per day, or considering the life of the computer, it's a real value at only one dollar a day.

When you finally get down to the bottom line of dollars and cents, make sure there is nothing else in the way of blocking the sale. You want a clear understanding of what your customer wants and needs, and you want to be able to handle any concerns they may have.

7. The P.C. Checklist (Positive Confirmation). When you have gone through your presentation and are ready to get positive confirmation, you will find this system helpful:

1. Ask a calming question: "Are you as pleased with what you've seen as I think you are?"

2. Wait for an answer and then turn it over to the customer by saying, "It's up to you, I'll work with you either way." This takes the sales pressure off.

3. Now give them a chance to make a choice by saying, "Would you rather begin with the entire lot, or would you feel better today starting with this split shipment?"

4. Now release it by saying, "Whichever you prefer will be fine with me." At this point keep quiet. Give your customer an opportunity to think. Silence here is difficult, but essential. You will weaken your position if you speak too soon.

Keep the Customer

So you've sold them. Now what? How do you keep them as loyal customers? Although this topic really has more to do with customer service, it's important to touch briefly on some thoughts to consider.

1. Stay in contact. Construct a definite plan for follow-up. Classify your customer by potential sales volume. Keep in touch by telephone, letters, facsimile, and notes between calls to keep posted on recent changes and needs.

2. Maintain accurate records. Get to know your clients well. Make special notes of birthdays, anniversaries, likes and dislikes, special interests and family names. Also, remember to record the amount, type and date of the last order.

3. Promptly respond to complaints. No one wants complaints, but when handled properly, complaints can provide great opportunities to develop long-term clients. Take each complaint seriously, and settle it promptly.

4. Show appreciation. Customers are people. Listen to them and show interest in their needs by helping them to reach their goals. Everyone likes to feel important and appreciated. Let your customer shine, this becomes simple when you are aware of who is really signing your paycheck.

5. Provide excellent service. Service makes the difference for loyal customers. As long as there is an advantage to working through and with you, people will be loyal to you. Make yourself indispensable.

There you have it. Keeping the customer doesn't have to be anything to be feared. When you do your job, when you show interest and appreciation, when you go the extra mile, it's like money in the bank, and the interest will compound itself many times over—it's called word of mouth. And that my friends, is what keeps your sales force alive.

EPILOGUE:
THE SALES LEADER

In closing, I suppose that if I were to capsulize the reason for anyone's success, in any endeavor, it would have to be that the person has a good self-image. I have seen people succeed, and I have seen people fail. I personally know people who take credit where credit is due, they made themselves successful and they're proud of it. But, I have never heard anyone say "I'm a self-made failure. I created this mess and I've got to live with it." Usually they point fingers, and blame something or someone else.

———— LIFE LINE ————

Self-image is the ultimate ingredient in achieving, and keeping anything in life.

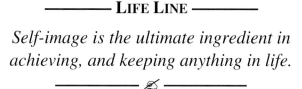

I would go so far as to say that the business of sales has more to do with your attitude than with your skills, but by combining the proper attitude and skills you are insured of true success. Unless an individual approaches a situation positively, the self-discipline required to gain the results you need to be successful will not exist. You see, if your image of yourself is faltering, if you can't imagine yourself as the sales leader, if you continually look upon yourself as average, then you will procrastinate, you will feel as though you are being used, and you will be doomed to mediocrity.

Yes, *self-image is the ultimate ingredient in achieving,* and keeping *anything in life.* With a positive self-image you will meet the world with confidence. You will attract to you all that you need to support your decisions. You will be respected. You will be responsible, and you will be rewarded.

We are all born equal, and become unequal. Not better, not worse than anyone else, just different. *Your desire to succeed,* your *willingness to accept change* as a normal and natural part of life, and your *interest in serving others* are three major traits in determining your success.

The attitude you hold will be reflected in the people you meet and in your experience. If there are a lot of negative thoughts, you better believe that there will be a lot of negative or limiting experiences. Success starts with conditioning our minds in a positive way. Positively think, speak, and become the success you want. Now, use these ideas, and enjoy the process.

─────── **LIFE LINE** ───────

A sale delayed is a sale not made.

─────── ✍ ───────

SECTION IV
REACHING
HIGH

Successful people form habits of doing things
that unsuccessful people will not do.

CHAPTER 24:
TAKE THE FIRST STEP

I suppose it can be said that the path to goal achievement is paved with good intentions. O.K., O.K., it's kind of a cliché but the point is, most of us want to think we're achieving, and moving forward with our lives. After all, we work hard, we support ourselves and our families, we're good members of society, right? *Right.* Sometimes, in our rush to pat ourselves on the back in appreciation for how hard we work, we forget to prod ourselves in the back to remind us we can achieve even more if we put forth a little effort. Goal achievement doesn't have to be a scary thing, you don't have to say swimming the English Channel is your goal! Losing a few pounds, getting a promotion at work, or getting on better terms with a family member could all be realistic goals. Goals need to be achievable to be realistic. But having goals is a real commitment, so don't pretend to have a goal unless you intend to make some effort to achieve it.

——— LIFE LINE ———

If you are sincere in your efforts, people will
want to help you reach your goal.

——— ✍ ———

I took a cruise to the Caribbean a while back. On about the second day of the week-long cruise, our cruise director asked, "How are you enjoying yourselves so far?" Some people said "Fine," others said "Great," some said "Lovely." The cruise director replied, "Our *goal* is for you to say 'excellent'. For us, good is not good enough. If something strikes you as just good, please ask a crew member to make it excellent." From then on, everyone paid great attention to how well the crew was serving us and (we had to admit) it was pretty excellent. The next night, when the cruise director said, "How's everybody doing?" the mass reply came back, "Excellent!" Of course, this has a lot to do with your expectancy. After a few days, we were all saying, "Excellent," to each other about almost anything. It got to be quite a joke among us, but the point is: we were noticing the smiling faces of the eager-to-please crew, and we were having a great time, so we *really* wanted them to feel they were reaching their goal. What this little story means is, the goal you set, and earnestly attempt to fulfill, is the attitude you present to those around you. *If you are sincere in your efforts, people will want to help you reach your goal!!* What a wonderful thought! You're not in this alone after all! You have all the help you need if you'll just reach out and take it.

Top Performers

There are known traits of successful people, traits that assist such people to regularly out-perform others. *Success can become habit-forming* . . . if you lock onto the proper behavior patterns and stick with them long enough.

After years of testing and observation, a research psychologist found that although high achievers tend to be a little different than others, for the most part, the characteristics of successful people can be learned. To begin with, top performers are not necessarily workaholics. So, you can drop that phony rationalization, "Why become successful? Most of those people are a bundle of nerves and die of a heart attack anyway." Don't kid yourself, you're not resisting success because you're afraid of a heart attack. In fact, the researcher also found out that successful people handle stress very well, and they are not often candidates for heart attacks. They take vacations and know when to stop working. Take a look at these six characteristics of successful people:

1. Top performers can see beyond their accomplishments. They avoid that comfort zone, the place where everything is safe and homey (though not all that rewarding). They are constantly trying to improve, and because of their drive they are almost always successful.

2. Top performers are guided by private goals that are all-consuming. These performers have a game plan which strategically allows them to continue until long-term goals are met. This means saying "no" to your friends once in a while when the popular thing is to go out for pizza. Staying home to study or otherwise attain your goal may not always make you popular but it could make you vastly more successful.

3. Top performers never attach blame to failure; instead they concentrate on solving problems. They learn how to identify a problem and set out on an organized course to solve it.

4. A top performer has the confidence to accept risks even after considering the worst possible consequences. That's because he or she knows any risk has more chance of turning into success rather than failure, if success is the goal.

5. Top performers are able to mentally review and practice their actions before events happen. That's a key. They rehearse every nuance of a proposal or presentation until they're satisfied it's what they want. They *psyche themselves up* just like any performer before a show or a big game.

6. Top performers approach new experiences in a challenging and artful way. To them there's no such thing as a routine job. Oh sure, they can follow instructions and take orders but once they're into a task, they make it their own and gauge their performance by their own satisfaction.

Top performers are driven by goals they set for themselves. Well respected and successful people have to be good team players, but they also have to work to develop their own personal skills and goals. They find ways to make the process as enjoyable as the results. Less successful people, on the other hand, might meet their goals, but they don't necessarily enjoy the work, or the method of task completion. They perform their job, draw their pay, and are content with the experience at that level.

Know Your Goal

Ask yourself what you are reaching out for. It's good to set your sights on something.

I remember a young girl came to my door one day selling magazines. I'm a pretty hard sell when it comes to door-to-door sales pitches but this girl was bright-eyed and enthusiastic about her presentation. I could tell she was nervous but she stood her ground and gave me the whole spiel that said if she sold enough magazines she could earn a trip to Europe. I never know if those things are on the level but I was intrigued because of her enthusiasm, and she frequently stated, "I know I will be selected to go to Europe." It was kind of like a mantra to her: she affirmed her conviction regularly. I didn't really want any magazines, but she was making a good case for them and she enticed me to ask some questions about one in particular. Well, okay, I'll admit it, I succumbed to her sales technique and ordered one magazine. She became more animated as she took my order and, as she walked down the path away from my door, she once again thanked me for making it possible for her to earn the trip to Europe. I don't know how she made out—I got my magazine and I hope she got what she wanted too. She had a goal, *and* a technique to keep her attention focused on it. At any rate, you can see what I mean about setting out on a realistic quest for an achievable goal.

We're all in the people business. Let's look at some points that will bring this together on a personal level for focus, self-expression and fulfillment. Also, for eliciting support from others who are involved in assisting us to reach our goal.

1. *Take responsibility for your own behavior.* Realize that you are not responsible for someone else's behavior. What goes wrong for you is your doing and your responsibility to change. What goes right for you is to your credit even if your part was nothing more than knowing the right people to involve to insure the successful outcome. And if we have goals we wish to achieve, most likely other people will be involved in your process of goal realization.

2. *Know that your self-worth is not dependent on someone else.* You don't need a certain boss or loved-one or mentor to make you a worthy person. Sure, having a special person in your life is wonderful and a gift to be cherished. But keep in mind, you are part of the reason that relationship is so wonderful. Take credit just like you take responsibility.

3. *Avoid arguments.* I don't mean you should suppress anger: anger is a necessary emotion. But, discussion is better than an argument. Communicate with the other person and relate in terms of "I" rather than, "You did this to me," this way they won't be on the defensive. State your own feelings, don't find fault or lay blame. Simply put, "It takes two to tango."

4. *Discuss with the other person what you plan to talk about.* Don't just rush in like a bull on the rampage, give the other person a chance to become part of the discussion. On the phone or in person say something like, "I need to talk to you, is now a good time? If not, you tell me when." That gives both of you time to collect your thoughts and avoid a confrontation.

Finally, ask yourself, "How are my relationships working?" If you want to improve your relationships, carry an image in your mind that is conducive to the life-style you desire to live. When you change your image and become confident about yourself, not only will you respond differently, but the people in your world will tend to respond positively toward you.

When you're striving to get ahead on the job, for instance, you might sense some inner ambivalence about making it big. Is it fear of failure? Is there a fear of being called "too tough"? Or, are you just playing it safe? There are all kinds of emotional roadblocks on the path to career success. These self-sabotaging ways of thinking can trap us into not achieving our career goals.

For instance, do you know the difference between assertion and aggression? Psychologists say assertion is being able to speak up, gently but firmly, when you feel wronged, or when you want something. An assertive person, when asked to do something on the job that isn't in their job description, can easily say, "I can't do that for you but I'd be happy to call someone to take care of it." An aggressive person, on the other hand, might get angry and snap back, "Do it yourself!" Aggression is often thinly-veiled hostility. Both people declined to do what was asked of them in different ways. The assertive response lets everyone know you'll stand your ground, and that you're not easily rattled by a challenge to self-esteem. The aggressive response exposes your sensitivity to such testing and tends to escalate negative feelings all around.

Depending upon how we feel about our ability to succeed, we aim high or low in our expectations or goals. A build-up of those expectations (plus ability) usually determines job status. Even if you are very bright, if you think you can't rise above a certain level, you probably won't. A woman bank executive I met said she never expected to land such an important job. Consequently, she didn't get it until she was well into her 40's. She admitted that when she was younger, she didn't think much of herself. She set her goals low because she didn't believe she could amount to much. As she matured she began to suspect she had a lot more on the ball than she was giving herself credit for. So, she went to school and got a master's degree in business. Now, she feels her job is right in line with what she's capable of doing. By the same token, overly high expectations can ruin careers, too. Some people set their sights on being the corporate president, when they're really best suited as a department head. When they can't fulfill their impossible dreams they become bitter and condemn themselves as worthless.

Expectations that are too high can cause stress and depression and might even paralyze job performance. You must determine what is real and achievable for you. That way, you can give adequate thought to setting and re-evaluating your goals one by one.

CHAPTER 25:
TAKE A RISK!

Taking a chance carries with it the unspoken fear, "But what if I fail?" This fear paralyzes many people, gluing them to dead-end jobs or inappropriate careers because they prefer the unhappiness of the known to the terror of the unknown. But risk-taking is an essential part of life, both professional and personal. Anyone who avoids risks won't advance their position, on the job or career, because high-level positions demand some degree of decision-making in which the outcome is often unknown. To face the risks in your life, why not sit down and make two lists. The first list is titled: *What I Lose by Risking a Change*. The second list is titled: *What I Gain by Risking a Change*. While you think you're too undecided to make an important change, you might surprise yourself by finding the first entry on your *Gain* list is, "Self-respect *because* of making a change."

Some people don't succeed in their goals because of repressed hostility toward authority. They don't realize that to command authority, you have to first be able to take directions. Still, some people resent advice, instruction, or criticism from those around them and tend to see orders from their boss in personal terms. For the most part, this anger against taking orders is a holdover from childhood, when we were forced to obey parents, teachers, and older brothers and sisters. By exploring and developing our own self-confidence (that could be a goal) we can overcome the "doormat" mentality, where everyone is stepping on you. Until we do, we'll do nothing more than resist authority, and we'll never achieve a position of authority.

Work With Your Team

Don't become a lone wolf in your quest to reach your professional goals. Be inclusive, rather than exclusive. You may be eager to shine as a star, but you still have to be a team player. We live in a communal society. Office politics and personal relationships demand a team approach, people who ignore this basic rule find themselves locked out of goal achievement forever. I remember meeting a very talented guy who was crushed because his promising career was cut short. He had it all: education, looks, ability. But he saw himself as *the* employee, not *an* employee. He was always late for meetings, stingy about sharing information or duties, and unwilling to play by the office rules. Eventually even the personnel officer couldn't help him because of his reputation for being uncooperative and he became virtually unemployable. Remember: in business and in life, you have to play on the team—no one says you have to like everyone on the team—you just have to play with them. If you don't particularly like someone you work with or socialize with, simply learn to get along as much as you need to for the time you spend together and let your happiness goals take over from there.

Power

Power is a concept, not a thing. You are powerful if others perceive you as being powerful. A successful person will always wind up with power of some sort, so fearing power can be a fatal trap. In your quest for success, first recognize that you deserve power, because your talents led you to it. Then, project that competence to others, and don't be afraid if they lean on you for support. Power also carries with it the strength to ride out mistakes. Power works two ways: it's not just what you can do, but what you can calmly accept. Knowing this can help lift you out of the power trap, Learning to sail over these traps and achieve your goals isn't easy.

You've probably spent a lifetime internalizing fears and mental blocks to success. So, don't expect to rid yourself of faulty reasoning overnight. Just spotting the traps, knowing where they are, is a big step in being able to avoid them, and in summoning the strength to break out of their hold. Once you penetrate and strip away old fears about being a successful person, those fears fade and are replaced by confidence. Then, no trap can hold you, and you'll be free to make the most of your goals. Part of goal achievement is making it happen.

Dana and I were in Portland some time ago. On the way in from the airport, I noticed *The Day The Earth Stood Still* was playing at a local theatre—you know, that 1951 classic science fiction film with Michael Renney, Patricia Neal and Gort!? Anyway, I told Dana, "You've got to see this film." We were staying at Lloyds Center. We called and found out the movie started in half an hour. I called down to the bellman and asked for a cab right away. We went downstairs and waited, and waited, and waited. More than ten minutes went by —no cab. We began to get edgy. "After all," I said, "you've got to be there for the beginning, that's when the flying saucer lands!" Right about this time, a Bentley pulled up. It was beautiful, it was chocolate brown in color; a chauffeur got out. He opened the door for these two lovely couples, dripping in furs and fine clothes. I said to Dana, "There's our cab." The bellman ran up and said, "Hey, where are you going, that's not your cab, your cab is yellow?" I told him there's no reason this couldn't be our cab to get where we were going. I approached the chauffeur and told him our dilemma. I asked if he'd take us to the theatre, and after thinking for a moment, he said, "Sure, why not." We got in and he drove us there straight-away. When he stopped in front of the theatre I asked, "Aren't you going to get out and open the door?" "Very well," he said. We got out—looking quite grand I might add—and I tipped him nicely. We saw the movie right from the beginning with the flying saucer, and when we came out of the theatre, there was our Bentley and our chauffeur. He opened the door, we got in, and he asked us if we'd like to go to dinner. He drove us to a wonderful seafood restaurant, McCormick & Schmick. After dinner, he drove us back to the hotel. We got out, said good-bye and that was that. Now, what we didn't know (and neither did the bellman since he was new on the job) was that the Bentley was a courtesy car for McCormick & Schmick restaurant. Anyone could have had a ride in the stately, chauffeur-driven car. You see folks, this thing beneath your nose is a mouth, and if you want anything to happen in your life you have to be willing to open it up a little. You've got to be willing to speak up for what you desire, what you feel you've earned, what you know you should have. Once in a while, you'll speak up and someone will tell you to *keep quiet* or they'll tell you *no*, or maybe they won't answer you at all. But, you'll never know until you ask. *If you don't ask, the built-in answer is "No."*

Decision-Making

Now, let's take a look at decisions. In the overall scheme of things, *it is more important to be decisive than to be right.* Please digest that a bit before you get your feathers up. It might sound strange and almost illogical, but you've got to take action. Non-action is deadly. I'd rather make the wrong decision than no decision at all because indecision is fatal; action is the key to success.

Decisiveness arises from confidence. People who are confident know they are able to make decisions. Therefore, they're more prepared to be leaders. Confident people tend to say, "My opinions are valid, though they may not be right in every case." Some people seem to be better decision makers than others. It comes from education, training, and experience: a process of acquiring skills. The commitment and motivation to acquire the necessary skills comes from desire. What if your opinion turns out to be wrong? It happens. But remember, there are good decision makers who are not good leaders but there are no good leaders who aren't also good decision makers.

Decisiveness doesn't mean becoming dictatorial. To be assertive you don't have to be curt, abusive, or short with people. It doesn't always mean you're right. It simply means you're taking action, and taking action is critical.

Don't let setting goals make you inflexible. Many people go into a project sincerely believing that their way is the *only* way. It's often more productive to present an idea as one possible solution, then invite other ideas, and mix everything together to form a plan. This way, everyone's goal is being met, and the whole team can get more enthusiastic about the project.

Another point. ***Goal setting involves ethics.*** When you set your goals you have to ask yourself if achieving them will be as valuable to your family, friends, co-workers, etc. as they are to you. After all, a promotion won at the cost of others is a bittersweet victory—and all the riches in the world won't comfort you if you've lost your home and health to attain them.

Goal achievement, just like any other project, is a commitment, and knowing what you want and where you're going will make your flight a lot easier. Studies indicate that only 5% of the population ever really succeed. Social Security Office records state the 95% of the people who file for social security cannot even write a check for $250 and have it covered after working 20, 30, or even 40 years. Only 3% of the population have written goals and only 5% have any goals at all. These statistics aren't meant to discourage you or shock you. They simply demonstrate the difference between "wanting" and "having". I'll bet if you stopped ten people on the street, nine of them would insist they had goals. Some would be delusions of grandeur, some would be routine things that you and I don't even think about, and one or two might even be realistic(!). But, the point is, everyone *thinks* they have goals, and yet it seems that only a few succeed. For some people, writing down their goals seems superfluous—they claim they know exactly where they're headed and don't need a list to help them through. For others, making a goals list is nearly impossible because they've set up all sorts of mental roadblocks to success. "Well, I guess I want to stay at this job and get promoted because I dislike my boss. But, if I got another job, I could take some night classes and get my degree . . . . Or, maybe my cousin and I will start that little side business we've been talking about; that would be great, unless the economy gets sluggish, then we might have to get part-time jobs . . . ." and so on. That kind of thinking is the fast track to nowhere. At some point you have to ask yourself, "Am I going through life with my hands on the steering wheel or with my eyes on the rear view mirror?" The process of being alive is entirely in the present, it's not a deferred payment plan. You can't collect brownie points for promising to *think about it tomorrow* like Scarlet O'Hara. Life is today. Goals are today. Goal achievement is this minute, not the next.

──────── **LIFE LINE** ────────

If you cannot imagine yourself having your goal,
it will not happen.

──────── ✍ ────────

If your life is in balance, your goals will be in balance. Take a good, long look at your life and its different aspects—mental, physical, material, emotional, and spiritual. Do you see any problem areas? If so, make a short list of goals to overcome these problems. Then, once you've conquered them, your life goals will seem easier to attain. If you cannot imagine yourself having your goal, it will not happen. If you can't imagine what it would be like to be the head of a multi-million dollar company, don't be concerned: you'll never have to worry about it because you'll never be there. But, if you start a small business in the hopes of making a decent living, and your product or service takes off, you'd be surprised how quickly you'll start imagining yourself in a penthouse office. A little taste of success can be a powerful motivator.

Goal achievement is a never-ending life process. In fact, the very action of plotting your goals is the first step in attaining them. You'll be closer to your desired goal simply by sitting down and putting it on paper. One gratifying aspect of achieving goals is that success is limitless, each time you achieve one goal you'll find another to take its place. And, the better you get at attaining your goals, the more you'll look forward to the next challenge. Goal setting helps you feel better; it makes you healthier because it fills your mind with positive energy and promise. Setting your goals will give you more time and less worry.

Whatever your goals, whatever your plans, please be sure to make one of your top priorities each day: *Be good to myself.* Being good to yourself should be easy but some find it harder than others. You have to get to *know* yourself first before you'll even know how to be *good* to yourself. If you've never been a particularly vain person, being good to yourself might be a day of pampering to make you look nicer with a new haircut, or some new clothes. Or, if you're an indulgent person, being good to yourself may be spending a day volunteering for a charity group. You decide. Whatever you do, remember: *There are no ex-goal setters.*

CHAPTER 26:
DO IT RIGHT OR DO IT OVER

Let's explore the ways in which time affects our lives.

———— LIFE LINE ————

Somehow we never have time to do it right,
but we always find time to do it over.

To put time into perspective, you've got to handle tension before it controls you. You may laugh at this, but we need to discover ways to maintain and increase our accomplishments without causing undue stress. In other words, making time work for us. Working smarter, not harder. Somehow we never have time to do it *right,* but we always find time to do it *over.* When surveyed, business executives cited that their number one daily concern was: *lack of time.* You know as well as I do that everyone has the same amount of time in their lives. There's no such thing as a 25-hour day or an eight-day week! Time management allows some people to accomplish great things, while others merely exist.

There's a saying in the computer industry that goes like this: Computers work at the speed of light. If you are disorganized in the way you do your job manually, and you transfer your work onto a computer, you'll be disorganized at the speed of light.

Smarter, Not Harder

Have you ever worked with someone who seemed busy all day long and, when quitting time came, they'd always sigh and say, "Well, I guess I'll be here late tonight finishing up these projects I'm working on." You start feeling guilty that you're going home on time. And you say to yourself, "Am I working hard enough; am I pulling my weight?" Then, eventually, you begin to pay more attention to your co-worker's habits and you realize that he or she isn't really accomplishing that much all day. That's why they stay late all the time: *they have to work twice as long to get their work done.* Maybe they're too easily distracted during the day, maybe they have developed a habit of procrastinating. Or, maybe they like the sympathy they get from others and can't think of anything better to do at home! It sounds silly but very often it's true.

——————— LIFE LINE ———————

Computers work at the speed of light.
If you are disorganized in the way you
do your job manually, and you transfer your
work onto a computer, you'll be disorganized at
the speed of light.

I know a lady who managed a scientific research facility. Her whole life was dedicated to this center and she would appear at staff meetings looking tired and somewhat disheveled and say, "I was here all night . . ." She would hardly ever acknowledge staff accomplishments except to say, "So-and-so has worked a week straight without a break and even brought a sleeping bag a couple of nights instead of going home." This manager's message was clear: in order to show me your productivity, you have to prove you're willing to give up the rest of your life. That's not management by objective, that's management by obsession! Don't assume that time management means cutting out your leisure time or spending less time away from your job. On the contrary: *when you can manage your time wisely your job will become easier and your free time more rewarding.*

 **LIFE LINE**

A focused mind produces order that allows wanting to become having.

Time and life are one in the same. Don't waste either. If you feel there is no room for advancement in your position or feel you are locked in to an incompatible relationship, you might want to take another look at your willingness to accept the responsibility that the new situation would demand. To get a clearer picture of your current situation, think about the answers to these questions, I'll elaborate on them later:

1. What are your lifetime goals?

2. How would you like to spend the next five years?

3. How would you spend the next six months if you knew that's how long you had to live?

4. If you knew you couldn't fail what would you do right now?

These are difficult questions but, if you can answer them honestly, you can plan to make time each day to take one step closer to reaching your goals. Writing it down is important because thought on paper is tangible. People can see it. Post your list where you'll see it often and it will help keep you on track.

——————— LIFE LINE ———————

You can lose a thousand dollars and get it back,
but lost time is gone forever.
——————— ✍ ———————

Cleaning House

It's a known fact that most people waste 80% of their time even though they seem to be perpetually busy (trying to do too many things that don't matter). They clutter their lives. Then, they can't understand why there isn't enough time to do the things they really want to do. A scattered mind produces scattered results. A focused mind produces order that allows *wanting* to become *having*. It turns dreams into reality. There's a saying, "Yesterday is a canceled check, tomorrow is a promissory note. Only today is cash in hand." You can lose a thousand dollars and get it back, but lost time is gone forever.

Both in work and leisure we need to set priorities. Wanting a promotion is one thing, managing your time to work toward that promotion is another. Wanting to paint your house or take a vacation is fine, but you have to set your priorities to enable yourself to reach your goal in the amount of time you have to make it happen.

There's a dry-cleaning store I know of with a marquee that is changed frequently with clever messages. I drove by the other day and the sign said, "When you kill time, you murder success." Killing time comes from all kinds of sources: procrastination, bad habits, or lack of good communication.

——————— LIFE LINE ———————

The secret of finding time to do the things you
want is to really want it.
——————— ✍ ———————

We've already covered some ground on why people procrastinate and we know it's a common problem. *Most people waste time—of* course I realize none of you do—but most people do. There are things you've been meaning to do for *years:* learn a language, visit a certain place, write a special letter, take a personal enrichment course. And yet, everyday the clock ticks away and we're distressed by a feeling of inferiority when we continue to delay action to move ahead. This is followed by a sense of inadequacy and fatigue. Pretty soon, we're saying, "Aw, I'll make that call tomorrow." or "Next week I'll set some time aside to do that." People take courses in time management and still end up having no time to do the things that are necessary for success. If you *really* want to get something done you'll find the time to do it. You don't need a time management expert to tell you how. Why, I'll bet if I put you to work selling lemonade on the street corner, and told you I'd give you $100 for every glass you sold, you'd be out there hustling! Or, how about if I promised you college students a one-year scholarship if you maintained a four-point average for one semester? You'd be cracking those books till daybreak. And, if you accomplished either of these goals, it wouldn't be because you suddenly got a whole lot *smarter;* you just got a whole lot more *motivated.* You don't get motivation like that from a textbook or lecture, you get it from identifying an extremely desirable goal and making up your mind to get it. So, you see, it's simple really: the secret of finding time to do the things you want is *to really want it.* Some say, "Good things come to those who are *prepared* to receive them."

Ask yourself this question: "What is my time worth to me?" If your answer is, "Nothing," you have some major problems, and we'll have to come back to you later. You may say time is your most valuable resource, but are you spending that resource wisely? Some people spend hours, even days trying to save a nickel, 50 cents or a dollar. They run around taking money out of this account and depositing it in that account for an extra 1/4% interest. Then, a few months later, they change accounts again because of some other new lure. They've made money on paper but wasted some very valuable time in the process. Awareness of your time is the key factor here. How often have you said, "I don't have the time."? when in reality the true statement is, "I've chosen to use my time differently." After all, isn't it all about choice? Even if you procrastinate, that's a choice. "I'll do it someday." I've got news for you: *"someday" is not a day of the week!*

"What Happened?"

All the tasks that face you in a lifetime fall into three categories: *I cannot, I will not,* and *I don't know how.* Identify the things you cannot do; is it important you learn how to do them? And, what about the things you've decided you will not do; is it because you fear them or loathe them, or just don't understand them? And, finally, what's the answer to the problem, "I don't know how." Is it that you don't know how to begin, you don't know how it will end, or you don't know how you got into this mess in the first place? There are three types of people: those who make things happen, those who watch things happen, and those who wonder, "What happened?"

In the final analysis, you'll be the one to identify your own reasons for procrastinating.

Eighty/Twenty

It doesn't matter how many academic degrees you might have, promise me now you'll work on your D.I.N. degree: *Do It Now.* Mastering this degree can be the most valuable of all. In business the 80/20 rule applies, that is: 80% of the phone calls come from 20% of the same callers, in short: 80% of your business comes from 20% of your customers. Everyday life is the same way: 80% of the time you make one of your favorite 20 recipes for dinner. And, 20% of all TV programs are the same ones watched by 80% of all TV viewers. And I find that these four examples convince about 80% of the people.

So, how can you put the 80/20 rule to work for you at your place of business? Here are ten useful tips on time management that will help you stay focused on the most vital tasks at hand:

1. *Consolidate similar tasks:* instead of making or returning business calls sporadically throughout the day, set some time aside to do it as one task. Frequent callers can be informed of the best time to reach you and you'll sensitize callers to develop a habit of calling you during times that are more convenient.

2. *Tackle tough jobs first:* start your day with the important work when your energy level is high and work your way down your list of priorities.

3. *Delegate and develop other people:* Break the "I'll do it myself" habit. Make sure business tasks are properly delegated, but remember—delegating doesn't mean dumping. When you delegate, you have a responsibility to make sure the individual has the skills and knowledge to do the job and you need to follow through to see it gets done right and on time.

4. *Learn to use idle time:* Instead of waiting for an appointment with nothing to do, review a report, read an article, or catch up on correspondence. Listen to self-improvement tapes or foreign language lessons on the way to and from work.

5. *Get control of the paper flow:* Decide immediately what paperwork can be streamlined, and what can be eliminated. Throw out junk mail and have other mail routed directly to the person who will carry out the task. Don't get trapped into sorting through all the mail because you're curious.

6. *Avoid the cluttered-desk syndrome:* If your desk is piled with paper and you waste time looking for buried items, clear your desk of everything except the work you intend to do that day. The chances are that you'll get it done.

7. *Get started immediately on important tasks:* Unfinished work is more of a motivator than *unstarted* work. By having started a job you have made an investment of your time and are more likely to complete the task.

8. *Reduce meeting time:* Sometimes the only reason for a weekly staff meeting is because a week has passed since the last one. Such meetings disrupt your work. Reduce the number and improve the quality of meetings. And always follow an agenda.

9. *Take time to plan:* The great paradox of time is that by taking time to plan, you end up saving time. Instead of spending your days fighting "fires" develop a schedule for doing things that must be done in the time available.

10. *Learn to say* "No": There will always be someone asking for a portion of your time. If your help is truly needed, give it and then get back to your own tasks. If a solution to the problem can be found without you, make a quick suggestion and return to work. Be open but be firm.

Associations

The person you are is largely comprised of the influences you get from the people you meet and the books you read. Therefore, your selection process is important to achieve your goals and manage your time properly. Choosing your friends and associates wisely is a critical factor in attaining your goals. Negative associations have caused many aspiring people to be passed over for a promotion, a raise, or a new opportunity. Negative people are ones who rob us of our time, energy, and reputation. Positive people, on the other hand, can enrich our lives, and can actually improve our present situation simply by their presence. These are action people, people with good judgment and decisiveness. But, you say, what about peer pressure? You want to be "one of the guys". That's natural, everyone wants to blend in, it makes us feel wanted; like we belong. Even strong individuals sometimes make decisions in a group that they would never think of making if they stood alone. Haven't you ever spent an entire afternoon doing something you really didn't want to because your mate, your friend or a family member wanted to do it? Yes, I think we all have. And, what about on the job? The most natural thing to do when starting a new position is to observe your coworkers. Their performance, habits, and their use of company time and materials quickly become your own. This would be okay if one could be assured of success by following the crowd. But, statistics show that more than 95% of people today do not enjoy where they are, do not have a definite goal in mind and are not aware of the steps necessary to accomplish a successful and constructive life-style.

If we do not take charge of our attitude, our behavior, and our environment; if we do not choose a direction that will be beneficial and constructive, then we've killed time and murdered success. It doesn't take any longer to make a positive decision than it does to make a negative one. Time is constant. It ticks away regardless of whether you're making a million dollars or one dollar. Those who make the worst use of time are the ones who complain most of its shortness.

So, choosing your peer group and maintaining a routine are more than just incidentals in life. Not so very long ago, people's choices about time were much more structured. Imagine how long it took the caveman to stalk a beast, kill it, drag it home, clean it, make a fire, cook it, and eat it. Now a quick trip through the drive-up window at your nearest fast food place and you're on your way in minutes!

Today, with all the social, economic, and physical mobility we enjoy, the opportunities for (and pressures of) making choices have multiplied. Instead of becoming overwhelmed by all the things you have to do, and the little time you have to do them in, consider all your options and how lucky you are to have them. Because, even today there are people out there with nothing, whose sole preoccupation each day is getting something to eat, just like the caveman. Take a few moments each morning to mentally see your day progressing as you wish. You'll find that your tasks will be accomplished much more smoothly. Time is your friend. Use it wisely and it will reward you ten times over. Waste it and it will pass you by like a stranger on the street.

We are all creatures of habit. Habits are pieces of behavior. Habits can help us or keep us from achieving our dreams.

New Habits, Better Habits

People form habits, and habits form futures. By replacing destructive behavior with constructive behavior, and consistently repeating the process, a new constructive habit is formed. You know that saying about teaching an old dog new tricks? Do you believe it's true? It depends on the trick, don't you think? I mean, if you're trying to teach the old dog how to get out from in front of an on-coming automobile, its learning powers greatly improve, right? Just because you're used to getting up at 6:45 every morning doesn't mean you couldn't get used to getting up at 6:15 and making good use of that extra 30 minutes. That 30 minutes a day equals an extra one working month a year. Think about it. You could start that exercise program you've been putting off. Or get to the office a bit early to handle a few items before the morning rush.

LIFE LINE

We all have the same amount of time: all there is.

If you have a plan for your time, there's no limit to what you can accomplish. How often have you or someone around you said, "If I only had more time . . . ." Well, my friends, the plain truth is *no one* has more time. We all have the same amount of time—all there is. Everybody gets the same 24 hours in a day. And yet, some people get so much more accomplished than others. Blaming time for your lack of success is simply an excuse for not succeeding. Busy people are able to find time for what they want to do, not because they have any more time than others but because they think in terms of "making" time by careful planning. You don't want to become a clock-watcher but you can easily change some habits to create extra time for yourself. Not enough time with your family? Schedule preplanned activities, you'll be surprised how they fall into place. No time for your creative pursuits? Spend only an hour cleaning house this time and devote the rest of your day to a favorite creative activity. The dust will still be there when you get to it!

The point is that when we begin to look at and utilize time in a more realistic and efficient manner, we respond to our needs and activities in a more confident and realistic fashion and *time becomes our friend.*

CHAPTER 27:
GET YOUR DIN DEGREE... DO IT NOW!

Many people come down with that dreaded disease called tommorowitis. But, escaping through procrastination is a fallacy, and it can become a habit.

Some of our habits are necessary ones: eating, sleeping, getting dressed, filling the car with gas, taking out the trash, and so on. But, there are ways even within these everyday chores to make time for success or enrichment.

The late Robert Kennedy was reported to have listened to Shakespearean plays while shaving. Breaks can be a good time to relax. But suppose you're not particularly tense or tired. How about learning a new word from your dictionary? Or mailing those bills you've been putting off. Or calling your dentist for an appointment for your annual cleaning. You can even make your sleeping hours more productive; get an appliance timer to start your coffee, or hot water so it's ready when you get up in the morning. Or, start a crafts project before you go to bed and, by the time you wake up, the glue will be dry and you can move on to the next step.

Each individual has his or her own set of personal ideas about managing time. Each person's expectations are different. Yet, each person does expect something. Think through your own personal reasons.

1. What things would you most like to gain?

2. What are your toughest time problems?

3. What would you like to accomplish with your time that isn't happening now?

Think about your expectations and put them down on paper. Now you have a list to work from, something you check, re-check, or review as needed. Remember, your list can be job-related or personal, but it's yours. Don't expect your list to match up with others in your office or even in your family. Paste a picture or some other reminder on your bathroom mirror. Each night as you brush your teeth (you did put that on your list, didn't you?) look at whatever reminder you've left and ask yourself, "Did I spend any time today moving toward my goal?" If your answer is yes, take the rest of the day off. If your answer is no, then take a few minutes before you go to bed to jot down a few mental reminders or specific goals for the next day. Some people even take it a step further by practicing a form of meditation in which they get into bed, turn out the lights, and take several deep breaths while repeating a goal over and over again in their mind. This sets up a subconscious thought-pattern which will direct the mind to think about your goal while you sleep. Pretty good use of time, huh?

──────── **LIFE LINE** ────────

Thank goodness for time; it
motivates us to change and grow.

──────── ✍ ────────

Visualize a sand timer. It's just like the reality we live in. All the sand in the bottom is the past. It's over; you can't even get five grains of sand back. You can feel sorry about what you said yesterday or, you can feel guilty for treating someone badly, but it's still over. Will Rogers once said, "Don't bring too much of yesterday into today." Just imagine getting up tomorrow with the same anxieties, fears, and resentments as today, that would be like recreating yesterday for the rest of your life. Oh sure, the weather and the world around you would change, but your mental attitude would stay the same. Thank goodness for time; it motivates us to change and grow. As I said earlier, insanity is doing the same thing over and over again expecting to get different results.

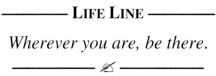

─────── **L**IFE **L**INE ───────

Wherever you are, be there.

Getting back to our reality timer here, all the sand in the top is the future, it hasn't happened yet. A lot of people think they have a lot of sand left so they're in no hurry to accomplish anything. Others fear their sand is running out so they become preoccupied worrying about it, and still never accomplish anything. You can't spend your time living in "What might be," or "What has been." You have to live in the here and now. Have you ever been talking with someone and realized they were not really with you? They stare off into space and you can tell they're neither here nor there! A good rule of thumb is: wherever you are, *be there.*

The 'Best Time' is Now

We actually live in an ocean of motion. We live here, in this small area of time where everything is happening *now!* This is it; there is no other time! Don't get caught up in the "After Theory." You say you've got real plans: after the kids go to college, after you find the right job, after you make your first million. This 'after' period never comes, but you keep on promising yourself that someday you're going to get what you want. Now, it's good to have plans and aspirations, but even if opportunity knocks more than once, it seldom sits on the doorstep awaiting your pleasure. Do the things you always wanted to *now.* Or, at least make the plans now. Not tomorrow! You will never have more time than you have today because today is what is real! Today is what's happening. Today is your life. An ancient Chinese proverb says, "A journey of a thousand miles begins with a single step." We all exist in a vast rhythm center. Our ever-changing universe is a series of on-going rhythms like the daily ocean tides, the monthly cycles of the moon, and the yearly changes in the seasons. Everything in our world functions on a rhythmic time schedule. Finding your own individual rhythm of time is a way to keep you in sync with not only your own cares, but with the world around you. Never look at routine as an uninteresting matter of duty. Think of it as your cosmic rhythm; the beat that keeps your own life in tune. There have been some very famous quotes about time throughout the ages. Some of the best known come from The Bible, you've heard, "For everything there is a season, and a time for every matter under heaven." And what about this passage, also from The Bible, "Live life then with a due sense of responsibility, not as men who do not know the meaning and purpose of life, but as those who do. Make the best use of your time, despite all the difficulties of these days." Those words, written so very long ago, are still as timely today as they were then.

Prioritize

Earlier I talked about procrastination. Let's take another look at this, in one way or another it is common to most people. Supposing you want to eliminate procrastination from your life. Sort your activities into three categories A, B, and C. A, must do; B, important to do; and C, nice to do. You can see right away that the C's would be nice to do, but if you have priorities things that must get done, and tasks that are important to do, these must be handled first. Put the C's in the bottom drawer; when it gets full, toss 'em, otherwise you'll be majoring in minors. Now you're left with the A's and B's, the must do and the important to do. It seems apparent that both must be handled, but where do you begin? With the A's of course.

"Must do" A priorities carry with them an immediacy, so begin with the A's, even if it's only a small beginning. Quite often the A priorities involve more time, more energy, and more skill than tackling the lesser important tasks, but it is imperative to begin them. Possibly you'll need to acquire some knowledge in order to proceed.

Maybe you'll need help, a new technology, and a definite plan of action. You must initiate whatever is necessary, and it boils down to "I cannot," "I will not," or "I don't know how." You fall into one of these categories, which one is it?

Identify Procrastination

Now, how can you identify procrastination in your life? Some of the traits are:

Waiting for the big deal: wishing or hoping for some big deal to fall into your life is one of the most popular versions. Thinking that a big breakthrough, personal change, or management change will prove to be the panacea, is common.

Recognizing a need, but not taking action: realizing the need and practicality to correct your health, but not taking action, is an area many have discovered. Excessive eating, smoking, drinking, realizing the need for exercise, all these are things known, but seldom acted upon.

Waiting for the right time: another sign of procrastination is desiring to relocate and waiting for the "right time". Certainly there are times when it may be easier to take action than others, but in general, if someone is really serious about making a change, they will plan a date and do it.

Constantly putting off: delaying the little things by putting them aside for another day, thinking they are unimportant and may go away. These can develop into virtual monsters. Of course, the priorities take precedence, but sometimes handling the small tasks can provide the mental freedom and the space to plan effectively.

Excessive planning: excessive planning is also a procrastination tool. Pre-planning, planning, post-planning: "Let's do anything so we don't have to start." Excessive planning may stem from a strong need to achieve without having the self-confidence to move directly toward the goal.

Living vicariously: living life vicariously, through others, is a form of procrastination. Often, parents will find themselves leading a life, essentially through their children. Their happiness seems to be gained only through the activities of their children. Using the child as a ploy, although unintentional as it may be, an individual has again created a non-action status. Vicarious management is similar, often causing non-action.

Ignoring the obvious: ignoring areas that need attention is still another. It is true that everything passes in time, but the success-oriented person acts with a total plan, moving toward a goal in a complete fashion, a direction with a well-designed purpose.

These are some of the areas to look for when identifying procrastination. Watch for them in yourself. Awareness is the key. When we are aware of these tendencies, we place ourselves in a better position to handle them, and eliminate them from our lives.

CHAPTER 28:
STRESS WITHOUT DISTRESS

How many people do you suppose there are all around the world who wish success came in neatly wrapped packages, handed over as gifts with no strings attached? The world is filled with these people . . . people who spend their lives wishing rather than acting. Just what is it that keeps so many people from acting? A few of the excuses we use are:

"I'm under too much pressure, I can't sit around and think about my future."

"I just don't have enough time to sit down and plan anything."

"My only goal is to make it to lunch today!"

Let's talk about stress. Stress is a necessary part of life. It's your body's chemical, mental, and physical reaction to stimulus, any stimulus, good or bad. Stress is part of what propels the track star across the finish line to win an Olympic gold medal. Stress is also what prevents people from asking for a raise or confronting a co-worker about an office problem. It may seem like stress is an unpleasant thing; it usually means sweaty palms, a racing heart, a lump in the throat, or butterflies in the stomach. And yet, you wouldn't want to go through life without stress because stress is the very thing that prepares us to handle situations that we are unfamiliar with or even fearful to us. When managed properly, stress can strengthen us for our next important challenge. *But*, when handled poorly, or allowed to get out of hand, stress can cause fatigue, disease and even death. My friends, our goal is to achieve stress without *distress*.

Life is Stress — Rejoice!

Life is a constant series of stress stimulators. If you were at one of my seminars and I asked you to get up and explain stress management, you might feel some stress, right? Well, I wouldn't do that to you . . . after all, you might be pretty good and that would cause *me* a lot of stress!

Remember when you were very small? Your parents and teachers would create situations just tough enough for you to learn new techniques for problem-solving. You might not have known it then, but stress is what helped you pull yourself up to take your first steps, or learn to swim, or win a spelling bee. Remember the feeling of accomplishment you had when you mastered a problem? That was your good friend, stress, causing the chemicals in your body to come alive and work together to see you through.

Don't give up on your old friend stress now! Make friends again and use stress to your own advantage. The Chinese symbol for "crisis" is actually a combination of two words: "danger" and "opportunity". In fact, most of the problems we face everyday are dangerous opportunities. Asking for a raise could lead to rejection, *or* it could earn you a promotion. Confronting a co-worker could cause a big fight, *or* it could win the respect of a new friend.

Asserting yourself is always a calculated risk. Many people find speaking in public tremendously stressful. And yet, actors, politicians, musical performers, and lecturers make a handsome living taking that risk.

"No Problem."

As we know, different people manage stress differently. In the Caribbean they have a wonderful way of dealing with stress. Their answer to everything is, "No problem." Whatever question you ask or problem you pose, the retort is, "No problem." My wife (Dana) and I were lounging by a hotel pool in the Bahamas. There was an outdoor bar nearby. A man came up to the bar and said, "My wife says this martini you made her has too much vermouth. I don't drink martinis so I wouldn't know." The Bahamian bartender responded with, "No problem, man," and quickly mixed another drink. Moments later, the same man came back with a ten dollar bill in his hand and said, "Now my wife says you used gin instead of vodka. I don't drink martinis so I wouldn't know. Let me start over and buy a new drink." Before the man had completed his sentence, the bartender had mixed yet another new drink, handed it to the man and said, "No problem, man. Take it and be happy." After the man walked away, Dana remarked how in control the bartender had been by not pointing out that a martini *is* made with gin. If he had wanted a vodka martini, the guy should have said so and saved himself a whole lot of trouble. I got to thinking about that incident. Here's a man on vacation; he's supposed to be relaxing and unwinding from daily pressures; the person closest to him, his wife, sent him into a potentially confrontational situation with little or no correct information. A total stranger, the bartender, who knew he could control this guy's destiny for at least a few minutes, minimized the problem and sent the still-confused tourist on his way.

So much of what we do in life has us depending on others. We can make that *dependence* an excuse for why we don't succeed *or* we can declare our in*dependence* and take complete responsibility for everything that enters our consciousness.

———— LIFE LINE ————

If you remember to think of your problems as opportunities, you'll want to control them yourself.

———— ✍ ————

Taking responsibility can be a scary thing. Sometimes it's comforting to know you can always blame your problems on someone else, isn't it? *But*, if you remember to think of your problems as *opportunities*, you'll want to control them yourself. Most people will wake up tomorrow thinking about the problems of today. There might not be anything wrong with that as long as you're evaluating your progress or validating your solutions. But there's no point in simply reliving *yesterday's* shortcomings, because it takes up valuable time you could be using to handle *today's* challenges.

———— LIFE LINE ————

Worry often gives a small thing a big shadow.

———— ✍ ————

Take Shelter or Take Action

Let's take a moment to talk about our thought process as related to stress and worry. No two thoughts can occupy the same mind at the same instant. Strive to make each thought count. Are there some negative, destructive or non-productive thoughts you would like to replace with a more positive train of thinking? What kind of thoughts are counter-productive 'worries'? What's wrong with worrying? It doesn't accomplish anything except creating more worries! *... I should put bars on my windows in case someone breaks in ... but then, how will I escape if there's a fire? I'd better watch my speed as I drive around this curve ... but if I drive too slowly, the guy behind me might hit me. What if it's cold outside; I'll catch a cold. What if it's too hot; I could get sunstroke.*

There's an old proverb which states: Worry often gives a small thing a big shadow. Research indicates that 40% of our worries never happen. Thirty percent are in the past and can't be helped. Twelve percent concern the affairs of others that aren't our business. Ten percent are about sickness, either real or imagined, and only eight percent have even a small chance of being justified.

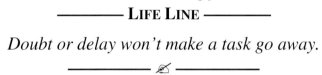

——————— LIFE LINE ———————

Doubt or delay won't make a task go away.

Okay, what are some other kinds of thoughts we could eliminate? Doubt is certainly a factor of worry. How often do we raise doubts about our abilities before we even attempt to accomplish a task? Or, how often have we raised doubts about other people's motives just because we didn't know those people, or because we were envious of them for some reason? Over and over again, it is a lack of positive action that causes us to doubt. Doubt and indecision go hand in hand. What's the real price of delay? If you have your doubts about going to see the doctor and you put off the decision to go, you might risk creating a serious health problem that could have been cured with simple treatment. At work, if you have your doubts about completing a report or project, you risk getting reprimanded or even fired! And yet, some people justify it by saying, "I work best under pressure." I've spent the last several paragraphs talking about ways to cope with stress and not distress and here's a statement from someone inviting pressure?! I think you can already see the folly of that logic. Anyone who tells you they deliberately delayed a project because they like working under pressure is fooling you and themselves. I always ask them, "You like pressure? Why not put your desk on a train track!" Now *that's* working under pressure!

Doubt or delay won't make a task go away. In fact, the actual work required may increase as time goes on. Have you ever put off filing your paperwork so long that every time you need a certain document it takes you ten minutes to sort through your "to-be-filed" stack? Or, have you ever put off filling your gas tank until you got stuck on the open road on the way to an important meeting? Or, have you ever delayed getting around to changing something in your business product or service until you were swamped with customer complaints? Answering the complaints takes twice as long as fixing the problem would have taken–*and you still have to fix the problem!* I think you get the point about doubt.

Fear

What other thoughts are bad for us and what can we do about them?

Fear is one. One cause of fear is non-action. But fear can be looked at as either positive or negative for we will either retreat, or we'll be prompted to take steps toward positive action. Fear is really an acronym for: *F*alse *E*vidence *A*ppearing *R*eal. Fear is caused by not working toward a solution. Many people live in fear that others will not solve their problems to their liking. Well, that's a self-fulfilling prophecy! If you put your problems in other people's hands, you're almost guaranteed they won't be solved as you would solve them. If you're afraid of catching poison ivy from the weeds in your yard, what have you done to remove them? If you're afraid of making a speech in front of people, what have you done to prepare for it? If you're afraid of dying from high blood pressure, what diet and life-style habits have you changed to prevent it? Now, don't get me wrong, it's healthy to fear death; it makes us drive a little slower on the freeway. And it's okay to be concerned about your family and your future. Keep in mind: confidence will always overcome fear. Have confidence in your actions and your ability to deal with problems. Fears need to be addressed head on. At the risk of sounding strange, you can set up a personal dialogue with your fears to bring them into perspective. It goes something like this:

Fear: I'm afraid!

Jim: Of what?

Fear: Of taking my drivers exam.

Jim: Why?

Fear: They're a pretty tough group at the DMV.

Jim: So, what's the worst that could happen? You could end up having to retake the exam.

By this time you shrug your shoulders and realize the old cliché is really true: *We have nothing to fear but fear itself.*

Many people avoid jobs that have been given high priority because they fear the consequences that will follow once they complete the job. Consider the sales executive who put off selling a new account because he was afraid how much it would add to his workload if he succeeded. Or how about the executive who refuses to acquire typing skills that are necessary for effective computer operation, still harboring the belief that typing is for secretaries. Don't let your emotions do you in. Worry, doubt, and fears that are not confronted, have no place in a body that's moving forward and making decisions.

Whatever the mind dwells upon, anything feared or revered, it multiplies, magnifies, and causes to grow, until finally the mind becomes locked in the fear. Focusing your mind firmly on your desires, and keeping it there can be quite a job. Can you do it for a week? Perhaps not. A day? Again, perhaps not. Even an hour can be difficult. It seems all we can really do is replace our thoughts moment by moment.

If then, we ever hope to better ourselves and our life situation, it would seem evident that we realize that there is no situation or cause external to ourselves that can affect our world. Be it job, family, or money, our thoughts are involved, and as long as we place our success or our failure on something "out there" like that raise, that person, or something like natural talent, then we will continue to be pushed and pulled, like puppets, by the world around us. Effective thinking takes practice.

CHAPTER 29:
LOOKING INWARD

So far we've covered a lot of ground about the nature of stress and how it manifests itself in our lives. Perhaps it's time now to talk about some concrete ways to manage stress. Research suggests that a healthy mind and body will accept stress more readily, and deal with it in a more positive fashion. To determine how "healthy" you are in regard to stress, ask yourself these questions:

1. Do I have a wide range of activities that I find enjoyable and fulfilling?

2. Am I flexible under stress?

3. Do I recognize the assets and accept the limitations of myself and others?

4. Do I treat others fairly, as individuals?

5. Am I active and productive away from my business or job?

If you answered 'no' to any of these questions, you might take some time to develop a more positive attitude about the specifics mentioned.

What I Like

You should be able to make a long, long list of activities you enjoy. They can be obvious things like breathing and being alive, or they can be more specific, like shopping, reading mystery novels, shopping, playing racquetball, or possibly shopping. The point is, what you enjoy about life says a lot about how you see yourself. If nothing is fulfilling or enjoyable to you it might be because you are unhappy with yourself for some reason. Be honest, find the reason and fix it. As you become more aware of your own needs for fulfillment, you'll find hundreds of ways to satisfy those needs. Start small: reorganize your files at work, give your house the best spring cleaning it's ever had, do an errand for a needy friend. Whatever task you accomplish, it will focus your attention away from your unhappiness and set you on a track toward positive goal achievement.

If you find you're not very flexible in a stressful situation, ask yourself what you really know about the problem at hand. Do you fully understand what's happening? Are you embarrassed or flustered? Or, are you just plain angry and want your way no matter how much stress it causes? Being flexible doesn't mean giving in or "eating your words". It simply means thinking before you react; taking into account all the variables of the situation, and keeping an open mind to another person's train of thought.

The more in control you are of your own thoughts and actions, the better prepared you are to compromise without defeating your own objectives. In fact, an astute thinker usually weighs the objections before posing an argument. In the practice of law, it is suggested, "Never ask a witness a question to which you don't already know the answer."

Turning Fear Into Fair

Recognizing the strong and weak points in yourself and others is essential to good communication. If you can dish it out but can't take it, think twice about calling attention to someone's shortcomings. If you have weaknesses, you can work on correcting them, but don't expect someone else to welcome your criticism without reservation.

Learning to treat others fairly is something we began in kindergarten. And yet, we sometimes forget that grown-ups have feelings too. Before you blow up at a friend or co-worker, take a moment to figure out what made that person say, or do, what they did. And, be mindful not to judge individuals just because you "don't like people from California" or you "can't stand guys with long hair" or you "just dislike it when elderly people get ahead of you in the check-out line". People are individuals and should never be prejudged because of a group they fit into.

If you give all your energy to your work and can't feel active or productive *unless* you're working, it's time to evaluate your priorities. Are you really working to form outside relationships and interests, or are you even trying? Are you hoping the world will notice how dedicated and selfless you are? If so, guess what? The world doesn't care because it's too busy being active and productive without you and your work! Your job doesn't make you worthy — you give your job, and everything else you do, a life and a worth. Don't hide behind your work and let it be your reason for living, or a safe haven to go to on weekends. Think of yourself as an active, interesting individual pursuing your hopes and dreams. Entertain new activities; you don't necessarily have to try skydiving, but at least allow your horizons to be broadened.

By considering these questions, you'll be more familiar with ways to relate to stress. As you go about your daily tasks, spend some time thinking about the thoughts you use to determine conclusions and to solve problems. Are they substantial? Are they rational? Concentration and rational thought go a long way toward managing stress. By concentrating on the job at hand, you are less likely to overlook something that could cause you stress: like an important deadline or a critical meeting. By thinking rationally, you'll remove patterns that lead to stress, induce worry, doubt, and immobilizing fear. Take for example these thoughts; do they sound rational to you?

1. It's essential that I be loved or approved of by everyone in my community.

2. It's a catastrophe when things aren't as I want them to be.

3. It's easier to avoid certain responsibilities than to face them.

These are irrational ideas. Why? Because they don't allow for the simple fact that people are human. The eyes of the world are much bigger than the eyes of just one person. Only you see your special view of life through your eyes. Each person views life with their own expectations, their own experiences. Your irrational thoughts exist only in your own mind.

Coping with Common Stress

To best cope with common stress in today's busy world, consider these coping skills:

1. *Do it now!* Don't let things drift.

2. Deal with tension. Don't avoid it.

3. Do something for someone else.

4. Handle the details, don't drown in them.

5. Respect yourself.

6. Maintain a healthy mind and body.

7. Get involved.

8. Seek humor.

9. Make your desires clear.

10. Live for today. Get rid of the "what if's".

Let's talk about coping with stress. First, we must learn to work off stress. If you're angry or upset, release tension through physical activity: take a brisk walk, go to the gym after work, or go home and mow the lawn. If you're at work or in a situation that would be difficult to leave, and stress becomes a problem, back off for a minute and take a few deep breaths.

I was going out of town one Friday evening and I stopped at a busy gas station to fill my tank. It was a self-serve station so I had to go in to leave my credit card before pumping the gas. There was a long line and the first person being waited on was looking around for any last item she might need like a magazine or a candy bar (which the attendant was calmly ringing up on her bill). The man behind me and I thought it would be simple enough for us to hand over our credit card and call out our pump number while this woman continued compiling her shopping list. But, when we stepped out of line and tried to hand over our cards the attendant severely chastised us in front of *everyone* and told us to "Wait your turn." I wasn't especially in a hurry, I just took exception to his lack of efficiency in handling the customers. Well, regardless of who was right, I ended up waiting with the rest of the crowd anyway. I guess the other guy must have been a little agitated . . . because when he peeled away he left most of the rubber in his tires at the gas pump.

Another way to cope with stress is to *talk out your problems.* Sometimes another person can help you see a new side to your problem, and a new solution. You can talk to a friend, family member, clergyman, teacher or counselor. Seeking professional help for problems is not admitting defeat; it's admitting you are an intelligent human being who knows when to ask for assistance. Seeking advice from others can give you fresh insight into your problems.

Avoid self-medication. By that I mean there are many substances: food, drugs, alcohol, caffeine; that seem to mask stress symptoms. But you have to remember that stress comes from within, not from without, and so does the ability to handle it.

Treat your body like your best friend. Eat well, get plenty of sleep, balance your work with recreation and relaxation. Your body really is your best friend; it takes you everywhere it goes and gives you something to take care of, kind of like a puppy.

Next, learn to take one thing at a time. It's frustrating to try to tackle all your tasks at once. Instead, break each task into small steps and handle them as best you can. Check your expectations every so often. Are they too high? Too low? You take your car in for a front end alignment after so many miles, don't you? And you might go to the chiropractor for a spinal adjustment, right? You align your bank balance and financial affairs with your CPA. So, why not align your expectations?

Even though you know you're right, give in once in a while. If you find the ones nearest and dearest to you are causing you stress, try giving-in instead of fighting. You may find the other person giving-in more often too.

And, finally, make yourself available. If you're bored and feeling left out, whose fault is that? Go where the action is! Instead of withdrawing and feeling sorry for yourself, get involved.

To put stress in perspective for you, here's a fun article called "How You Can Tell When It's Going to be a Stressful Day". You might have heard some of these but play along with me, won't you?

−You find a major network news team waiting for you in your office—cameras rolling.

−Your birthday cake collapses because of the weight of the candles.

−You tune into the news and they are showing the emergency routes out of the city.

−Your twin sister forgot your birthday.

−Your boss tells you not to bother to take your coat off.

And you know it will be a stressful day when your income tax check is returned stamped **"INSUFFICIENT FUNDS"**.

Author unknown . . . but troubled.

CHAPTER 30:
YOUR SUCCESS EQUATION

Henry Ford once said, "You can't build a reputation on what you're going to do." Imagine where the world would be if its great civilizations only *thought* about doing great things? Consider for a moment man's milestones in communication. It took early man 3000 years to get from basic gestures and speech, to simple picture language, and eventually an alphabet. And yet, in a little under 200 years, we've gone from carrier pigeons and the Pony Express, to FAX machines and cellular phones. Two-thirds of the advances in communications have been made in the last six percent of the time span. What does this mean? Are our goals better than those of our caveman ancestors? Not necessarily—but we've escalated our thinking process with our development. We've learned to achieve more each generation. You can just imagine what our children's children will accomplish.

Having Goals Helps You Live Longer

Learning to set goals is the key to progress, no matter how big or small. In rest homes for the elderly it's been noted that the death rate drops drastically before holidays and special occasions. It appears that many of the elderly, who might have otherwise lost the will to live, set a goal to make it through to just one more Thanksgiving, or until one of the grandchildren graduates. The point is: having something to live for makes life more valuable. Very often people will say that they're not interested in material things; they'd prefer to seek happiness, love or peace of mind as a goal. Eleanor Roosevelt said that happiness and peace of mind are the *results* of having goals—they are not the goals themselves. So, how do we attain the goals we seek? First, we must learn how to set goals. It's important to realize that before we can obtain something we cannot see, we must understand how to obtain those things we *can* see.

Regardless of the goal you set for yourself, remember that something for nothing equals nothing. Whatever you want out of life, you must first decide what you are prepared to give up for it. For every goal you set, you must be prepared to shift gears a little to achieve it. If you did nothing different you would remain right where you are, and of course the goal would never be reached. Set your priorities; only you can decide what's most important to you. And, if you cheat on your priorities, only you will lose. Get rid of the "Big Put-Off". You know, the "never put off 'til tomorrow what you can do the day after" syndrome. It takes zero energy to do nothing. What you don't do doesn't exist. You see; you either do something, or you don't. You can never "should have done" something yesterday. "Should" is an excuse word that provides people with an acceptable excuse for not doing something. Remember the Olympic boxer who missed his bus and arrived too late to compete for a medal? He can say, "Gee, someone should have told me my bus was leaving." Or, "I guess I should have paid more attention to the time." The excuse doesn't really matter because the event is in the past and all the "should-haves" in the world aren't going to bring it back.

Moving Towards Positive Change

With the proper belief and the action to follow it up, you can have just about anything you really want. It's just as easy to form a habit of *doing* something as it is to get in the habit of *not* doing something. This phrase from Hamlet is so appropriate, "Refrain tonight, and that shall lend a kind of easiness to the next abstinence, and the next more easy, for use can almost change the stamp of nature." Put off, put off, and put off, and all of a sudden it becomes so easy not to do it. In other words, the habit of *not* doing is formed, rather than the habit of doing, which successful people form.

Fear can be the monster motivator. Even if the new situation we're looking toward is for our advancement and betterment, the fear of change is often too overpowering. We become complacent in our everyday ways. We get in a rut. But, my friends, *a rut is nothing more than a grave with the ends kicked out.* Set up a desire for the goals you want to achieve. Then, persist! History reveals that where there was no vision, people perished. Order seems to be nature's first law. And, advancement into all things is nature's great purpose. Nature does not seek disease, depression, or failure. Life means growth. Growth in turn requires change, and as we move through life in a positive way, we see our goals successfully unfold before our eyes.

In the workplace there's a definite link between goals, behavior and training. In your office, for instance, each person has his or her own personal career goals. Then, each department may have its own set of goals. The people above and below you on the totem pole have goals. If your goals are all reasonably similar, the flow of work is probably meeting company expectations. If everyone's goals are at odds with each other, there may be a more serious problem. If you're a manager, it might be your responsibility to determine how everyone's goals play a part in company operations. Programs may be in place to help evaluate these conditions. But what if it's not your job to worry about company goals? Maybe you've never even considered your company's goals. Whether or not you are in a management position, it is your business to find out what the office goals are. If you don't, you could be working toward all the wrong aspirations. Let's say you work for a real estate developer and your goal is to become the sales manager or top producer. You've spent hours or months studying and preparing to be able to handle that job only to find out the company has sold its interest to another firm, and now only needs customer service support, not sales people. Now you have to begin again, or get another job. Company goals may not always be obvious. But, department goals are certainly a matter of record for all employees who express an interest in being part of the process.

Even setting your own work-related goals will have outside benefits. You'll present a more organized appearance and will probably understand others' goals more clearly. Research indicates that motivation to achieve goals is greatest when the possibility of success is near fifty percent. Goals set too high or too low will not motivate an individual to achieve them. In a sales force, goals that are unattainable, or not worth attaining will produce less than stunning results. Sometimes training can be the problem. Managers set goals with the overall company performance in mind. But, if an employee doesn't have the right tools to properly carry out the job, the manager's goals might be useless. If you see a need for something that would help you, or your associates better achieve office goals, why not suggest it? Or, take your own course for improvement.

Job skills are a valuable investment and will follow you wherever you go. Oftentimes I hear employees complain that they've taken all sorts of initiative and were never thanked, or even acknowledged by their boss. Your job performance is your achievement; only you need to appreciate it. Sure, rewards are welcome. But, you'll gain more by not expecting others to recognize your achievements. Live your life for your own enrichment and purpose. Once you've mastered this technique, you'll display a confidence that demands recognition and reward.

When setting goals, consider internal as well as external aspects: be more accepting of others, cultivate a sense of humor, be a good listener, also; don't limit your goals to things you know could be accomplished. *Don't limit yourself.* When the United States vowed to send a man to the moon by the late 60's, we didn't know how to accomplish it — it had never been done. There were many unknowns. And yet, on July 20th, 1969 we all watched Neil Armstrong and Buz

Aldrin walk on the moon. Following that were the next steps of Pete Conrad and Alan Bean of Apollo 12.

Goals + Thought and Action = Results

Goal setting alone will not get you what you desire. There are two more important steps: Thought and Action. Thought determines what you want and action determines what you get. Earlier I mentioned a method of goal achievement, I call it the 7 + 1 Plan. Let's take a more in-depth look at those points for your own personal application to demonstrate how your commitment to excellence can become a reality.

1. *Write it down:* The physical act of writing something down creates perspective. Your thoughts will be focused on the words written on the paper in front of you. A focused mind initiates creativity. You might jot down additions to your goals, or even embellishments. You might put the paper down and look at it again tomorrow with new insight. You may keep it by your desk, or near your chair where you watch TV and refer to it while your mind is at ease. You might even doodle on the same page. But, whatever you do, having it written down will let your mind zero in on the right area of attention.

2. *Be specific:* Paint a clear picture for your mind to grasp. What you've first written might be bold, or it might be vague. Take this second step to specify exactly what you want. Before any desire can become a reality, it must be clearly stated. Give your mind the details it needs to fully visualize your goal. Set the scene for success. When a company launches an advertising campaign to sell a new product, the ad agency first determines who the product is for. A target market is determined by researching the trends and needs of different consumers. Expectations are made specific; we want to sell more snow shovels in Alaska, or we think inner-city residents would like a new type of game their children could play in a small patio or side yard. It would be foolish for businesses to develop new products without an intended audience in mind. So, determining the specifics of the goal you desire is important.

3. *List the benefits and satisfactions:* You'd be surprised how many people can state their goals, but stop short of listing the

rewards. What better inducement to achieving a goal than a visual reminder of the benefits you'll receive once you get there? Focus on your whims, your secret yearnings, your deep-seated desires. List anything and everything you can that would make your goal more satisfying. This step serves another purpose: it allows you to vent the unspoken desires that are lurking beneath the surface. Your goal might be "beating Roger at racquetball". One of your satisfactions might be, "I've always thought Roger was arrogant and I want give him a challenge." Getting these excess emotions out now is healthier than harboring them until you perfect your racquetball game, and you may find more respect for Roger.

4. List the losses and dissatisfactions: Bring your apprehensions out into the open. Face the fact that not all goals will be reached. By committing these thoughts to paper it's easier to deal with them. Prove to yourself that the change you seek is truly needed. Weigh the potential losses or dissatisfactions in order to validate your goals. Write down what the impact will be if the goal is *not* reached. Be careful not to make this your excuse list. Instead, make this your reality check list. Desiring a change means confronting your status quo. Succeeding in making a change means having to say "good-bye" to some parts of your status quo. Face up to these losses and they won't seem so formidable.

5. Make the choice: Take a good long look at your benefits and losses lists. By evaluating the two you will clear up many of the blocks in your path toward your goal. Weigh your options. Make a decision and go for it! The longer you wait to hop on the success plane, the further away it gets. Pretty soon, you're running twice as fast and working twice as hard to get to the same place you could have reached by flying. Conquer the spiritual doldrums of indecision. Rid your life of worry, doubt and fear. Making a decision is seldom wrong. If a course of action becomes difficult, or unproductive, simply make a new course. By not taking action you take the risk of wrong *and* right out of your hands by doing absolutely nothing. You can't expect results if you don't make decisions.

6. Set a date: Challenge yourself. Put some dates on your goal-setting plan. Use these dates to propel your goal-setting into goal achievement and personal enrichment. Life is a constantly changing set of milestones. Each time one is achieved, another rises to take its place. You have no trouble setting dates for your vacations; you know when payday is coming; you're aware of your birthday. So why not set dates for your goals to be achieved? Again, writing down the dates makes them more tangible. Review and re-evaluate your timelines as needed. You fully expect to meet your deadlines at work because your job depends on it. Create those same expectations for your goals. Don't take less from yourself than you'd take from others. Be your own taskmaster. Impress your goal dates on your memory, and when you begin to feel yourself slipping, remind yourself that the time is drawing ever nearer for you to satisfy yourself with achieving your goal. Believe that you have the character to follow through on a resolution long after the mood in which it was made has passed.

7. *See the end result:* During our waking and sleeping hours, we have one of the most powerful forces ever conceived at our disposal: mental imagery. Our minds are capable of creating mental images so real that sometimes we don't even know the difference between fact and fiction. Instead of wasting this powerful force on idle fantasy or conjecture, why not practice visualizing the end result of your goal. Get into the habit of filling your mind with the images of you enjoying the success of your goal. When you come home from work, relax and sit back in an easy chair for a few moments and train your mind upon the achievement of your goals. Play out the success scenario in your mind over and over again whenever you get the chance. Create new story lines for your success dream and the dream will begin to take shape. Directing your thoughts can carry the capacity for materialization. See yourself the way you want to be. Like they always say: seeing is believing. Point in fact, the reverse may be even more true: believing is seeing!

Those are the seven steps in my 7 + 1 goal-setting plan. Before I recap the + 1 step, the final step, let me share a little story with you. An elementary school teacher greeted her class one morning with a series of commands written on the chalkboard. She told the students to put their books away and follow the directions on the board. The first direction read, "Read everything on the board before moving to the next step." Subsequent steps said things like: draw a picture, stand up and put your hands on your head, hop on one foot, and so on. The last item on the board said, "Ignore all the previous instructions." Everyone in the class completed all the silly steps before realizing what the last step said. They ignored the directions. I brought this story up to point out the reason my goal achievement plan is called 7 + 1. The last step is *so* important, you need to heed it well, before (and while) you heed the rest. The last point is: *act silently*. Like those school children, you could faithfully follow all the steps in the plan only to find that you've overlooked the most important piece of information available to you. Act silently. Up until this point, the plan is good for simply goal setting. But adding this essential final ingredient transforms the process into decisive achievement.

Go about attaining your goals quietly and purposefully. Focus your attention on the actual achievement, not on convincing yourself, or others that you can do it by talking about it all the time. Movement through life is visible because of accomplishments, not words. Others can't make your goals any more attainable simply by agreeing with your plan, or listening to your intentions. In fact, the more you share your strategy with others, the more dissipated it may become. Keep focused on your own goal. Discipline yourself to stay on top of your goals with no outside incentive. Make your own personal accomplishment the incentive to succeed.

CHAPTER 31:
USE FUN AS YOUR VEHICLE

A long time ago, I discovered, "A service rendered is a benefit received." For years I remembered that saying but could never quite figure out what it meant. Eventually, as I grew older and experienced life, I came to realize what it means: the simple act of doing something creates a reaction. Everything we receive in life is the direct result of what we've done in life. And, how much we receive is in direct proportion to how much we've given. Getting rewarded for performing a service is not the main issue; it's how we feel about this service, combined with how we feel about ourselves that determines the value of the return.

Personal Value

To increase our prosperity we must enlarge the inner value we have set on our actions. Before anyone else will believe we are worth more, we must be convinced. Money is really only an indicator of how much service we have provided.

Separate yourself from your actions. Look at yourself as an outside person would see you. What kind of attitude do you portray? Analyze your walk, your speech, your actions; do they speak of success? Ask yourself what you need to bring or enhance a success perspective into your life. Challenge yourself by experiment. Take a new course of action in your life; if it works, *don't fix it!* If it doesn't work, take another course. Keep experimenting and fine-tuning until you find the right combination for success.

——— LIFE LINE ———

If you don't know where you're going,
it's going to be really tough to get there!

Don't sell yourself short. You may be surprised to learn you can change your behavior more easily than you thought. It all boils down to how important the new behavior is to you. Be honest. Don't claim you're going to try to do something if you know you won't. The premise for "I'll try," is "I can't." Make your actions clear. "I will run a mile after work." "I will not be attending the party." Not, "I'll try to be more careful," or "I tried to be there but something got in the way." Only you can decide where you're going and how you'll get there. And believe me, if you don't know where you're going, it's going to be really tough to get there!

Make sure your actions portray the actions of someone who has already arrived. Don't fritter your time away. Sure, it's easier to go with the program, to be with friends and fit in with the crowd, but you need to ask yourself what crowd you want to be with when you reach your goals—then stay on track to get there.

Be prepared to find what you seek. If you get in an airplane with no direction in mind, you might fly in circles all day. But if you believe in your destination and picture yourself there, you'll find that getting there can be half the fun. When you walk into life with eyes open, you can expect to see a variety of experiences. Some you'll like, some you won't. But having seen them will make all the difference when it's time to choose your life's path.

If you are envious of someone for whom life seems so easy, stop and think: maybe his life seems easy because he worked very hard to make it that way. We used to always tease my mother about putting all kinds of cold cream and preparations on her face. "Your face looks fine, Mom, why do you put all that goop on it?" She'd say, "My face looks fine *because* I put all this goop on it!" I guess she was right, or at least she believed it—and it worked!

You can apply this same idea of accomplishment to your work simply by studying your current position. The traditional approach to a position is to develop job descriptions. You, or another responsible party, determine what duties your job covers. This way you will know what's expected of you.

The *Goal Effective & Time Efficient* approach places the emphasis on *results* instead of *activities*. With this approach, you view your job in terms of what it can achieve instead of what kinds of activities it entails. Why not choose to live your life this way also? Taking the same minimum requirements for the *Goal Effective & Time Efficient* system, ask yourself these questions:

1. Does my life include specific goals?

2. Have I prepared a written list of goals I believe in?

3. Does my list include how I will measure my success?

4. What might block my path to accomplishment?

5. What are the actions steps I will take?

6. Are my results systematically determined at regular intervals and compared with the original goals?

7. When I have not progressed toward my goals, do I identify the problems and correct them?

8. Are my goals at each level related to the goals at the level above and below?

The great importance of a goal achievement plan is that it forces us to learn about ourselves; it stretches our capabilities. We have to learn to develop skills to effectively measure our performance. We have to learn to anticipate real problems which could threaten the achievement of our goals, and take steps to cope with these problems.

Your goal achievement plan (like your life) must be balanced. It must take into account the long-range outlook rather than be a reaction to the immediate problems confronting you. In the traditional goal setting approach, four kinds of goals are reviewed: regular work goals, problem-solving goals, innovative goals, and development goals.

The first: **regular work goals,** refers to the activities which make up the major part of your job responsibilities. The goal might be to operate more efficiently, improve quality of production, or increase productivity.

Problem solving goals refers to ways you can eliminate office problems or shortcomings. Problems are first defined and then solutions or goals are applied.

Innovative goals: these are goals that don't necessarily refer to an existing problem but outline creative ways in which an operation can be more effective.

Development goals recognize the importance of developing employees and co-workers. You know you can do your job more effectively with support and the proper training; development goals assist you in making sure you and the people around you have developed the right skills and attitude to keep projects running smoothly.

Proceed with Desire

Assuming that you have set a goal and you have made a commitment to move in that direction; how do you know for sure that the goal you have set is right for you? Earlier I said that you can have just about anything that you really want; you can, but you could get yourself into a lot of trouble if you bring things into your life that are really not right for you.

A major factor in reaching a goal is desire. If you are striving and fighting to assist someone else in reaching their goal, that's nice, that's kindhearted, that's being a good person and we'll pat you on the back for it, but *you must not lose sight of your own desires.*

Sometimes it is possible to get the desires of your loved ones mixed up with your own.

Isn't it great that we are all different and have our own desires? What a world it would be if we all wanted to be zookeepers, surgeons, or accountants. Life speaks to us through desire; whenever you desire something, that's life knocking at your door saying, "I'd like to do this through you. How about it?" The rest is up to you. If you don't pay attention to your desires and fulfill them, no one else can. If you don't sing your own song, it won't be sung.

Is it Right: Is it Fun?

The first step in deciding whether the goal you set is right for you is quite simple. Ask yourself if you really desire to achieve that goal. The next step is to look at the ease with which your goal is accomplished. If everything falls your way, if there are no blocks and no barriers, if everything moves smoothly, the path to your goal is easy. If a thing is easy it will also probably be fun to do. The ease of reaching the goal is a determining factor in whether or not it is right for you. If accomplishing the goal flows easily from the desire, it is probably right.

Persistence is important, of course, and if accomplishing a goal doesn't come easy, you can work at it until you reach it. If you are proceeding with great difficulty; experiencing great strain, resistance, and frustration, you may be pursuing something which is not right for you. To clear this up we have to go back to the beginning, back to the desire. If you truly desire something, you will also desire the way it is to be accomplished. You will not have to fight your way to the top. The way to the goal may still be difficult, but your outlook will be considerably different. My own rule of thumb for measuring the rightness of goals which prove difficult to reach is to ask myself, "Is it fun?" If it is, I'm probably on the right track; if it's not, I fall back and take another look at it. Possibly the goal is right but the method of accomplishment is wrong.

If you are living each moment out of your true desire, enjoying it, loving it, and above all, are excited about it, you will be pursuing your goal in a natural, orderly way. Setting a goal and living in the present moment are not contrary to one another at all. They are a perfect blend, a natural blend. Enjoyment is the key. Your goal may be right for you whether it is easy or difficult to reach, but the way must be enjoyable. Success will be the result; for the press of nature in all that she does is for expansion and fuller expression. Advancement into all things is nature's great purpose.

─────── **LIFE LINE** ───────

Don't pity yourself for what you don't have,
praise yourself for what you do have.

─────────  ─────────

In the end, all forms of goal setting and goal achievement are based upon the integrity of your conscious decisions. If what you desire is worth more to you than the time or money it will cost, let go of the time or money and *get it.* You must believe in your own good sense. You may not be as attractive or smart as the next person but you have your own valuable traits. If you didn't, why would you expect anyone to hire you, or to love you, or to trust you? Don't pity yourself for what you *don't* have, praise yourself for what you *do* have. Stay on target and make adjustments as you need them but keep moving forward! Always respect personal integrity. If you keep all your promises, fulfill all your commitments, you'll attract people who act the same way. Redefine your goals regularly. Keep a note pad with you at all times so you can force yourself to make descriptions of what you want. Act as though you *are* and you will *be*. Write it, read it, repeat it, and you will believe it.

Goals are the windows to your future. The future will happen with or without your goals. But having goals and achieving them makes the prospects for a successful future brighter than they were before. Maintain your goals like you would any other precious commodity. With the right amount of determination and direction you can parlay a good set of goals into a lifetime of prosperity and enjoyment.

EPILOGUE:
REACHING HIGH

There you have it: a practical outline for changing significant areas of your life. Used in part, these suggestions can help you clear up many areas of dissatisfaction; used in their entirety, they can alter your entire life course.

Andrew Carnegie once offered a 25 million dollar suggestion: He said, "Take one good idea and use it." If you heed his advice it will be much to your advantage. While I will be the first to affirm that we have available to us limitless power, I will also acknowledge that if we dive, head first, into all areas that we think need attention, disaster may very well result. Therefore, I suggest this: pick one or two good ideas from this section and use them first. Directly apply the ideas you choose into specific areas in your life. In the beginning it might be helpful to pick an area that has not totally fallen apart; your emotional involvement will not be as great, and you will probably have an easier time tackling it.

In using these guidelines, please do yourself a favor, hold on to the ideas, as applied to your particular situation, for at least one week and observe the changes that take place. When you see the dynamics of *you* in action, there will be no turning back. Also remember that you will make the changes in your life as only you can make them—your course will more than likely be different from anyone else that you know.

Whenever you see that someone else has something, is doing something, or is being something—that you desire to have, do, or be—don't envy them. Realize that all they did was put the picture in their mind, and through the natural laws of life, it was made available to them. You, too, can put the picture in your mind and it can be yours. You will accomplish this feat, whatever it may be, in your own unique way. You are the best *you* there can ever by. Trying to be like someone else will only put you second in life; no one can express life exactly as you can in your own unique way, nor can you express it as someone else. It's just not possible.

Also realize that you must do it. No one will be solving your problems for you; you must take control of your ship and fly it. A club, a friend, a spouse, or even this program will not do it for you; you must do it. When you commit yourself to that, the wings of freedom are yours.

Whatever you choose to do, remember that through goal-oriented persistence you can achieve what you set out to do. It is your right to fly.

SECTION V
GETTING
RESULTS
THROUGH
PEOPLE

Leadership inspires vision.
Exemplary leadership transforms
vision into substance.

CHAPTER 32:
WHAT DO YOU SEE IN OTHERS?

Few areas in business have been talked about or written on more than managers and management skills.

Many have analyzed, dissected, inspected, and charted anything and everything, and what do they have to show for it? Well, we've got a lot of charts. We also have a lot of statistics. Mostly though, I think a mass of information has been created that is thick, complicated, and sometimes hard to follow.

What I want to do—what I'm going to do—is to cut this down to the bare essentials; the basics. I want to share ideas that we can all relate to from a business standpoint, but moreover, from a personal standpoint as well. Because what managers do is manage people, not charts, sales figures, inventory books, nor buildings; but people!

People who, in turn, take care of the books, the buildings, and the charts.

So, let's start off right now with stating clearly what a manager does. A manager gets the job done by utilizing other people. That's it. Sounds easy, but textbooks are filled with how to, how not to, and solutions for . . . and yet no one can offer a prescriptive remedy for how to maximize the utilization of employees. It is to this end that this Management/Leadership section is devoted—to take the best, to eliminate the useless, and adapt the balance for you.

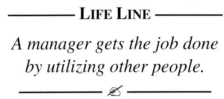

LIFE LINE

A manager gets the job done
by utilizing other people.

I'm not going to delve into the entire spectrum of leadership styles that lie between authoritative/dictatorial and humanistic/permissive. And there are dozens of styles that lie between these two polarized ends. Every manager has his or her own particular style, and each can be effective to accomplish results. Which one makes you most comfortable? It's not a crime today to be a dictatorial type, again it is only important that you know your own style.

Research tells us that *managers tend to bring employees within their departments who function best under the manager's style of leadership.* But until such time as you can readily identify yourself as a leader, the confidence necessary to improve, or become a leader will not happen.

The Performance Chart indicating the traits of leadership is one which I developed. The chart graphically depicts the attributes a high-performance manager must have. *A manager who possesses all but one trait will still be ineffective.* It would be just as if the driving engine of your aircraft were shut down.

Preflight Checklist for
HIGH-PERFORMANCE
LEADERSHIP

An individual who is insecure and uncomfortable would find it extremely difficult to display trust, one of the key ingredients of the Performance Chart. It follows also that someone looking to become more effective in delegation must surround themselves with capable people, and be willing to release the reins. Also they must refrain from making value judgments on those who say they are not comfortable working with that style of management. Economically, for the company, this is a valuable insight.

—————— LIFE LINE ——————

*Managers don't have to know everything, but
they do have to know where to
go to get everything they need.*

—————— ✍ ——————

An individual who is unwilling to delegate authority will find it impossible to display trust; their own capabilities and limitations would make them highly suspect. An example: a manager may read research on everything, then ask a college graduate to compile a product sale analysis, only to find out that (with his educational level and current knowledge) he can't read the report the college student has prepared.

Managers don't have to know everything but they do have to know where to go to get everything they need, and be willing to delegate authority, and trust that the task will be completed with satisfying results. Understanding this simple idea, I approached several of the most successful managers I know and accumulated a list of traits; characteristics common to all good managers. I then developed the Performance Chart which shows just how these characteristics build and interrelate. The simple components of the chart clearly display what it takes to be a good manager and an effective leader. To begin with, *a good manager knows the capabilities and limitations of the people she works through. A high-performance manager listens, and has compassion for her team,* for her team is made up of people, and an effective manager never forgets that it is people who get the job done, not machines.

It's important here to note that when I speak of a team, I am using that term not to refer to a small group of people gathered together to accomplish a particular task. I am using the word "team" as meaning: people working with people; people serving under one corporate roof, all striving to reach out for and achieve the corporate goals.

A good manager exhibits ethical standards that can be evidenced in his private life as well as his professional life. *A high-performance manager can make decisions.* She doesn't sit on the fence for days or weeks trying to gather more and more information. High-Performance managers show all of these qualities by example in every aspect of their own lives. And it is this very aspect that can separate a manager from a leader. Whatever he says to you holds true for himself as well. And as a result, *a high-performance manager exhibits trust,* trust in herself and trust in the team she works through.

As you begin to associate with the traits on the Performance Chart as your own personal traits, you evolve as the skills of implementation develop. So do the people around you evolve, as does the work you all do together. And as this trust develops and builds between manager and worker, it fosters growth in the employees, and in their capabilities.

Now, the traits on the chart are not necessarily equally weighted. For instance: gaining knowledge does not necessarily correlate with the ability to have compassion. But no one item can be taken lightly. On the Performance Chart, "listen" means to *really listen.*

Let's take a closer look at the individual components of the Performance Chart.

Discernment: Abilities and Limitations

People are different. Says who? We all know that every teenager looks alike. People jump on the first fad, and suddenly everything's the same. Unfortunately, management sometimes operates similarly. *Managers tend to manage so as not to rock the boat.*

Well, in reality, it's true. People are different, and it's also true that not everyone is going to approach their work in the same way that you do, and there is really no need to and I'll tell you why.

Number one, *they may have a better idea* about it than you do. Their approach may be in such a way that it shows you something that you wouldn't ordinarily see. This causes us to look at a problem in a different light. The more approaches to a problem, the more possible solutions that exist.

Number two, *they may be able to see the difference between what is important and what isn't.* If a member of your team can quickly see (and separate) the unimportant from the important, it means you will not have to invest as much time on the project. And subsequently, you get to the solution a lot faster.

Number three, and this may not seem as important but it is; *their way of doing something reflects a creative part of them.* "He's just filling out forms," you may say. And that may be true, but everyone likes to think that he or she matters—makes a difference. And if they feel that, then it shows up in the quality of their work. After all, they're doing this for themselves as well as you and if *they* look good, *you* look good and this, of course, has a snowball effect, and soon everyone is feeling good and looking good.

But you say, "Okay, everyone is different and I accept that, and allow them to do the job in their own way. What can I say? What can I do? I need to get my expectations met without getting myself in my own way. I don't want to cut off their creativity, or present an attitude that they don't count, but how do I get the work done that has to be done?" Fair enough question.

Matching Team Members and Talents

As I said before, a manager manages. As an example; consider that the manager of a baseball team would never think of starting a game with his best hitter on the pitching mound. He may be a terrific hitter, highest R.B.I., and home runs, but what he can't do is pitch. And so it goes throughout the rest of the players on his team. Each member of the team has a specific talent and a specific role to play. There are infield players and outfield players. There are starting pitchers and relief pitchers. *It's the team manager's job to know what each can do.* The same thing holds true for managing in business.

You, as a manager, have to know the members of your team. Who excels at paperwork and who doesn't; who's more patient with clients and who has the shortest fuse. And I'm sure you know who to call on to handle problems with the copy machine. Some people have a knack for fixing it quickly.

Knowing the team players makes all the difference in the world when it comes to managing.

Everyone has abilities and limitations and it's the challenge of the manager to discern in his own mind which person matches best with the job. Only in this way can a manager utilize his team to best advantage. Only in this way can a manager know where a team member is strong, and where he needs help . . . and only in this way can a manager know where to place the team member.

Which brings up another aspect: teaching. A high-performance manager knows the potentials of his team members and recognizes when training can help a member grow past his own perceived limitations through learning.

A good manager knows that she has to spend some time *showing* as well as *telling* someone on her team how to do something. Growing requires learning and the effective manager will promote learning with the people she manages. Teaching them either through herself, or a seminar, is an excellent way to show that she cares about them. It also gives a manager the opportunity to pass on information and experience that they've learned themselves.

Showing and telling are important attributes of teaching. Equally important is the process of evaluation, for it is true that, when properly implemented, this is the attribute that allows the individual to gain confidence in that which was just learned.

When a fellow employee comes to you with a problem related to the job, he looks to the manager to either solve that problem or point him in the direction of the solution. So, it's up to you as the manager to be open and willing to help out.

Don't be afraid to do this. This kind of openness goes a long way in terms of building trust between yourself and the other employees. One way of being open to a person's needs is by being a good listener and asking them to share their thoughts on a solution first.

Why are We Doing This?

This leads us to our next idea and that's motivation. Motivation is perhaps one of the strongest qualities that a manager brings to his employees. The obvious purpose behind motivation is to get everyone built-up and focused so you can all achieve the goal that you have in mind.

This not only helps them, but it helps stimulate you as a manager as well. If you get your team charged up to go out there and accomplish the job at hand effectively, you watch the results and begin to feel charged up yourself and continue to pass that same enthusiasm back to your team to start the next project. And so it goes, onward and upward from project to project. With this kind of motivation, problems turn into challenges and challenges offer opportunities for growth.

Here are eight principles of motivation that can help move people in the right direction. These principals will work for you and when applied, they will assist people to confidently step forward for greater accomplishment and reward.

1. Participation. Motivation to accomplish results tends to increase as people are given an opportunity to participate in the decision-making process. Input becomes output; participation translates to understanding, and understanding increases goal achievement.

Don't be afraid to actively seek feedback; encourage ideas. As I said before, the difference in people often results in them looking at a problem in a different way, allowing for a new and better way of dealing with a situation.

2. Communication. Motivation to accomplish results tends to increase as people are kept informed about matters related to those results. Let them know what's going on. Keeping people in the dark only repels them. How would you feel if you were sitting in the waiting room, and your boss and your co-worker went into the office and closed the door behind them?

Talk, make notes, listen, brainstorm. Unless everyone on your team is psychic, I don't know of any other way to get things done effectively than to keep the lines of communication open.

3. Recognition. People, all people, like to *hear* that they're doing a good job. And they want to feel recognized for the contributions that they're making. This only increases their desire to contribute more. I mean, we're not asking for a banquet dinner in their honor. We're just talking about simple recognition. "Hey, great job Steve!"

A comment, a memo, a phone call; any or all of these has relevance. Use them.

4. *Delegation.* Delegation means turning it over to someone else. When this is done, people like to have some authority of their own to make decisions affecting the final outcome. If you allow them to share in the decision process they feel like a greater part of the whole.

I like the statement, "When the best leaders' job is done, the people say, we did it ourselves." Allowing people to become involved in the decision-making process, and having them feel significant, is one trait of a leader.

5. *Reciprocated interest.* Fancy term—simple meaning. It means that the good manager shows interest in the results along the way, every step of the way. The M.B.W.A. system of management is appropriate here. Management By Walking Around. See and be seen. Comment, and listen to comments.

Constant, positive feedback is important to the individual and the team. You, as manager, are the captain of the ship, but it takes the effort of your entire crew to get you to the destination. Don't miss an opportunity to let them know how they are getting you there.

6. *Know your people.* Know where their specific talents fit and utilize that talent to best advantage for both the individual and the team. Remember, the dynamic hitter on a baseball team isn't very effective on the pitching mound.

Know your people, and maintain the business separation. That defined line between boss and buddy-buddy is a thin one. Use caution and confidence, and you will come out a winner.

7. *Awareness.* Motivation increases as people are made to feel as part of a team. People desire a sense of belonging, they need to feel important as a person.

Again the corporate esprit de corps (the sense of direction, a feeling like we're all in this together) is important. People will tend to do more for the good of the team, than they will for the boss as an individual.

Be aware of the up days, the down days. People are not robotic, they are feeling individuals. Don't just tell them, *show them!* Show them how their part fits into the whole picture and how the picture accomplishes the goal in mind.

8. *Motivate up, down and across*. People tend to get "up" for a job when they see that other people they work with are "up" for their jobs. Don't just settle with motivating the dead wood, work with everyone around him. This can be done by showing that you, and every one else is there to help when he needs it. He is likely to help *another* when the time comes, and this only raises the support of the group. All for one and one for all.

Everyone has a potential for growth; the ability to move beyond where they are today. It's your responsibility as an effective manager to know the abilities, and limitations of each and every member of your group, to utilize their talents to the best possible degree, and train or teach them in other areas where you know they can benefit. And if they get better and grow, so does the team, and so do you.

CHAPTER 33:
GUIDING AND DIRECTING

Tapping the potential for growth in your people can be effectively accomplished through training. Because of its significant impact on the bottom line, many of the examples here will focus on customer service. Some companies that recognize the value and importance of top-flight customer service have invested as much as 2% of gross sales in ongoing training for their executives, managers, and employees.

Corporate education has three phases: executive education, where senior management learns its roll; management education, where those who must implement policy learn to do so; and employee education, where employees learn their jobs and how their performance contributes to superior service.

Where does training begin and end? Top corporate leaders in customer service believe the process begins during the selection process and continues through until retirement. Each year everybody attends at least one week of class to maintain and reinforce the commitment to the customer. Coincidentally, companies that implement these training programs also lead the field, or is it a coincidence? These companies also lead their industries in productivity, cost effectiveness, profitability, and overall management effectiveness.

Effective Training

Here are some of the considerations in establishing an effective training program:

1. People learn what kinds of questions to ask superiors and superiors are taught how to respond. There must be a basic understanding or language, if you will, for people to communicate about the job. If you provide a clear concept of each member's job function and corporate policy, employees will be better equipped to communicate.

2. Formal training is centrally developed and locally implemented. By developing training centrally, you can insure uniform policy and expectation. It's easier to direct the orchestra if you're all playing the same music. Local implementation allows employers to address their own specific requirements based on their own unique environment.

3. There is diversification in the kinds of training offered including management, human resource development, and motivation. No training program can be one-dimensional. That sounds more like brain washing! Training needs to develop employees in every facet of their jobs from the technical to interpersonal skills.

4. Supervisor training is mandatory. Being a supervisor is more than knowing how to do the job or having the seniority. Supervising means coordinating and motivating a group of diverse individuals based on an expectation level set by senior management. Not an easy task, nearly impossible without substantial training.

5. *"Behind-the-scenes" employees are extensively trained to motivate and sustain service attitudes,* stressing how their performance indirectly affects customers. Everyone is part of customer service. The complaint department relies on every other division to cooperate in solving a problem, whether they have customer contact or not. It has to be a team effort.

6. *Heavy phone-users receive special training.* When you "meet" customers by phone, your contact is usually extremely brief, but the impact of it will be reflected in every other interaction the customer has with the company. This is a very specialized position that can make or break your customer service chain, and the customer's first impression.

7. *Training creates a spirit of teamwork.* Everybody is involved with, and responsible for, customer service. If departments are not working as a team, the service chain cannot hold up. Commitment to service is not just words, but a team philosophy and lifestyle. Research bears out the fact that companies who spend the time and money for training are able to create the service edge needed for today's marketplace.

Staying on Top

Keeping people sharp can be a challenge. Basically, you can expect what you inspect. Mystery shoppers can be used in almost every retail business to evaluate everything from cleanliness to customer service. Some companies utilize mystery shoppers to enhance the service standards of its sales associates. The mystery shopper has a list of service expectations that he uses when interacting with sales people. The results are then submitted to the personnel department for the appropriate response, a ten for great service or below five for less than adequate. Department managers are encouraged to train their staff well, because awards for excellent service enable the manager to provide the necessary recognition. *It will always work to your advantage to observe potential problems and correct them before the customer has to register a complaint.*

Disney is a premiere company for employee training. If you are hired to take tickets, you'll receive days of training! *For ticket taking?* The Disney posture is that every employee (cast members) should be prepared to assist the guests (not customers) at the park. Ticket takers need to be able to respond to questions about park directions, timing of events, special services provided, and must know where to find information quickly if they don't know the answer.

Every employee at Disney, from top corporate executives to clean-up crew, must pass Traditions One before going on the job. There they learn not only Disney philosophy and tradition but how each division relates to the other and the part every person plays in the overall workings of the park.

It's interesting to note that once a year executives get out where the action is. They put on the costumes, drive the monorails, sell the hot dogs, and do all the things that make the park work for the guests. This firsthand experience with the guests can be energizing because that is where the business is alive, it also gives the executives the opportunity to experience and observe what line employees do everyday.

Evaluating Your Training Program

In establishing an employee training program, it is essential that you continually evaluate its effectiveness. Be sure that you know what will be changed after training and how you will measure the change. Also consider what new skills employees will need to learn to implement the changes you desire.

You may want to ask yourself some of the following questions about your training program:

1. Which parts were most, or least effective and why?

2. What was, or was not, learned and retained?

3. How did the training help the employee do his job more effectively?

4. Did customer satisfaction and profit increase and to what degree?

5. What difficulties were there in applying what was learned?

6. What would you add, or delete from future training?

Measuring Training Impact

When you are measuring the effectiveness of the training program, you may want to include some of the following areas:

1. Turnover in management and staff; did it increase or decrease?

2. Communication within the company; the improvement or deterioration can be measured through well thought out surveys.

3. Operations; are departments better managed and more effective?

4. Personnel costs; is turnover decreasing and are the costs of recruiting, selecting, hiring, and training increasing or decreasing?

5. Customer complaints; are they increasing, or decreasing, and what is the nature of the complaints?

Education and training is essential at every level for a forward thinking organization. Anyone at any level can add significant input to the system. It's like fine tuning an airplane. If the machine is not in good working order, it's very risky business. If employees and managers do not have a clear idea of how to perform their jobs and an awareness of how each one impacts the success or failure of the business, you'll find it very turbulent and risky in today's extremely competitive market.

Here are some of the essentials of training:

1. *It must be ongoing and comprehensive for all levels of the corporation.*

2. *Each job must be clearly defined.* People need reinforcement and encouragement in the training process as they master each task.

3. *Performance must be reviewed and evaluated* according to the specific job requirements.

4. *The training program itself must be constantly re-evaluated* and updated to provide the best techniques available.

5. *The results of employee training must be measurable* not only in dollars and cents, but in employee effectiveness and satisfaction.

The establishment of clear, concise job descriptions and performance standards and the support training to implement them is critical to establishing superior results. If these things do not exist in your industry, it's time to take a good look at what you really want to accomplish. The commitment to the long term goal will provide ample rewards, not only in increased profitability, but in the satisfaction and productivity of everyone. The process will require that you ask some hard questions about job descriptions and performance. Create your own if necessary. After all, isn't it time we all took responsibility for our positions?

You will need to continually ask if your programs are successful and make changes when they are not. But what could be more exciting than watching your business increase and your employees become a more effective team? Obviously some things that apply to McDonald's will not apply to computer sales, but the basic premise remains the same: treat your customers and your employees as you would like to be treated and you'll establish a loyal, ever-increasing customer base.

CHAPTER 34:
ATTENTIVE LISTENING

The greatest managers in the world can't manage anyone if they can't communicate. And by communication I mean more than just talking. Actually, the talking part shouldn't take more than about twenty percent of a manager's time.

The high-performance manager knows how to be attentive and listen eighty percent of the time. All effective communicators are good listeners. They listen carefully and patiently. *They listen not just to the words but to the feelings behind the words. They listen with respect; with concern.* And even if they don't like what they hear, the high-performance manager encourages the members of her team to speak openly and honestly.

Sometimes—many times, a manager must allow a person to just blow off steam for a while in order to get to the real issue. The effective listener learns how to make the person talking feel relaxed and comfortable enough to share what's really on his mind.

——————— LIFE LINE ———————

[High-performance managers . . .]
listen not just to the words but to the feelings
behind the words. They listen
with respect; with concern.

——————— ✍ ———————

Listen and Learn

Enhanced learning is predicated on concerned listening, and a manager cannot learn what is really going on without listening carefully to his people. Varying degrees of listening are required depending upon the nature of the unit, group or bodies to be managed. For the purpose of our discussion, you want to look at those types of units where employee participation and interaction are absolutely essential to the goals and objectives established by the company.

Listening is as easy or as difficult as you make it. Actually, more than anything else, listening expresses being there with someone. Not just a body in a room, but being present and aware of what the other person is thinking and more importantly, what the other person is feeling. Now, I know what you're thinking: "What does listening to someone's feelings have to do with managing the work that they do for me?" Plenty.

If you can hear how someone feels toward a project, you can get a pretty clear idea what kind of attitude they have about the work that they're doing for you. If they express a lot of irritation behind the words you can bet that the irritation is going to come out in their work, and they're probably not going to do the job as efficiently as you'd like.

But listening to the feelings behind the words is only one part of listening. Another aspect for the high-performance manager to consider is listening with an open mind.

I've come across so many people who listen, and then you see this change come over their face. And the change comes because they've heard something—a phrase or word—and all of the sudden they're not listening anymore, because now they're waiting for an opportunity to jump in to comment.

Whenever you see people react like that, there's no point in going any further because they won't be listening to anything else you have to say. They're too busy waiting to rebut what you've just said.

Being a Good Listener

Listening with an open mind means just that. *Your mind is open and clear to any new thought or idea.* Maybe there's something that can be looked at in a new way—maybe there isn't. However, if you don't give a team worker a chance to express that idea and express it the best way he can, you can cut off any further ideas that he may have in the future. And those ideas, the ones he isn't sharing with you, those could be the significant ideas. Listening with an open mind is always important.

The next characteristic of a good listener is *showing your attention.* Sitting there, like the great stone face is not going to encourage anyone to share much of anything with you. If you're too busy to listen actively, postpone listening. It's just that simple.

When you do listen, *let the person know you care about what is being said* by showing it: smile, nod, or even a few verbal queues: "All right," and "Okay." A listener can also show interest by having eye contact with the speaker.

This doesn't mean that you necessarily agree with what is being said. What it does mean is that you are actively listening to what is being said, and your responsiveness shows this.

Next, listen for the positives rather than pointing out the negatives.

So many times it becomes tempting to point out what we don't like rather than pointing out what we do like. Remember, as part of a team, being a team leader means encouraging the positives. A simple phrase to this effect might be, "Let's try it and see if it works!"

If a suggestion appears unworkable to you, rather than making it wrong, the encouraging manager might say, "We've tried this before and it hasn't worked very well. Maybe we can make some slight changes in our approach to get the results we want."

Mental Notes

Another aspect to consider in listening is: *make mental notes.* Taking time to write things down, particularly in the early stages of a relationship, can be distracting to someone who might find it difficult to talk. In order to show you care, it's really important to express that you do by just sitting and focusing on them completely. However, you can achieve this goal and make mental notes as well.

The best way I know to do this is to ask yourself some questions during the listening process:

1. Is the matter work-related or personal?

2. Are they clear about what they're talking about?

3. Are they asking for help or making a comment?

4. What can I bring to this situation or should I refer them to someone else?

These can be simple yes and no questions that can be followed up in your mind with simple words or phrases that summarize whatever they are talking to you about.

Most importantly, *follow-up your listening by summarizing what you believe you just heard as quickly and simply as possible.* This shows the speaker that you are paying attention as well as clearing up any questions you might have.

This last part is critical. *Ask questions if you're not clear about anything,* and keep asking until you are clear. So many people I meet are afraid to ask questions for the simple reason that if they do, the very act of asking shows that they weren't paying attention or bright enough to understand in the first place. This couldn't be more incorrect and the successful, high-performance manager creates an atmosphere of trust and confidence and openness to ask questions, no matter how they may appear.

Okay, let's go back over these listening points:

1. Be there for the speaker.

2. Listen to the feelings as well as to the words.

3. Listen with an open mind.

4. Show your attention by smiling or nodding every once in awhile.

5. Listen for the positives.

6. Make mental notes.

7. Ask questions about anything that you're not clear about.

The last point I want to make is *practice!* Like anything else, good listening requires practice, so allow time to practice consciously every day.

Listening can tell you a lot about the person talking to you, and a high-performance manager needs good information about the situation and the people that she works with. Sometimes, in the long run, good listening skills can be the most effective tool a manager can use to make the right decisions.

CHAPTER 35:
AN INSIDE JOB

Referring to the Performance Chart, another characteristic I believe is necessary for a high-performance manager is compassion. Compassion? Compassion. *Compassion!* Now, don't confuse this with being amorous. But what does this mean exactly? And what does it have to do with managing people?

Compassion is not a subject you're liable to find in any book on management or leadership. At least I've never come across it. And yet, I believe it is as important as the bottom line, decision making, and motivation.

Quite simply, without compassion, a manager is managing *things* not people and sooner or later the people he manages will realize this and it will show up in the quality of work you all do as a team.

All right, so what do I mean by compassion? Is it feeling sympathy for someone? Sometimes. Is it feeling sorry? Perhaps.

More than anything else, I believe compassion is feeling. It's the humanness of being able to be with another person and not as an authority figure, boss, worker, employee.

It's also understanding, helping, listening, teaching, learning. It's treating ourselves and everyone around us in a respectful, caring way. It's recognizing that we're all on the same flight together and understanding and respecting the role of our fellow man as well as our own.

Work is what we do, but it is not who we are. It's only a part of who we are. And I believe it's important to remember that, in order to keep a perspective on things. A good manager knows that of the people who work with him, he respects the humanness of others and responds in kind.

You say, "Okay, all right. I hear what you're saying, Jim, but how do I put this into something tangible, something I can use as a tool with the people I work with, every day?"

Demonstrating Compassion

I've come up with four points: no, I don't think I want to call them points this time. I want to call them ideas. Ideas seems a better word in this case because compassion encompasses so much and is such a personal characteristic of each individual that I believe it's important that everyone develops his own "style", if you will, to demonstrate it.

Okay, so here are my ideas about demonstrating compassion:

1. *A manager teaches:* He passes on what he has learned in his experience. Most of us want to grow, to learn, and get better at what we do; a manager encourages this and shows this as well, by passing along his own skills to others. And, most important of all, he does this without reservation or obligation. Almost with an attitude of, "Here's an idea that I've picked up, see if you can use it." Through this process, he learns himself. You may have heard the phrase that we teach best what we need to learn most.

In the teaching process he learns just what is true for himself. What works and what doesn't. He learns about the other person. How quickly they are able to understand and apply what he has taught. Mostly, he learns how to really give of himself, and in that way he begins to create an atmosphere of trust and openness.

2. *A manager helps:* After instructing her fellow worker, she watches and listens for ways she can further encourage and help that member of her team reach another level of performance. And many times this means giving constructive feedback during the teaching and learning process. Notice I said, "constructive" feedback, and not criticism. It's easy to point out what someone did wrong. It takes great care and patience to point out what has been achieved, as well as possible alternatives to further that achievement.

I like the statement, *"Go out and catch someone doing something right."*

3. *A manager accepts people as they are* and not as he thinks they should be. This can be difficult. I know. But what this really means is not trying to fit a square peg into a round hole.

Robert Frost puts it this way, "We love the ones we love for who they are." Not for what we want them to be, not for what we think they should be, not for what we know they can be, but for what they are. Many people look at others and mentally say, "If only you were more like me, then I'd love you so much more."

Changes are inevitable. Changes in a situation; changes in people. They happen every day. A good manager is aware of the changes and is flexible; looking for alternatives, and then implementing those alternatives.

The last idea I'd like to present regarding compassion is:

4. *A good manager looks for the balance:* The balance between the needs of the company and the needs of the individuals working in that company. The balance between teaching and getting the job done. The balance between personal distance between his team and being accessible. The balance between the demands of the job and the human beings doing that job . . . and this is not always easy.

Well, welcome to the world of the manager.

This last point though, that of balance, is probably the most difficult because it will change on a constant basis and most of the time the manager will seem to be in a constant state of juggling: people, feelings, attitudes, judgments, decisions, work load, ups, downs. But this is a manager's job.

A manager is put in a position to make things happen, get things done and get them done now! But without a basic sense of compassion, he becomes a machine. A machine that sifts, weighs, files, documents, distributes, and orders.

The compassionate manager is always aware of the juggling act and yet maintains a sense of balance, harmony, and humanness. The people on her team recognize the job she has and know that (because of her actions) she is approachable, understanding, and they can learn by her example.

The high-performance manager develops compassion for another by sometimes putting himself in the other person's shoes and seeing what it feels like, seeing what it means to the job at hand and then coming up with alternatives to deal with the situation, any situation.

They don't demand—they ask. They don't posture themselves as the ultimate authority, they encourage suggestions and alternatives. They never feel threatened, but remain open to ideas.

Compassion Enhances Intuitive Decision Making

Now that the employee is open, displaying a healthy compassion can only lead to enhanced intuitiveness related to other employees.

When a manager develops a sense of *feeling* with his team, develops understanding; that understanding helps strengthen his own feelings or hunches that come up in future work. Now, he doesn't have to explain all of this process. It's not a manager's job to explain how he gets things done. His job is to get them done. However, I believe that when he reaches out with his feelings towards his workers, he begins to develop certain instincts, and these instincts on how to act and react to situations can be just as valuable as the knowledge that he gains from the facts.

The point I'm making here about intuition is: don't ignore it. Learn to trust it more and more, soon you will rely on it.

Sometimes, we get so involved with the problems of the day and the pressures and stress placed upon us as managers to perform, to get the job done as quickly and effectively as possible that we lose sight of others around us. Sound familiar? We lose sight of their work, their problems, their achievements, their words, their thoughts, their ideas, their feelings, and eventually, their lives. When this happens, when the humanness of people working around us disappears or becomes invisible to our conscious awareness, in that moment we lose the ability to be compassionate. We lose the opportunity to share with another our struggles, hopes, challenges, and fears. And if we cannot share the "down" times, then the "up" times seem empty somehow.

Everybody has a story. Everybody has a fight, both internal and external at one time or another. The compassionate person understands this and extends himself in a way that shows. She listens, and in that listening the compassionate manager recognizes herself and her own difficulties and begins to gain a saner perspective. She realizes that there is more to her life than her own problems and difficulties, and in that realization she becomes closer to others and everything begins to make better sense.

Together, we can find answers. Together, we can move forward toward a more sensitive, compassionate environment.

CHAPTER 36:
ETHICS CHECK

A lot of people talk about ethics—but ethics isn't talk. A lot of people have opinions about ethics—but ethics isn't opinions. Quite simply: ethics is what we *feel* is right and what we feel is wrong; what is fair behavior and what is unfair behavior.

It's also not necessarily a rigid code of behavior that you live by, which is not to suggest that you be wishy-washy, either. It *is* to suggest that particular situations call for different behavior. I believe ethics come out of the way we were raised as children. What you were told growing up and the accumulated experiences along the way.

When we're children growing up we tend to see things very simply. "You can't do this." "You can do that." Yes, no, right, wrong. But as we get older, see more, hear more, experience more, things get a little more complicated: situations, people . . . it's not as black and white as it used to be. What's more, we don't have Mom and Dad around telling us what is right and what is wrong. *We* have to tell us what is right and what is wrong, and because the world is so complicated and involves more than just us, our sense of right and wrong changes, or rather evolves to another level.

Lying: Grownups do it Better

When you were small, your parents told you, "Don't lie, or you'll be punished." So, you learned quickly that if you lied, you would get punished. You were taught that lying is wrong. But as you grew up you learned that it isn't always that clear cut.

Example: someone asks you, "What do you think of my new dress?" You take a look and immediately dislike the dress. Do you tell her the truth? But, wait a second, I left something out here, you also know that this friend of yours has just lost her mother a month earlier, her husband has left her, and she's currently undergoing psychotherapy to help lift her self-esteem. Now what do you say to her when she asks about the dress?

Assuming that you are a caring individual it becomes a little more difficult, doesn't it? How do you answer in situations like that? Would you be justified, in your own eyes, to compromise your sense of right and wrong by lying to her and saying you liked the dress when you really didn't? Not really. Alternatively, you could be truthful with your response by moving beyond the question and saying, "New clothes are really fun aren't they? And that color in the rose print is very striking." *Sometimes it's good to move beyond the question.*

What do you do when your best friend and you are up for the same promotion at work? You're both equally qualified, with the same amount of time with the company, and would both be able to handle the new duties of the post equally well. Except, you know something about your friend that the boss or no one else knows. You know some negative piece of information that might have some bearing on the outcome. Do you share it with the decision-makers? Is it essential that anyone know, or are you just looking for something to create an opportunity for yourself?

——————— LIFE LINE ———————

The ethical person (essentially)
walks like he talks.

——————— ✍ ———————

What are Ethics?

The older we get, the more complex the situations become. How do we deal with them? What is the right choice here?

I'm not here to tell you what that right choice is. That's up to each one of us to decide in his or her own heart. I am here to (hopefully) bring an awareness to the hundreds of little choices we all make every week, and to point out that many of these choices do involve (and help mold) our sense of right and wrong, and that's what creates our standard of ethics.

Ethics is what a prudent man would do. Ethics are what we show people about ourselves. We've all seen people say one thing and do another. The ethical person (essentially) walks like he talks. He has taken the time to think and feel about a person or situation and come to a decision and then behaves in a way that shows others that he is consistent with what he says. And I believe that it is this consistency that, over the long run, shows the ethical standards of a person.

Few decisions in business are as black and white as they were when we were kids. There simply are too many other factors involved. The ethical manager is aware of these factors and consistently acts in a way that demonstrates his sense of right and wrong. That sense of consistency builds reliability and trust. We've seen how she acts and how she reacts and we can then begin to trust that she will act in a similar way about other people and situations.

And for the members of her team, this consistency is important. For consistency in ethics sets the tone, the atmosphere, for most of the ethical behavior of the others on her team. I'm talking about predictability, and in a broader sense, conforming to the standards of conduct of a given profession.

———— LIFE LINE ————

A manger is accountable for all her actions and those of her team, period!

———— ✍ ————

"I Don't See a Problem Here."

There are managers (and I'm sure you'll relate to this) who, when faced with a situation, simply bury their heads in the sand rather than point out some action that is wrong in his department. "Ostrich" management, I call it. They bury their head deep in the sand and hope that the whole thing just goes away.

The only problem with this is: when you bury your head in the sand and can't see the world around you, there's just one thing exposed . . . and sooner or later that thing's going to get kicked and I don't necessarily mean from upper-management either; I mean in the morale of the team. The team of an ostrich manager is going to kick back, somewhere down the line, where it's going to hurt most. You don't know where and you don't know when, but believe me, they are going to kick sometime.

You can't mention ethics in management without talking about accountability. In management, especially, they go hand in hand. A manager is accountable for all her actions and those of her team, period! She's accountable for the smooth running of the operation. She's accountable for the productivity of the department. She's accountable for getting the job done in an effective manner and ultimately, and certainly most important to the people upstairs, the manager is accountable to the bottom line: money! Money coming in and money going out.

Accountability means responsibility, being liable for or counted on to get things done. And I don't think you can really be accountable for anything unless you are first accountable and honest with yourself. If you are truthful with yourself and others, that makes the job of being accountable to others easier. You develop reliability and dependability when you're honest with yourself and others, and those things speak loudly about your standard of behavior; when that happens, we then see your standard of ethics.

Ethics Check

As I said earlier in the book, I'm not here to tell you what I think and feel is right and wrong in the work place, or what you should or your shouldn't do. People are different and those differences will come up from situation to situation. But I do think it is important to take another look at the ethics check that was presented in an earlier chapter. This will offer another perspective into your actions to help determine what your ethics are and how you can begin to be more aware of and ethically handle situations that arise.

Don't let the simplicity of the F.E.E.L. system deceive you.

F: *Does it feel right?* Inside each of us, lying deep within is something that calls us to action, or restrains us from acting. This element or character of our being has been termed everything from *gut feeling* to a *sense of knowingness.* It is what guides the emotionally stable person to determine right from wrong, good from bad, it guides us to be accepted or rejected. An example would be the reactions of your peers to your behavior. Would you have peer acceptance for your behavior and actions? Would you feel guilty in front of them? Would you want your behavior printed on the front page of your city newspaper?

Your feelings are a valid and valuable tool when determining your ethical direction. Learn to trust them and use them wisely.

E: *Is it equitable?* When you use the word fair, what does that mean to you? To me it means just and honest. This concept probes deeply into the values we established as a child. Although each culture may relate differently to what is fair or unfair, a standard base to rely upon has been established many years back in the ***Golden Rule.*** Do unto others as you would have them do unto you.

E: *Is it emotional?* Is there resentment involved? How about jealousy, envy, disappointment, distress or spite? When we talk of emotion, this is different than gut feeling. An emotionally-backed action can, and most often will back fire. We're not talking pure altruism here, but you can be certain that if you are able to get your base-self out of the way and elevate to a higher level of expression, the odds are in your favor to achieve a result for the good of the whole. Remember, your head and your heart are inside your body to work together. Balance is the key.

L: *Is it legal?* For a lot of people this can help make the decision very simple.

One thing you want to be careful of here is the comment many people use to justify an action or unethical stand, the expression: "Well, everybody does it!" *Doesn't work. Unacceptable.* Saying that "everybody does it" simply shifts the focus onto someone else, and now you are saying that you're going to use someone else's standards to make a decision instead of your own. And this may not be right for you.

Notice, I'm coming back to right and wrong, again. I think this is important. Because ethics really is what we determine is right and wrong. Just like a parent to a child.

As a matter of fact, maybe it wouldn't hurt to try framing a situation in this parent/child context. Would you tell your child to do a certain action, knowing that it could hurt someone else? Take a look at your situation in this light, and decide for yourself.

Okay, let's take a last look at this question of ethics with a quick summary of thoughts.

A manager shows ethics, they don't just talk about them.

She shows them in her behavior.

The ethical manager is accountable for his actions, of himself as well as his team. What they say is what they do.

A manager sets the tone for ethical standards and behavior in her department and needs to be aware of this, and act accordingly.

A manager takes responsibility.

A manager accepts the blame for employees, for he knows that he is the one responsible for those under his direction.

A manager gets the job done in an open, honest, and effective manner and shows this by example.

Ethics is a matter of making choices. Little decisions that we make and carry out every day. In the long run, it's the little decisions that accumulate and grow and determine just how ethical we really are.

What kind of choices do you make? What are the choices made by the people around you? Are you willing to live by *their* choices? Are you willing to take responsibility for your choices, all of them, personal as well as professional? And are you willing to make changes in the choices you don't like? Think about it. *The choice is yours.*

Chapter 37:
The Power of Decisiveness

So far, in discussing management skills, I've talked about knowledge: knowing the capabilities and limitations of a worker. I've talked about feelings: the feelings of compassion a manager would have toward those workers. And I've talked about morals: the ethical standards that a manager simply *must* develop and demonstrate in order to more effectively lead his team by example.

It's time now to get into an area that is not only the most tangible of skills, but a most important one as well. I'm talking about *decisiveness.*

When we speak of decisiveness, it is important to identify the problem, and insure that there is a communality of thinking on the true nature of the problem. As in many of the areas we have discussed, this too is, in degrees, dependent upon the decisions being made.

To quote Lee Iacocca, "If I had to sum up in one word the qualities that make a good manager, I'd say that it all comes down to decisiveness."

A manager can have all the other characteristics I've been talking about here and have them in abundant supply, but if he can't make decisions, he can't manage. It's that simple.

——————— **LIFE LINE** ———————

"If I had to sum up in one word the qualities that make a good manager, I'd say that it all comes down to decisiveness."
–Lee Iacocca

A manager makes decisions everyday. Some are big, most are small. I believe that if we get in the habit of becoming more aware of how we make decisions about small things, the everyday things, then when the big decisions come along we won't feel as anxious, frustrated, or (possibly) confused.

Decision Enhancers

I've made a list of some points to consider that help examine decision-making skills more closely.

1. *Be clear on what you're making a decision about.* The first step may seem obvious, but think about it a moment. A good way to do this is to answer the five basic questions: who, what, when, where, and how? *Who* does this situation involve? *What* does the situation involve? *When* and *where* does it have to take place? And finally, *how* are all these things supposed to happen?

Being clear about these points will keep you focused on the main issues and prevent you from wandering and spending time looking at something or someone that really isn't relevant to the decision of the moment.

2. *Be aware that you might blow it.* Mistakes; always a tough one for me. Who likes making mistakes? I know I don't. And I also know that I'm going to make them sometimes. Knowing that, and accepting that, are two different things. Now, I'm not suggesting that you go around with the conscious attitude, "I'm going to make a mistake sooner or later, so the heck with it." I am suggesting that it's okay to make a mistake. I don't mean *lots* of them.

Everyone expects decision makers to make a mistake now and then, and hopefully, they won't be too costly. Just because you make a mistake doesn't mean you are that mistake! Think about this: mistakes are not failures, they're aids to learning. We become more aware of ourselves and the situations we work with on a daily basis through our mistakes.

Being aware that you can make a mistake can take the pressure off of you long enough to calmly look at a situation and then make the appropriate decision.

—————— LIFE LINE ——————

Fear is really only an acronym for
False Evidence Appearing Real.

—————— ✍ ——————

Looking at the decisions from an attitude of fear can only set you up for making one mistake after another. As I've said before, fear is really only an acronym for *F*alse *E*vidence *A*ppearing *R*eal. So don't preoccupy yourself with what was or what might be.

3. *Don't get hung up on the facts.* Once all the facts are in, it's obvious to everyone what the decision should be, but that's not always the background that a manager operates from. Many times a manager simply does not have the time to wait for *all* the facts. Set yourself a time frame to work in and look for as many facts as possible, and then make your decision.

4. *Check your feelings.* That's right, I said feelings. Believe me, they're sometimes just as important as the facts. Hunches are not random. They're the result of your background and experience stored in your subconscious. Don't be afraid to use them. It's good to balance these with your head, however.

5. *Break down your thoughts on paper.* Putting the various elements of the decision down on paper lays it all out in front of you so you can see everything at once. This way, you can add, subtract, contrast, and compare: who, what, when, where, and how.

6. *Make small decisions first.* Especially if it's a big decision, it's very helpful to answer a lot of small decisions with simple yes and no answers. "Can this be done in the time required?" Yes or no. "Will she be better at doing it than him?" Yes or no. By going through the path of making a lot of little decisions, sometimes the big decision becomes more clear when it's time to make it.

7. *Ask around.* Along with acquiring all your facts and figures, it doesn't hurt to get a little feedback from some of the people on your team. This encourages their own growth and tells them that you consider their opinion important.

Remember, you always have the final responsibility for the decision, but many times you can see things more clearly from a slightly different perspective and this may lead you toward a more effective choice.

8. *Have fun.* Now, I know what you're thinking: "Fun? Decisions? Is he kidding? The business of decisions are not fun, they're work. They are things I have to do." Well, if you always frame them in the context of something you "have to do", an obligation that has to be performed without the slightest element of enjoyment, then after awhile the whole process becomes emotionally draining. And the one thing you don't want is to allow the decision-making process to drain you. This is the time when you need all the energy you can get. Especially regarding important decisions.

I'm not suggesting that you be careless and lighthearted about something that is serious to the company and the people that you work with. I am suggesting that you lighten-up just a little during the whole process. By doing this, you allow your creative energy to flow more and your creativity can cause you to make some excellent decisions.

9. *Know that you can change your mind.* Most decisions can be altered, and most are adjusted after they're put into effect. Knowing this can sure make a manager more comfortable with the whole process. And he can communicate this to his team by saying something like, "Let's do this and see if it works." This sends a clear message that he is willing to get in there and try something, and if it doesn't work, he's willing to change or alter the situation to find something that does work.

What's more, the manager's credibility remains intact. He is not put on the spot all the time to perform and have his performance judged as either right or wrong.

Nothing is cast in stone. So, don't be afraid to change your mind when new information, insight, or feelings enter the picture.

Thinking about these points, going over them in my head, right now, I'm reminded of all the decisions I make, that we all make, every day. What to wear? What toothpaste to buy? What movie to rent? What to eat for dinner? And we seem to handle those decisions without many problems.

Now, not for a minute am I comparing a choice of toothpaste to a multi-million dollar proposal for a shopping mall, but I do think that if we can become more aware of how we make the little decisions, and are willing to remain open to what we can do to make better, more effective decisions, then the *big* decisions will also be well made.

A championship baseball team comes to the play-offs after making thousands of little decisions over the course of 162 games, not just one.

CHAPTER 38:
YOU DON'T HAVE TO
REINVENT LEADERSHIP

Referring again to our Performance Chart, of characteristics important for successful management, one trait that perhaps speaks more loudly than anything else: *action!*

Actions speak louder than words. (How many times have you heard that?) Well, it's true. You can tell more by what a person *does* than by what they say. And as far as a manager's ability to manage people, it's important to remember that a good manager, the effective manager, must be able to show her team *by example.*

Every time I think about this idea, I'm reminded of a commercial that I like for Porsche. Maybe you've seen it on television. The commercial starts off with the driver hitting the gas and then, bam, the car takes off. A close shot of the speedometer shows us how fast the car is accelerating. Another shot shows the car taking a tight, clean line around a corner. Yet another shot shows the ease of shifting from one gear to another as it continues scorching down the straight-away. Finally, the car comes to an abrupt stop just in front of a neatly painted, white line. And then the narrator says: "Porsche, there is no substitute!"

———————— LIFE LINE ————————

All great leaders have displayed patterns
of success that can be repeated.

———————— ✍ ————————

That's how I feel about being an example. There is no substitute for showing your team. Show them with your behavior the attitude you want them to have; the motivation you want them to feel; the performance you want them to express; and the ethics you want them to demonstrate.

All great leaders have displayed patterns of success that can be repeated.

Management by Example

General Patton would not ask his men to march day and night for forty-eight hours without getting out there and doing it himself. All high-performance managers must (yes, I said *must*) be able to inspire loyalty by *showing it first!* They must be able to teach as well as to learn. They must be able to encourage growth in every member of the team. And ultimately, by doing this, the high-performance manager shows that he cares about his team as people, because *a manager manages people*–not things.

The good manager must be able to care about his people. Without demonstrating that care, the respect he receives will diminish. His credibility for asking anything of his team is gone if he doesn't show that he cares.

Okay, let's take a close look at some of the traits of exemplary behavior:

Loyalty: The dictionary defines loyalty as: being faithful to one's obligations. But I believe that you can be faithful to your obligations and not necessarily be loyal.

My feeling is that loyalty shows up at crunch time, the time when the schedule has changed, and a situation arises that causes you and your staff to make an additional effort. A little something extra. The loyal team member doesn't hesitate to do what is asked of him; doesn't question, complain or argue. The loyal worker just gets in there and re-doubles his efforts to get the job done because he respects the manager he's working with. Notice, I said "with" and not "for". That's the feeling we desire to create.

Loyalty is like money in the bank but it can't be bought at any price except one: showing that you, the manager, care and are loyal to your team.

It's being there for them as much as you can. It's listening, it's supporting, it's encouraging, it's teaching. These are some of the ways a manager demonstrates loyalty toward her team. She's got to believe in the people she works with in order for them to be ready, willing, and able to turn around and believe in her.

Teaching: By teaching I don't just mean the job in front of you. We've covered this before. It's understood that the effective manager is capable, and willing to teach any member of his team what he himself has learned from experience, and how that experience applies to the job at hand. More than that, the good manager teaches his team the very qualities that he demonstrates and wants from his staff: discipline, honesty, openness, communication, decisiveness, balance; all of the characteristics we have been talking about, and most of this teaching is done *by example.*

The question is, of course, how does a good manager teach these qualities? Think back a moment to some teachers in your life, teachers who you felt made a difference. What was it about them that made that difference?

I know that the significant teachers in my life were always ones who caused me to think about alternatives, caused me to realize that there is something more than just what's in front of me, allowed me to grow through experience, and stretch myself beyond my normal limits. They always encouraged—never criticized; always talked—never lectured; and always helped—but never did it for me.

The truly high-performance manager never forgets for a moment that she is both teacher and student. That she learns as much as she teaches about the individual, the team, and herself.

And, of course, I've already started talking about the third quality of creating a good example and that is:

Allow for growth in others: A high-performance manager shares her experience about the job with a team member and then steps back and allows that person the space to swim around and develop their own strokes, their own approach, and a way that works best for them. It is this flexibility in attitude that a worker appreciates, and comes to enjoy most about a manager. And it is this attitude that causes a worker to develop respect for her manager.

Lastly, let's talk specifically about:

Caring about people: An exemplary manager cares about his team. You've heard me say this in one form or another throughout everything that we've talked about, and I know you're probably getting tired of my saying it, but there's just no other way of saying it. Showing that you care about your team member means that you have respect, that you're sincerely interested, that you feel that they do make a difference. And that's the biggest bottom line in any approach to managing people: *managing by example.*

Caring about people also means that you set boundaries and create direction for your team. That means that you clearly establish what is acceptable behavior in the work place and what is not. Everyone needs structure, something that they can count on, something that tells people what they should be doing and when they should be doing it. And it covers everything from what time you come to work, to what is expected on the job, how paperwork is to be turned in, how to talk to a client, and so on.

The effective manger gives feedback along the way to help strengthen and improve the structure because it is the structure we all cling to that helps us get the job done as efficiently as possible. This is caring about people. It's called showing respect for the job.

Managing by example means cooperating. It means teaching. It means learning, and it means allowing for growth in others. It means showing loyalty toward the team you work through so that they can then show loyalty to you and the job you're all there to do. It means caring about people.

Management's responsibility is to set the example: there is no substitute.

Trust

We have another characteristic on our Performance Chart to talk about here, and that is *trust*.

Trust would have to be the cornerstone of any relationship, business as well as personal. And let's make no mistake here, trust in a business relationship is just as vital as trust in any personal relationship. Without trust a manager has no real bond with his team. Without trust a manger is managing things not people.

So, what is trust? Trust accepts, and believes. Trust allows. Trust has faith, and enhances. Trust talks freely. It listens with an open mind. And I believe trust is in short supply today. And I think the problem is that everyone wants to *be* trusted but nobody wants to trust *first!*

Trust isn't something that walks in and just happens. It builds over a course of time. However, in terms of a manager managing people, the high-performance manager has to learn to trust almost immediately. Once he accepts the job, once he accepts the people on his team, that acceptance means that he trusts them. That first step in trust then allows the other team members to turn around and trust him.

"Do I Trust Myself?"

Let's start with the basics, and basically speaking you can't trust anyone until you first trust yourself. (". . . here we go again. Trust myself? Of course I trust myself! What's he talking about?") Do you really? Here are some questions I've come up with that you might ask yourself:

1. Do I trust my feelings?
2. Can I trust my feelings enough to act on them?

3. Am I willing to trust others around me?

I think if you can honestly look at your answers to these questions, you might be able to gain a little insight into your level of trust with yourself.

To begin with, trusting yourself means being honest with yourself. One way of checking honesty with *yourself* is to see how honest you are with *others*.

Here are some more questions to help you.

1. Are you able to talk to upper-management openly and honestly about what's going on?

2. Are you able talk with your team and talk to them openly and honestly about their level of work? Are you able to tell them honestly when you're happy and when you're not?

3. Are you able to admit your own mistakes?

These aren't easy questions to answer especially when hurt feelings and egos can easily get in the way. But, if you can look at your level of honesty with the people you work with, and know that it is through a consistent level of honesty that you are going to be most effective, then you are on your way to developing trust and being an effective manager.

Looking at it from the other side for a moment, we can see that lying simply takes too much energy and effort. How do you keep all the stories straight? How do you remember all the stories you've told? And how do you ever begin to trust anyone if you constantly hide behind lies yourself?

What does trust feel like? Confident, dependable, loyal, honest, safe. I think that creating a safe atmosphere is one of the most important things an effective manager can do for her team. The high-performance manager allows her team to feel comfortable enough to share what's going on and trusting that no matter what, it's going to be okay; *we* can work things out, *we* can get the job done.

Trust is certainly not something that is easily gained—but you better believe that it can be lost in an instant (and take a long time to rebuild).

Making the First Move

The high-performance manager learns how to develop trust with her team by making the first move. And here are some thoughts about doing that.

1. *Be willing to accept what a team member says he will do and see what happens.* If you give them a task and have explained it, trust that the job will get done and stick to that attitude of faith until facts prove differently.

2. *Keep checking-up to a minimum.* Do you feel that all delegations have to be checked on? There is a difference between checking up on something and not allowing a worker the space and the time to do their job. The high-performance manager knows that difference, and respects it.

Perhaps hardest of all:

3. Be *willing to take a risk.* You have to risk trusting someone else in the same way that they have to risk trusting you. And if you, as the manager, make the first move you'll be surprised at how much your team will begin to respect and trust you.

Trust is an attitude, a belief, a good feeling of dependability, safety, openness, and honesty between people.

When we trust others more, we become more open and honest ourselves. That's the way trust works. Helping to create that feeling of safety can make all the difference in the world in motivating people to do the things that a manager needs to get done, to inspire the loyalty you want to inspire, to manage effectively and to feel good about yourself.

CHAPTER 39:
MANAGER OR LEADER?

At the beginning of this section I mentioned that few topics have been talked about, or written on, more than management. It's true. I think that in any given week there is always some new book or seminar circulating that's emphasizing the need for better, more efficient management skills in the business community.

What I have endeavored to do here is to bring a common sense approach to this whole idea of management by stressing the basics, and by synthesizing those basics down to a simple component: the Performance Chart.

This reminds me of a when I was in the military service. I was sent to active duty for the Berlin crisis back in the early 60's. Paul Horning and Boyd Doular of the Greenbay Packers were in my unit. They showed films of Vince Lombardi coaching the team to repeated victory. Paul said that each season Vince would sit the team down and say, "Alright men, let's start from the beginning. This . . . is a football." And Paul would say, "Wait a minute coach, not so fast."

As I'm thinking about this now, it's interesting to note that the Performance Chart is based on some very simple principles available to man. They are used in most every aspect of our lives every day, every hour, every second. Its primary use, in one form or another, is to get us from here to there as easily and quickly as possible. Like the principle of action/reaction used by jet and rocket engines.

And that's what I'm reflecting back on now, the basic components of management that are used on a daily basis to get us, *all* of us, from here to there as easily as possible.

——————— LIFE LINE ———————

Motivation increases as people are made to feel part of a team.

——————— ✍ ———————

The high-performance manager is discerning and knows the abilities and limitations of his team. He needs to know where the greatest strengths of his team members lie and how to utilize those strengths to the best advantage. Most importantly, he needs to know where teaching can bring out new potentials in a team member, potentials that will not only help the individual grow, but the team he works with as well.

I've talked about how motivation becomes a very strong part in bringing out, and developing, the potential abilities of a team member. Knowing that, it follows that motivation increases as people are made to feel part of a team, a team of people all working together to get the job done. If you are one who lacks motivation, then you will lack the ability to inspire others. You will need to capture a sense for adventure and curiosity. Dale Carnegie said, "Act enthusiastic and you will be enthusiastic." What can you lose? Give it a shot.

I mentioned how *the high-performance manager needs to have good listening skills,* and that she listens eighty percent of the time not just to the words spoken, but the feelings behind those words. And that *showing* that you listen demonstrates that you, as a manager, care.

Are you one who listens? I mean *really* listens? If not, use my 100% present concept. Experiment with this. When you are listening to someone, really focus in on them with your total presence. You can tell when you have someone's attention, can't you? And you can tell when you don't—right? Well . . . do you think it works in reverse also? Of course it does. Have you ever been at a party talking with someone, and suddenly you notice them leave their body? And you say to yourself, "Come on back, I want to talk with you." The beneficial irony of my 100% present concept is that *it generally takes less time to really focus your listening than it does to be a scattered listener.*

An actively caring manager is a compassionate manager. And I've mentioned more than once that a manager manages people—not things—because it is *people* that the manager works through to get projects successfully accomplished, not things.

The compassionate manager is understanding, helpful, and a student as well as a teacher. The quality of compassion itself is simply: treating ourselves and everyone around us in a respectful and honorable way. It's looking beyond the moment of the job to the person who does the job, and feeling empathetic at the times when it's needed most. And that's a "bottom line" that never shows up on any bookkeeper's ledger, but it's just as important as all the facts and figures that stand up front.

Are you a compassionate manager? I might suggest that you take a moment to reflect upon your own thoughts and ideas. Sometimes simply asking yourself the question that you don't know the answer to is a good place to begin.

I've talked about ethics and just how important I feel ethics is to all of us today; how we can examine our own ethical standards that we demonstrate; and learn to adjust, refine, and change.

I mentioned the F.E.E.L. system that I use as a simple test:

F. *Does it feel right?* What are your inner feelings telling you?

E. *Is it equitable?* Is it a win/win situation or is somebody losing?

E. *Is it emotional?* Are you examining the situation objectively, from *all* sides, or is it emotion-backed, meaning: is your decision or behavior motivated solely by your emotions?

And finally:

L. *Is it legal?* Are you violating any city, state or federal laws as well as any company policies?

To emphasize again, *good managers show ethics more than they talk about them.* They show them in their behavior and treatment of everyone they come in contact with, from the valued client to a member of the cleaning crew.

The ethical manager is accountable, and responsible, and as a result is dependable to their team and the company they work with.

Have you had a question about your ethics while reading this section? Have you really taken a moment to examine where you feel right and wrong begins and ends? As I said before, I can't tell you what is right for you, this is strictly a personal decision, I can only ask you to give it some thought, remembering that you, as a manager, will set the tone for your people.

I've discussed decisiveness. And emphasized how important a truly decisive manager is to everyone he works with. *The decisive manager is clear on what the decision is* that he has to make. She doesn't get hung up on the facts. She checks her feelings knowing that hunches are the result of past experiences stored in the subconscious. She breaks down the various elements involved in the decision on paper in order to clearly see what can be added or subtracted from the circumstance at hand.

——— **LIFE LINE** ———

*The good manager shows
her team by example.*

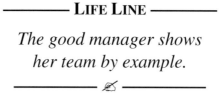

We've talked about the importance of making small decisions every day along the way, and by looking at how we make those small decisions we begin to take responsibility, and are more consciously aware of the choices we make every day. Ask yourself, "Do I like the choices I make? Am I willing to live by them? What do I need to do in order to change them?" The skilled manager isn't afraid of running these questions over in his head on a regular basis to check himself, and his reasoning.

Actions speak louder than words. And it's important for the high-performance manager to know and demonstrate all the characteristics we've been talking about. The good manager shows her team by example. Showing them in her behavior the attitude she wants them to have, the motivation she wants them to feel, the performance she wants them to express, and the ethics she wants them to practice. It's called: walk like you talk. All great teachers have led by example. And this brings up another point that I wish to talk about, and that's leadership.

Evolving: Manager Becomes Leader

Notice that I have not linked the words "manager" and "leader" and the reason is that I don't believe a manager is necessarily a leader. Many managers are appointed, promoted, and rewarded simply because of longevity. If they were not rewarded, dissension might occur among the ranks.

This may be an unpopular point to make, but I really believe that simply because someone is in the position of managing people, that job does not necessarily make him a leader. This is where the Peter Principle gained its notoriety, "In a hierarchy every employee tends to rise to their level of incompetence."

In a working situation, a worker may follow the instructions of a manager simply because he's the one in authority, the one in charge. But would he *follow* that person's lead under different circumstances? Think about it for a moment. Think if you were with a group of friends, camping-out somewhere, and your manager was part of the group, and somehow the group got lost. Now, the circumstance facing you is: not only how to get out, but how to survive. Under those circumstances, would you follow your manager's lead then?

High-performance management comes through education, training, and experience, which leads one to define and refine the knowledge and skills necessary to gain competence. A person can be trained to be an effective manager, but you cannot train someone to be a leader unless they are willing to step forward and assume the leadership role.

As with most things in life, it must be fully realized that virtually nothing holds true in all cases. That being said, *a manager may not necessarily be a good leader but a good leader can usually be an effective manager.*

A leader is one who confronts, challenges, and risks. A leader is someone who is always thinking of ways to help the team. *Always!* And this is clearly evidenced by the way he postures himself. Always checking on the welfare of others. Always a concerned listener. Always there when you need him. Always demonstrating an optimistic, open and honest attitude about people.

A leader is someone who is always willing to be out front, take complete responsibility, and effect changes along the way for the betterment of everyone, and not just to look good.

A leader has the best interests of the company, and the people on his team, always on his mind because he knows in his heart as well as his head that the company is made up of people, and in the long run that's what counts: *people!*

All right, so how does a manager become a leader?

Well, one way is by following the characteristics I've outlined on the Performance Chart. And by diligently looking for ways to improve yourself, and the quality and effectiveness of the people you work through, both as a team as well as individually.

And this brings us to our last characteristic on the Performance Chart that we've discussed, and that is *trust!*

Like I've pointed out, without trust you might as well break out the jackets and man the lifeboats because it's only a matter of time before the ship goes down, because nothing effective is going to happen; no growth. And where there is no growth in the individual there is no growth for the team or for the company they all work through.

With trust, everything is possible. A manager that knows and expresses this quality also recognizes its long range importance. Trust is the substance that creates a bond between the manager and the team she works through. Trust accepts, believes, and allows. Trust has faith and enhances. Trust listens with an open mind. Trust talks freely. When a manager learns to trust others more, she learns to become more open and honest herself and it is that openness that creates a feeling of safety. That atmosphere of safety can have a great impact on the morale and motivation of the people comprising her team. Nothing can take the place of trust. What's your trust level?

Those are the seven characteristics of my Performance Chart. The *magnificent seven,* if you will.

To recap briefly, a good manager:

1. Knows the abilities and limitations of his team.

2. He is a concerned listener.

3. He has compassion for people.

4. She exhibits ethics in her professional life and her personal life.

5. She is decisive.

6. He shows by example.

7. The effective manager demonstrates trust.

Every part of the Performance Chart develops, strengthens, and builds these characteristics in both yourself as a manager, and the team you are working through.

As the Chart progresses, the people evolve. And as the people develop, so does the quality and effectiveness of the work you all do together. It becomes better, brighter, clearer. It inspires more ideas which generate more work, and this causes everyone to reach higher to tap the potential within themselves.

A good manager, a high-performance manager, cannot help but see this progress as upward movement, and know that when one of his team leaves or is promoted, that he helped take an active part in the growth of that worker, and this inspires him to see the potential for growth in the team member that takes his place.

There are always more challenges to face, new obstacles to overcome. But the high-performance manager knows that with a solid foundation of characteristics, she can handle any situation that comes her way and knowing this makes her job—*everyone's job*—a lot easier, more productive and, yes, even fun!

——————— LIFE LINE ———————

When the best leader's job is done the people say, "We did it ourselves."

——————— ✍ ———————

EPILOGUE: GETTING RESULTS THROUGH PEOPLE

To be successful in your own terms, whether in business or your personal life, requires techniques that are effectively tailored for a specific task. This section has offered guidelines intended to enhance the personal development of every individual. The basic premise is that the more an individual becomes aware and uses his potential, the greater his quality of life. So, both individuals and corporations can benefit by exerting a more positive influence on those surrounding them.

From an observer's standpoint, I believe that it has been made clear that many people place the reasons for their successes in life outside of themselves. Personal success is directly related to business success. The degree of success lies directly within the responsibility of those who are in control. Worker productivity, for instance, reflects the attitudes of management, and such attitudes surround the business with either a positive or negative atmosphere, the effects of which reach far beyond the walls of the company.

Many strive for success, measured in their own terms, but few achieve it. Success in business and in personal life is something that, on the surface, often appears to be instant—all of a sudden a person or a business has made an impact on the world. But people usually fail to realize that behind that so-called "instant success" lie years of focus, dedication, and discipline. With the tools offered here, the ingredients needed to experience fulfillment are found to be rather simple (which is not to be confused with easy, which is most certainly not the case). If success were easy then all people would be successful, all people would be financially well off, and all people would be glowing examples of health—but they're not. So, the need to approach this area of success with a game plan and a reliable measure for fulfillment is mandatory.

The mere fact that an enormous number of businesses are virtually "out of business" within two or three years of their inception is evidence enough that there exists a need for direction toward increased stability. The Management/Leadership ideas expressed here allow you to investigate and evaluate various areas of your personal and business life, offering guidelines to get results where you need it most. Any emotionally stable person interested in self-improvement and business advancement will find that the system, used in part or in total, offers a means for expansion and fuller expression in the direction of their own individual desires. Explore the ideas, implement the techniques and enjoy the adventure.

A

accountability, 25
Aldrin, Buz
    Astronaut, 224
Allen, James, 78
Armstrong, Neil
    Astronaut, 1st to
        walk on moon, 224
associations
    personal, 198
Attitude, 15, 38, 47,
    54, 119, 198, 230,
    251
    from fear, 277
    non-survival, 79, 119
Aveda Corp., 26

B

Bacon, Francis C., 131
balance, 188, 219, 232
Bean, Alan
    Apollo 12 pilot, 225
behavior, 19, 24, 27,
    37, 153
    and habits, 199
    and values, 23
    Carl Jung, 84
    code of, 267
    demonstrate, 272
    in crowds, 10
    self-defeating, 31
    styles, 83
    types, 94
Ben & Jerry, 25
Bentley, 185
Berne, Eric, 89

body language, 91, 94,
    141
brainstorming, 7, 48
burnout, 39
    symptoms, 40
    ways to conquer, 41

C

C.L.O.S.E., 164
Carnegie, Andrew, 235
Carnegie, Dale, 290
Celestial Seasonings, 26
change, 77, 110
    acceptance, 173
    habits, 37
    interpretation, 71
    James Allen, 78
    looking for, 79
    opportunities, 47
    positive, 223
    risking, 183
    vs. values, 27
    William James, 52
clothing game, 148
Cohen, Ben, 25
communication, 1, 6, 14
    breakdown, 60
    clear, 157
    CLOSE, 164
    effective, 71, 93
    etiquette breach, 92
    motivation, 246
compassion, 9, 13, 80,
    261, 262
    demonstrate, 262
    understanding, 11
    vs. knowledge, 243
complaint, 63, 212